D1481725

Existential-Phenomenological Readings on Faulkner

Existential-Phenomenological Readings on Faulkner

William J. Sowder

UCA Press
1991

For
Bobby (1915-1963)

For
Ann, Lee, and Ann Miller

TABLE OF CONTENTS

Acknowledgments

A grant made possible by the Cooperative Program in the Humanities, which was sponsored by Duke University and the University of North Carolina and which was financed by the Ford Foundation and participating colleges, played a significant role in bringing this study to publication.

Chapter VIII of this monograph, "Lucas Beauchamp: Eye of the Storm," was first published as "Lucas Beauchamp as Existentialist Hero" in *College English*, November 1963. "Copyright by the National Council of Teachers of English. Reprinted with permission." Chapter I, "Benjy Compson and the field of Consciousness" first appeared in the *Journal of Phenomenological Psychology*, Spring 1988. ChapterX, "Young Ike McCaslin: Travels in *Terra Incognita*," was published first in *Heir & Prototype: Original and Derived Characterizations in Faulkner*, ed. by Dan Ford, University of Central Arkansas Press, 1988. Chapter V, "Colonel Thomas Sutpen and the Original Choice," appeared first as "Colonel Thomas Sutpen as Existentialist Hero" in *American Literature* in January, 1962. This article then was published in *On Faulkner: The Best from American Literature* in 1989.

Key To Abbreviations

AA William Faulkner, *Absalom, Absalom*. New York: Random House, 1951.

A Gabriel Marcel, *Ariadne*. Trans. Rosalind Heywood in *Three Plays*. New York: Mermaid, 1965.

AF William Faulkner, *A Fable*. New York: Random House, 1954.

AILD William Faulkner, *As I Lay Dying*. New York: Random House, 1964.

AR Jean-Paul Sartre, *The Age of Reason*. Trans. Eric Sutton. New York: Bantam, 1959.

ASJ Jean-Paul Sartre, *Anti-Semite and Jew*. Trans. George J. Becker. New York: Schocken, 1965.

B Jean-Paul Sartre, *Baudelaire*. Trans. Martin Turnell. Norfolk, CT: New Directions, 1950.

B & H Gabriel Marcel, *Being and Having*. Trans. James Collins New York: Harper Torchbooks, 1965.

B & N Jean-Paul Sartre, *Being and Nothingness. An Essay on Phenomenological Ontology*. Trans. Hazel Barnes. New York: Philosophical Library, 1956.

B & T Martin Heidegger, *Being and Time*. Trans. John Macquarrie and Edward Robinson. New York: Harper & Row, 1962.

C Albert Camus, *Caligula*. Trans. Stuart Gilbert in *Caligula & Three Other Plays*. New York: Vintage, 1958.

CA Jean-Paul Sartre, *The Condemned of Altona*. Trans. Sylvia and George Leeson. New York: Vintage, 1961.

CF Gabriel Marcel, *Creative Fidelity*. Trans. Robert Rosthal. New York: Noonday, 1964.

CS William Faulkner, *Collected Stories of William Faulkner*. New York: Random House, 1950.

DGL Jean-Paul Sartre, *The Devil and the Good Lord*. Trans. Kitty Black in *The Devil and the Good Lord and Two Other Plays*. New York: Vintage, 1960.

E Jean-Paul Sartre, *The Emotions. Outline of a Theory*. Trans. Bernard Frechtman. New York: Philosophical Library, 1948.

EA Jean-Paul Sartre, *Essays in Aesthetics*. Trans. Wade Baskin. New York: Citadel, 1963.

E & H Karl Jaspers, *Existentialism and Humanism*. Trans. E. B. Ashton. New York: Russell R. Moore, 1952.

EDS *Existentialism from Dostoyevsky to Sartre*. Trans. and ed. by Walter Kaufmann. New York: Meridian, 1956.

ES Karl Jaspers, *The European Spirit*. Trans. Ronald Gregor Smith. Kent, England: S C M Press, 1948.

F Albert Camus, *The Fall*. Trans. Justin O'Brien. New York: Vintage, 1956.

FM Karl Jaspers, *The Future of Mankind*. Trans. E. B. Ashton. Chicago: Phoenix, 1961.

GDM William Faulkner, *Go Down, Moses*. New York: Modern Library, 1942.

GP Karl Jaspers, *General Psychopathology.* Trans. J. Hoenig and Marian W. Hamilton. Chicago: U of Chicago P, 1963.

H William Faulkner, *The Hamlet.* New York: Random House, 1940.

HV Gabriel Marcel, *Homo Viator.* Trans. Emma Craufurd. New York: Harper Torchbooks, 1962.

I Edmund Husserl, *Ideas. General Introduction to Pure Phenomenology.* Trans. W. R. Boyce Gibson. New York: Collier, 1962.

IID William Faulkner, *Intruder in the Dust.* New York: Random House, 1948.

IM Martin Heidegger, *An Introduction to Metaphysics.* Trans. Ralph Manheim. Garden City, NY: Anchor, 1961.

K Jean-Paul Sartre, *Kean.* Trans. Kitty Black in *The Devil and the Good Lord and Two Other Plays.* New York: Vintage, 1960.

KG William Faulkner, *Knight's Gambit.* New York: Random House, 1949.

KJP Karl Jaspers, *Philosophy.* Trans. E. B. Ashton. Chicago: U of Chicago P, 1964-1971. 3 Vols.

LIA William Faulkner, *Light in August.* New York: Modern Library, 1950.

LPE Jean-Paul Sartre, *Literary and Philosophical Essays.* Trans. Annette Michelson. New York: Collier, 1962.

M William Faulkner, *The Mansion.* New York: Random House, 1959.

M & C Karl Jaspers and Rudolph Bultmann, *Myth and Christianity.* Trans. New York: Noonday, 1958.

MB, I Gabriel Marcel, *The Mystery of Being,* I. Trans. G. S. Fraser. Chicago: Gateway Edition, 1960.

MB, II Gabriel Marcel, *The Mystery of Being,* II. Trans. René Hague. Chicago: Gateway Edition, 1960.

MG Gabriel Marcel, *A Man of God.* Trans. Marjorie Gabain in *Three Plays.* New York: Mermaid, 1965.

MMA Karl Jaspers, *Man in the Modern Age.* Trans. Eden and Cedar Paul. New York: Anchor, 1957.

MMS Gabriel Marcel, *Man Against Mass Society.* Trans. G. S. Fraser. Chicago: Gateway Edition, 1962.

MS Albert Camus, *The Myth of Sisyphus.* Trans. Justin O'Brien. New York: Vintage, 1955.

N Jean-Paul Sartre, *Nausea.* Trans. Lloyd Alexander. New York: New Directions, 1964.

NE Jean-Paul Sartre, *No Exit.* Trans. Stuart Gilbert in *No Exit and Three Other Plays.* New York: Vintage, 1949.

NPS William Faulkner, Nobel Prize Speech

OGH Karl Jaspers, *The Origin and Goal of History.* Trans. Michael Bullock. New Haven: Yale UP, 1953.

P Albert Camus, *The Plague.* Trans. Stuart Gilbert. New York: Random House, 1947.

PE Gabriel Marcel, *The Philosophy of Existentialism.* Trans. Manya Harari.

New York: Citadel P, 1966.

PF & R Karl Jaspers, *Philosophical Faith and Revelation*. Trans. E. B. Ashton. New York: Harper and Row, 1967.

PI Jean-Paul Sartre, *The Psychology of Imagination*. Trans. not given. New York: Citadel P, 1963.

Po Albert Camus, *The Possessed*. Trans. Justin O'Brien. New York: Vintage, 1964.

PP Maurice Merleau-Ponty, *Phenomenology of Perception*. Trans. Colin Smith. New York: Humanities P, 1966.

PrP Maurice Merleau-Ponty, *The Primacy of Perception and Other Essays*. Ed. James M. Edie. Trans. Arleen B. Dallery, *et al*. Evanston: Northwestern UP, 1964.

PW Karl Jaspers, *Philosophy and the World*. Trans. E. B. Ashton. Chicago: Gateway Edition, 1963.

R Max Scheler, *Ressentiment*. Trans. William W. Holdheim. New York: Free Press of Glencoe, 1961.

R & A Karl Jaspers, *Reason and Anti-Reason in Our Time*. Trans. Stanley Godman. London: SCM Press, 1952.

R & E Karl Jaspers, *Reason and Existenz*. Trans. William Earle. New York: Noonday P, 1955.

Reb Albert Camus, *The Rebel*. Trans. Anthony Bower. New York: Vintage, 1956.

RFN William Faulkner, *Requiem for a Nun*. New York: Random House, 1951.

S William Faulkner, *Sanctuary*. New York: Random House, 1932.

S & C Maurice Merleau-Ponty, "Structure and Conflicts of the Child Consciousness," *Bulletin de Psychologie*, XVIII (November 1964), 171-202.

S & F William Faulkner, *The Sound and the Fury*. New York: Random House, 1956. (Reproduced from first printing, 1929.)

Sart William Faulkner, *Sartoris*. London: Chatto & Windus, 1954.

SB Maurice Merleau-Ponty, *The Structure of Behavior*. Trans. Alden Fisher. Boston: Beacon P, 1963.

SG Jean-Paul Sartre, *Saint Genet*. Trans. Bernard Frechtman. New York: Mentor, 1963.

Sit Jean-Paul Sartre, *Situations*. Trans. Benita Eisler. New York: George Braziller, 1965.

SNS Maurice Merleau-Ponty, *Sense and Non-Sense*. Trans. Hubert L. Dreyfus and Patricia Allen Dreyfus. Evanston: Northwestern UP, 1964.

SP William Faulkner, *Soldiers' Pay*. London: Chatto & Windus, 1957.

SS Albert Camus, *State of Siege*. Trans. Stuart Gilbert in *Caligula and Three Other Plays*. New York: Vintage, 1958.

St Albert Camus, *The Stranger*. Trans. Stuart Gilbert. New York: Vintage, 1942.

T William Faulkner, *The Town*. New York: Random House, 1957.

T & S Karl Jaspers, *Truth and Symbol*. Trans. Jean T. Wilde, William Kluback, and William Kimmel. New York: Twayne, 1959.

TE Jean-Paul Sartre, *The Transcendence of the Ego. An Existential Theory of Consciousness*. Trans. Forrest Williams and Robert Kirkpatrick. New York: Noonday P, 1957.

TF Jean-Paul Sartre, *The Flies*. Trans. Stuart Gilbert in *No Exit and Three Other Plays*. New York: Vintage, 1949.

TR Jean-Paul Sartre, *The Reprieve*. Trans. Eric Sutton. New York: Bantam, 1960.

TS Jean-Paul Sartre, *Troubled Sleep*. Trans. Gerard Hopkins. New York: Bantam, 1961.

U William Faulkner, *The Unvanquished*. New York: Random House, 1965.

VC Gabriel Marcel, *The Votive Candle*. Trans. Rosalind Heywood in *Three PLays*. New York: Mermaid, 1965.

WIL Jean-Paul Sartre, *What Is Literature?* Trans. Bernard Frechtman. New York: Colophon, 1965.

WP William Faulkner, *The Wild Palms*. London: Chatto & Windus, 1954.

WW Karl Jaspers, *Way to Wisdom*. Trans. Ralph Manheim. New Haven: Yale UP, 1954.

Z Friedrich Wilhelm Nietzsche, *Thus Spake Zarathustra*. Trans. Thomas Common in *The Philosophy of Nietzsche*. New York: Modern Library, n.d.

PREFACE

Faulkner's characters and the existential phenomenologists were made for each other. These characters in the range of their actions, in their diverse ethical, moral, and religious views, in the difference in their social status and other attributes are so various that heretofore they have required a multiplicity of critical approaches. Existential phenomenology can change this. As a philosophy of consciousness it covers the whole human spectrum. Albert Einstein was setting forth the perfect existential-phenomenologist dictum when he commented that "the eternal mystery of the world is its comprehensibility," and Karl Jaspers, the first to use the term "existential," expressed the same notion when he wrote, "an Existenz I do not meet outwardly does not exist for me" (*KJP* II: 144). As Jaspers made clear, the spiritual world of men is as accessible to precise description as the natural. Jaspers' basis for this claim lies in the definition of consciousness as given by the founder of the modern school of phenomenology, Edmund Husserl. This definition serves as a basis for all major claims of the existential-phenomenologists. First, Husserl makes clear the unparalleled importance of consciousness in the affairs of men: "Consciousness" . . . "is 'consciousness' through and through, the source of all reason and unreason, all right and wrong, all reality and illusion, all value and disvalue, all deed and misdeed." Then he defines the act of consciousness in perhaps the most elegant and fruitful thirteen words in all psycho-philosophy: "It is intentionality which characterizes *consciousness* in the pregnant sense of the term" (*I* 231, 222).

With this almost divine insight (It could have come right out of the Old Testament: it makes man responsible for his every action, without excuse: he *intended* to do it) phenomenology delivered consciousness from the vagueness that has always plagued it. No longer are we enveloped by a "state of consciousness," a cloudy realm floating at will everywhere and nowhere (*MB* I: 215, 225). Instead we know, as Husserl explains, that consciousness in order to be conscious must be conscious of *something*. We can perceive *it*, imagine *it*, conceive *it*. Sartre's famous affirmation that "existence precedes essence" (*B & N* 630) is another way of saying that consciousness in order to intend must have something—phenomena—to intend. This affirmation, in turn, inspired Sartre's most widely known existential-phenomenologist concepts: free choice, responsibility, anguish: man is free to choose that which he intends and thus is responsible for his intentions: the choice is made in anguish, as we shall see in Chapter V. For Sartre as well as for other existential-phenomenologists, human consciousness-as-intentionality is equated with human intention, and whatever the differences in their approaches to this reality, the existential-phenomenologists have set for themselves the same goal, namely, the describing of the human being in the *act* of being—the act of *intending*.

This was also Faulkner's goal. He wished, he said, to reveal his characters in motion, to catch in action the essence of their being. Faulkner was alluding to this essence when he explained that he often used characters, dropped them for a time, and revived them again. Over the years he might, he suggested, forget certain details about the characters, even get some of the details wrong, but this did not matter. The characters would remain the same, for there was a certain "facet" about them, Faulkner maintained, that was changeless, that made them what they were. It was this facet, Faulkner believed, that held all of the other facets together.[1] Phenomenally, the facet is the fundamental intentionality holding together all other intentionalities. Karl Jaspers had this intentionality in mind when he wrote that every man embodies "only one phenomenal form"; that is, a form which is "genuine," "no mere front" (*KJP* I: 286). The phenomenologist Ludwig Binswanger calls the form the "transcendental category,"[2] Sartre calls it the "original choice," but whatever the terminology, this existential consciousness is the ground phenomenon of our lives anterior to all other phenomena. The purpose of this study is to bring together a representative selection of Faulkner's characters and four of the acknowledged major existential-phenomenologists, Jean-Paul Sartre, Maurice Merleau-Ponty, Karl Jaspers, and Gabriel Marcel, in a way that will made clear the unifying phenomenon.[3] (At times I also call on Husserl, Heidegger, and others for special assignment). One character, Benjy Compson, holds a special place in the study. His is a consciousness grounded in the fractional perceptions of idiocy and thus a consciousness whose intentionality is much different from that of the other characters. Using Merleau-Ponty's phenomenology of perception, we see precisely how this exceptional being intended the world he inhabits and how his intentionality differs existentially from that of other human beings. No longer are we tempted to read our thoughts into this consciousness "blasted empty and clean forever of any thought" (*H* 98), as several critics have tried to do. We can establish Benjy's world instead of setting up our own.

This tendency of the existential-phenomenologists to include exceptions is one of the reasons they are so useful in the study of Faulkner's characters. Like the characters, they are a variegated lot who often quarreled among themselves. Although Merleau-Ponty and Marcel agree on the importance of the physical body in human existence, though Marcel endorses Sartre's analysis of bad faith as well as his description of carnal love, and though Marcel and Jaspers are together in their meaning of spiritual love, more often than not they are in disharmony. Marcel opposes much that Sartre proposes, Merleau-Ponty joins Marcel in disparaging Sartre, Sartre is critical of Heidegger. Jaspers seems to be the only one above the strife: he is impressed with Heidegger but has little or nothing to say about the others. Yet, out of these disagreements comes a powerful fact: the combined weight of this varied comment on human existence is enough to balance that which Faulkner has revealed in his characters. To repeat, and it is worth repeating, the existential-phenomenologist investment in human existence is equal to Faulkner's genius for creating human characters. If this is true, one finds in the existential-phenomenologist approach to Faulkner's characters what he looks for in vain in other critical approaches, a unified critical theory incorporating all of the characters. Other approaches—mythological, symbolical, Freudian, Jungian, religious, sociological, formalist, to mention a few—throw light on one or perhaps several of these characters to the neglect of all the others. Existential-phenomenology brings the whole congregation under one tent.

Another advantage of existential-phenomenology is that it combines great flexibility with great economy. In concentrating on acts of consciousness rather than on physical action, the existential-phenomenologist critic can eliminate the unnecessarily detailed plot summaries that inflate much Faulkner criticism. Furthermore, this economy is achieved without the distortion of characters evident in some of the other approaches—forcing parallels between such characters as Benjy Compson, Joe Christmas, Mink Snopes and Jesus Christ, for instance. Faulkner was doubtless referring to this kind of critical hyperbole when he complained about the "erudite professorial symbolism [that] gets into everything."[4] The symbolists as well as other critics all too often use Faulkner's characters as excuses for setting forth elaborate theories, while Faulkner himself saw these characters as living, dying, struggling "in the moil and seethe of simple humanity"[5]— "Dasein," "everydayness," as Heidegger calls it (B & T 533, 536). The existential-phenomenologist critic attempts to restore to Faulkner's characters their everydayness, attempts to rescue them, if you will, from the vacuum of myth, symbol, archetypes, and other artificial forms. In short, he attempts to treat each character as an authentic human being, not a figment of the critical imagination. More than anything else, I suppose, existential-phenomenology is an attempt to restore in Faulkner criticism human meaning and value, a restoration outside the narrow confines of any particular race or religion or society or moral or ethical mandate and in terms of human consciousness itself, the bearer of all meaning and value. Finally, the existential-phenomenologist attempts to close the gap between literature and life, for, as Gabriel Marcel writes, quoting Charles Du Bois and echoing the Novel Prize Speech,

> Literature is nothing but . . . life itself when it reaches its fullest expression in the soul of a man of genius. Life and literature, far from opposing and contradicting each other, are bound together by the closest and most intimate of ties. Literature would have no content were it not for life; but were it not for literature, life would be but a waterfall, that ceaseless waterfall in which so many of us are submerged, a waterfall without meaning, which we merely accept, which we are incapable of interpreting; and literature carries out the functions of a hydraulic belt with regard to this waterfall, catching, collecting and raising its water. (HV 214-15)

One further note: each chapter can be read separately, for it is a unit within itself. More profitably, however, the reader should recognize a progression in the chapters, a movement (roughly like that in Faulkner's own works-in-the-making— what Faulkner was talking about when he said that "the whole output or sum of an artist's work had to have a design")[6] flowing from darkness to light, from chaos to order, from ignorance to knowledge, despair to hope, evil to good, unbridled passion to passionate reason, and, most importantly, from the minimal consciousness of an idiot through stages of increasing complexity and awareness to the consciousness of the existentialist supreme being: a humanist miracle.

Notes

[1] Fredrick L. Gwynn and Joseph L. Blotner, *Faulkner in the University* (Charlottesville, VA, 1959) 24.

[2] Ludwig Binswanger, *Being-in-the-World*, trans. by Jacob Needleman (New York P 1967), 31.

[3] In Chapter I, I treat Benjy Compson and Merleau-Ponty's Phenomenology of the Body; in II, Flem Snopes and Jaspers and Marcel's Techno-

logical Man and Instrumental Reason; in III, Joe Christmas and Sartre's Pride, Shame, and Fear; in IV, Mink Snopes and Sartre and Merleau-Ponty on the Emotions; in V, Thomas Sutpen and Sartre's Bad Faith and the Original Choice; in VI, Quentin Compson and Merleau-Ponty's Phenomenology of Time; in VII, Faulkner's Romantic Women and Sartre on Female Sexuality; in VIII, Lucas Beauchamp and Sartre on the Look; in IX, Young Ike McCaslin and Jaspers' Encompassing and Authenticity and Marcel's philosophy of Intersubjectivity; in X, the Bundrens, Jaspers Encompasing and Marcel on the Mystery of the Family; in XI, the Generalissimo and Marcel's and Jaspers' Existential Phenomenological Religiosity.

4 Gwynn and Blotner, 279.

5 *Ibid*, 243.

6 Paul Levine, "Love and Money in the Snopes' Trilogy," *College English*, 23 (Dec. 1961), 196.

Chapter I

BENJY COMPSON AND
THE FIELD OF CONSCIOUSNESS

Many critics consider *The Sound and the Fury* to be Faulkner's greatest work. Through the "voices" of three members of the prominent Compson family of Jefferson, county seat of Yoknapatawpha County in Mississippi—Benjy, an idiot; Quentin, his suicidal brother incestuously obsessed with their promiscuous sister, Caddy; Jason, the oldest brother who is a cheap sadist and congenital liar, and Dilsey, the majestic mammy who devotes her life to the family—Faulkner explores the Compson's moral and social disintegration. The compositional center of the novel is the Benjy section. This, the first section, from which the other three evolve, extends over the thirty or so crucial years in which the tragic unraveling takes place. Benjy is a stroke of genius, a megaburst of creative energy activated by close observation. In the Deep South, as elsewhere, many rural areas and small towns seem to have their quota of idiots. Faulkner in his own Oxford neighborhood had for years passed a home with an idiot enclosed by an iron fence like the one enclosing Benjy in the Old Compson Place. Doubtless, this unfortunate and others like him served as models for Benjy as well as for Ike Snopes, the idiot-as-lover in *The Hamlet*. Once Faulkner spoke of Benjy as being

> [w]ithout thought or comprehension; shapeless, neuter, like something eyeless and voiceless which might have lived, existed merely because of its ability to suffer, in the beginning of life; half fluid, groping: a pallid and helpless mass of the mindless agony under [the] sun, in time yet not of it save that he could nightly carry with him that fierce, courageous being who was to him but a touch and a sound that may be heard on any golf links and a smell like trees, into the slow bright shapes of sleep.[1]

On April 7, 1928, Benjy's thirty-third birthday, we follow him from early morning until bedtime as he moves around in the community. Lacking any sense of sequential time, devoid of the cognitive processes, unable to make moral or social distinctions, and at various times accompanied by a succession of body servants (Luster, T.P., Versh, Caddy, Dilsey, and others) Benjy takes us first to the town golf course, which in better times had been part of the Compson property and now lies adjacent to it. He is accompanied by Luster, who is looking for a lost quarter, and hears a golfer yell, "Caddie!" The name immediately evokes an image of his sister long since departed the country—*His* Caddy, and he begins to moan. The moaning occurs often, as Benjy, omitting all transitions for changes in time and place, runs after a fleeing child, attends services at a Negro church, is a child sniffing at a perfume bottle, is unable to put his cold hands into his pockets, listens to a toilet flush. . . . We are almost as confused by these actions as Benjy: for clarification we can turn to phenomenology.

The chief contributions of the phenomenologists to literary criticism are their efforts to formulate an operative definition of consciousness and, more important for this book, their efforts to define perception, one of the most abused terms in the English language. This consciousness has become a catchall for other consciousness. Its misuse is especially notable in comments on Benjy Compson. Confusing perception and cognition, a critic writes that "we assent to this judgment involved in Benjy's perception that [Caddy] smelled like trees" and then compounds the error, writing that "only in his section of the first three in the book can we be perfectly sure that what the mind perceives actually occurred."[2] Failing to consider that Benjy, like Ike Snopes, was "blasted empty and clean forever of any thought" (*H* 98), a critic writes that an idiot's "'thoughts' are a good deal more fragmented and incoherent than Benjy's,"[3] and others compare him favorably with characters like Ike McCaslin, Sarty Snopes, and Bayard Sartoris as well as with the angels in Heaven and Jesus Christ.[4] These critics who endow

2

Benjy with intellectual, moral, and religious powers beyond his capacity have accepted the false premise that Benjy's world was present to him the way it is present to other human beings. His world is different from ours not only in the quantity of material at his disposal but also in the phenomenological structure of that material. His effort to bring order to the world was pathetic but unsuccessful, and however much we pity this being who remained "three years old thirty years" (*S&F* 87), we only add to the confusion when we try to force him into our world instead of witnessing his. In order to understand this victim of what the compassionate Ratliff calls the "primal injustice" (*H* 98), let us begin where the phenomenologists would have us begin, with Benjy's consciousness and not our own. Specifically, let us begin with the phenomenology of perception as set forth by the late Maurice Merleau-Ponty.[5]

For this existential-phenomenologist, perceptual consciousness, like all consciousness, is best described as a phenomenal field that reveals itself as a figure in coalescence with a background (*PP* 13). I am sitting in my room looking at the front of a bureau (figure) appearing against the ground of my bedroom wall. I shift my gaze to the drawer of the bureau, the ground of which is the front of the piece and therefore, the formulation of a second visual field. I shift my gaze to the knob of the drawer, with the drawer as ground and therefore, a third field and so forth. Although the perceptual field holds the world together for us, no field is ever complete. I am looking at the front of the bureau, but the back of the piece, which I cannot see is also a part of the field, and phenomenologically, coexists with the front. So do the bottom, top, and all the other parts of the bureau that are hidden from view (*PrP* 12-18).

Adding to the complexity of the perceptual field is the phenomenological fact that the same object can offer a multiplicity of configurations. I am looking at the wallpaper in my room. The ground of the paper is white with brown vertical stripes, upon which small figures, spaced at irregular intervals, give the impression of flower blossoms on a garden fence. When, however, I reverse ground and figure, the blossoms suddenly appear to be floating in a garden *enclosed* by the fence. Because of the multiple possibilities offered by the perceptual field, there are multiple chances for error (*PP* 297). I glance up from my desk and look at the moon (figure) rising above the horizon (ground) that includes trees, a church, and the church steeple. Low on the horizon, as the moon comes up, it appears to be much larger than it will appear to be once it moves away from the immediate ground to a place in the sky, both moons equally erroneous as to actual size. We can compound the error to the point where, perceptually, we do not know which is in movement, the moon or the steeple. All we have to do to create confusion is make the moon ground and the steeple figure: the steeple moves, the moon remains stationary (*SNS* 50-52).

In brief, perceptual consciousness is inexhaustible. It is a consciousness of endless perspectives (*PP* xxi), one vulnerable to inaccuracies, contradictions, and inconsistencies, and if Merleau-Ponty had gone no further with his description than this, he would have taken us no further than the Gestaltists, the empiricists, and the early phenomenologists. Merleau-Ponty's major contribution to our understanding of perceptual consciousness was to divest perception of all mentalistic processes and to place it where it properly belongs, in the body. Objects taken in their true identity, Merleau-Ponty insists, are taken not through the intellect but in the configuration of a sensory field revealed by the body. As I look at my bureau, I do not perceive projections of profiles of the piece, as the mentalists would have it (*SNS* 51). My eyes go straight to the bureau. I see it with them, not with my mind. My body with its senses, then, is the source of my orientation in the world. To say that a human being has access to a perceptual field is to say that his body is an opening upon and has access to the inexhaustible world of odors, colors, noises, tastes awaiting some sort of ordering (*PP* xvii, x). In the study of those persons who, like Benjy, move about in bodies of human beings but who are without mental capacity, this theory is all-important, for it allows us rare insights into a consciousness that could not bring figure and ground together in a way that makes perceptual sense. In treating Benjy with compassion, and yet without destroying his credibility, let us begin with the least complicated of the sensory perceptions and thus the one he handled most competently—his sense of smell.

Odors fill the air with indeterminate forms, they come from all directions at once, they are ubiquitous, but what the olfactory field loses in specificity, it more than makes up for in ease of access (*PP* 223). The survival of mammals, possibly the survival of man, can be traced as much as anything else to this ease; certainly one of the reasons Benjy was able to cope with the world as well as he did was his keen sense of smell. The simplicity of this field lies, first, in the physical fact that the nostrils are continuously open; to smell requires the most passive of efforts, an ability to breathe. Secondly, there is a minimal "separation" of figure and ground, a fact that adds to the ease with which this field can be constituted. Benjy could tell through his nose that the Compson servants were likable, for their rich body odor was inseparable from their bodies (*S&F* 363). He breathed and it was the Negroes' bodies which he suddenly possessed. Their odor was for him a part of the black body in precisely the same sense that their hands and feet were a part (*B* 174). Coursing through Benjy's body, the strong odors fused his body with theirs. He was no longer alone; he had friends. The pungent covers on T.P.'s bed, in which Benjy sometimes slept, gave him the boy's joyous presence (*S&F* 34), and the odors inhabiting Versh's cabin—a delicious combination of fireplaces, meals cooking, and unwashed bodies— smelled home (*S&F* 33). Benjy's sense of religion was founded, for the most part, upon his sense of smell. As he sat in the Negro church, the hairoil, cheap cologne, and body odors emanating from the members of the congregation formed a perfect and perfectly happy coalescence between his body and theirs. He was a member, too. (*S&F* 36).

Above all, Benjy reveled in Caddy's odors: "She smelled like trees" (*S&F* 51). Caddy was not perfect though, and the imperfection made its way through Benjy's nostrils. In an effort to quiet the restless boy, Caddy had sometimes offered him her perfume bottle. On one of these occasions, Benjy was afraid that she would leave him, and Caddy had taken "the stopper out and held it to my nose. 'Sweet Smell Good.' I went away and I didn't hush" (*S&F* 51). Phenomenologically, Caddy had made a bad situation worse, for she removed herself even further from the distraught boy. The odor of perfume is evanescent, it is amorphous, that is to say, it is all ground. Like ground, the essence of perfume publishes itself as a sort of absence. Benjy's fascination with and pleasure in perfume can be explained by this structure of its field: the odor teases and tantalizes, figure always on the verge of emerging from ground but never quite doing so. The field exists, as it were *à regret*, and Benjy breathed this regret (*B* 173-74). As Caddy held the bottle to his nose, the odor was making its escape from the bewildered boy even as it gave itself. Figure was there only to vanish, melting away on the spot. Quentin was wrong to say that Benjy did not like the smell of perfume (*S&F* 219). He disliked it no more than he disliked Caddy; he was puzzled by it, as he was puzzled by her gesture. Instead of her arms around him, solid as branches and smelling like leaves, she offered him the opposite: something like perfume, there and not there. No wonder he did not hush.

Because of his powerful olfactories, Benjy seemed to possess supernatural powers. Negroes in Jefferson looked upon him with awe, and they gave good reason for his extraordinary insight. It was his nose. He knew when his grandmother died, because he smelled it, Dilsey said (*S&F* 111). Roskus agreed. The distracted boy, the Negro believed, had sensed that his grandmother and father were dying (*S&F* 38)—had brought the figure of death out of the ground of odors of sick rooms. Almost as wonderful, he did not have to listen in order to understand. He smelled what Roskus had told about—that "*bad luck*" permeating the Compson family (*S&F* 34). Listening to Benjy moan one morning as they were leaving for church, Dilsey again gave credence to his ability to raise perceptual sense to extrasensory levels. Once under way he would stop, she said: "He smellin hit" (*S&F* 360).

The odors of Negroes, perfume, and sick rooms and death which filled Benjy's body were accompanied by sounds. The aural field, like the olfactory, is continuously open, but it is more complex than the olfactory (*PP* 212). Sounds, like odors, can easily be classified as good or bad, a classification that even Benjy could make. The sounds of the Negroes singing in church made their soothing way through his body, just as did their odors (*S&F* 366). The cacophonous sounds of his mother crying had the opposite effect: they tore into his body with such force that they made him cry too (*S&F* 78). A myriad of other sounds lying outside these simple extremes seem to have been lost on Benjy. Speech sounds were especially troublesome. He was, for example, unable to distinguish between statements and questions. Falling inflection, the aural ground for statements, and rising inflection, the ground for question, were beyond him: "'What is it.' Caddy said. 'What are you trying to tell Caddy. Did they send him out, Versh'" (*S&F* 5). Benjy also had great trouble with the meaning of words themselves, even the simplest.

The human body is a living instrument that vibrates to all sounds, especially the sounds of the human voice. We give words phenomenal value through the way our bodies receive them. The spoken word has a physiognomy because we take toward it, as toward a person, a certain attitude which appears the moment the word is spoken. I hear the word *warm*, and a sense of warmth invades my body; *hard* brings a stiffening. For the human being, then, sensuous sounds are, before anything else, physical events; only later do they receive cognitive value (*PP* 235-236). Benjy's body was phenomenologically deaf to all but the simplest sounds; his body could provide words with neither physiological nor conceptual significance, as we see when Versh warned him against going outside in the December weather: "It's too cold out there" (*S&F* 3). *Cold* made no vibrations in Benjy. It was as if his eardrums were acoustical stripping, figure suffocated in a spongy ground. Only when he went out of doors would cold mean anything, but even then he could not make a connection between his cold hands and warm pockets. *"Keep your hands in your pockets,"* Caddy said (*S&F* 3), command sinking without a trace to the bottom of aural quicksand, along with all the other linguistic debris. The best way to move Benjy was not by voice but by touch, as Caddy knew so well.

Touch incarnates. It is intimacy incarnated, for it delivers the body to the thing touched. Unlike odors and sounds, which we have at a distance, the tactile field cleaves to our skin, hair, tongue; we cannot distance our bodies from it. This field brings home, as no other field does, the phenomenological fact that we go to the world through our bodies. More than any other sense, touch involves all of the body. I touch satin and my whole body feels smooth. Ice sends shivers over me. In touch, the parts of the body become one part, carried along in all its organic simultaneity (*PP* 316-17). No wonder, then, Benjy was forever touching and loved to be touched. Touching, his body was at last fully conscious of the world: touching fences, weeds, flowers gave him things (*S&F* 1,15,397); touching Versh, T.P. (*S&F* 5,8,11) and, best, Caddy gave him other human beings. For Benjy's sake we would like to believe, as critics tell us, that he served as Caddy's active conscience,[6] but the truth is just the reverse. Caddy used Benjy as her conscience, reading into his actions her own guilt. Unlike Quentin, who was greatly concerned with Caddy's immorality, Benjy had no thoughts about her morals, one way or the other. His communication with her never went beyond the perceptual level. She was his through their bodies, "her arms around me and her cold bright face against mine," her hands rubbing "my hands" (*S&F* 3,5). Benjy continually reached out to Caddy. He held onto her dress, and he cried when Charlie fondled her (*S&F* 57). Someone else was touching her and he was not—that was all. Benjy was closer to Caddy than he was to anyone else because she was the one who touched him more than anyone else and more importantly encouraged him to touch her. When Caddy was not there, her slipper was. Benjy loved this object because, like Caddy it felt smooth and because it *looked* like something he wanted to touch. Like Caddy, it invited him to touch it.

Our greatest perceptual concern, as well as that of the phenomenologist and the creative writer is the field of vision and for good reason. For the human being the world is made to be seen, and what brings the visual spectacle to life is color. Colors are that part of the visual field which, more than any other, deliver the world to the body. That is why we are so aware of them. Before we notice geometric configurations of objects, their sizes and shapes, colors have already called forth from the body physiological responses inherent in the phenomenological structure of colors themselves (*PP* 224,304-05). This response invariably involves touch. When we look at colors, there is no distinction between touch and sight (*SNS* 15), as Benjy shows when he looks at Caddy's slipper. This object, which members of Benjy's family and a covey of servants used as a goad, a threat, and a tranquilizer, had once been white but, over the years, had faded to a soft, dirty yellow (*S&F* 395), a color eliciting from the body a desire to stroke (*PP* 209). Out of the soliciting yellow, the smooth touch of satin, came the soothing yellow-satin-Caddy, and stroking it-her, Benjy was absorbed, borne along easily and restfully and effortlessly, at peace with himself and his world.

Our bodies take up our abode not only in yellow but in all other colors, each one speaking its own phenomenological language, enticing from the body a variety of responses, and none more enticing that red. The red field is a command to touch. Here, figure and ground coalesce in such a manner that, phenomenologically, the body *does* touch (*PP* 209-11). Before I have any comprehension of a red dress, of a red light, my body has already taken up residence in them, as Benjy's in the flag on the golf course and in the tie adorning Miss Quentin's lover, but the red grabbing him first and and holding him longest was fire. One of the few ways to pacify the disturbed boy was to set him before a fireplace, letting him follow the flames up and down the walls of Roskus' cabin and around the walls of his mother's bedroom. The red flames made Mrs. Compson's rings jump, jump so high that they landed on Caddy (*S&F* 1,59,34,75,76), and Benjy landed there with them. Red drew him fascinated onto his mother's red and yellow cushion, into Caddy's eyes. He crawled with *"the bright, smooth shapes"* into Caddy's hair, into Versh's glowing face (*S&F* 8,88,69,34). He could not resist red flames, even in the countenance of an enemy, and so he made his way into the eyes and mouth of Miss Quentin, Caddy's illegitimate daughter whom she had named after her brother, the only man she ever loved. He opened his mouth to swallow the match flame Miss Quentin's lover offered, and at last he followed red to his death when he set the old Compson Place on fire and perished in it (*S&F* 82,59 *M* 322).

One of the dangers in a phenomenological analysis of perception lies in the impression that sensory fields operate separately. Nothing could be further from the truth; each field blends into all the others in a manner similar to the working together of my muscles and bones in the typing of these words. Benjy's immersion in the slipper is a good example of the blending of the senses, in this instance, sight and touch. Perceptual reality depends upon the harmonizing, and the miracle of the body is that it senses "automatically" which fields are necessary for the perception of any particular object. Unfortunately for Benjy, this miracle did not always take place, as he discovered when he burned his fingers on the black fire door (*S&F* 72). The door did not *look* hot. So perfectly do the sensory fields blend that we can substitute one for the other. This substitution, synesthesia, is a cliché with poets, painters, and other artists who recognize the organic nature of the sensory fields (*PP* 222-34). There is no way of knowing, Faulkner himself suggests, "where seeing stops and smelling begins, or hearing stops and seeing begins" (*KG* 26); our "eyes" sometimes go "a little blind with the strain of listening" (*S* 177). With

Benjy synesthesia was not a rhetorical device. It was an act of desperation, the attempt to provide himself with some kind of perceptual information, any kind, and in desperation his frantic body used the first sensory field available, not the most appropriate. Thrashing wildly Benjy smelled "the clothes flapping," heard "it getting dark" (*S&F* 15,89).

As these examples suggest, Benjy's substitution of one sense for another nearly always involved the visual field. Of all the perceptual fields, vision is not only the most important. It is the most complicated. It offers the greatest number of possibilities, but it is also the hardest to effect, for of all the fields, vision is the one most dependent upon an adequate constitution of space. Although space affects the olfactory and auditory fields, odors and sounds coming from a distance, it is not of paramount importance for these senses. Neither does space have much effect on certain visual fields—colors, for instance—and because of this, we can see a spot of green on the horizon long before we can make out the pine trees. Color may breathe life into the visual field, but in separating one object from all other objects, space delivers the world from chaos (*PP* 222-24).

Ordinarily, we have no trouble with space, for our eyes adjust to the object at which we are looking in exactly the same way that our eardrums adjust to sound, automatically. Benjy, on the other hand, had as much difficulty focusing properly as he did hearing properly. For him vision was monocular, figure detached from ground. In this two-dimensional world, images floated vaguely in front of things, having no "real place" in the world (*PP* 233). Giacometti used his knowledge of space as the basis for his sculpture. He forces viewers to see the objects he created in the way he wanted them to be seen: one step too close to his figure or one step too far away, and binocular spatiality became monocular, the visual field in collapse (*EA* 47-49). Objects at a distance were for Benjy what Giacometti's figures are for the uninitiated. They float vaguely in front of things; they have no established place in the world. This is disclosed in Benjy's continual misuse of the preposition *on* for the prepositions and adverbs of spacial depth: the flag flapping "on the bright grass," the bird slanting "on it," trees black" on the sky" (*S&F* 2,56). While feeding Benjy, Luster teased him by moving the spoon just enough to change depth, causing the boy to bite the air (*S&F* 345). In these instances, the field that should have been constituted in depth—figure coalescing with ground—is given in two dimensions, figure on a flat ground.

The well-known mirror scene gave early indications that Benjy would have difficulty with spatial depth. At about the fourth or fifth month, an infant can recognize the reflection of another person in a mirror, but when the other speaks, the child is startled and turns to look at him. He cannot understand how there can be two persons but only one voice; later, when he is about a year old, he will find out why. Just as intercommunication of the senses is given to the body as part of its definition, so is the perceptual knowledge that the world is readily accessible to it. A child will, for instance, naturally and without thinking, hold a watch up to his ear to hear why it ticks, and so, naturally and without thinking, he will discover why there is only one person and one voice. He will crawl to the mirror and inspect it. Instinctively extending his hand, he will touch the hard surface of the glass and not a person. This discovery is a critical one, for at this stage in his perceptual development he becomes aware of the illusion of depth, as the child now shows. Naturally, without thinking, he turns to the person, placing him with the voice. The person is in space where he belongs, not in the mirror (*PrP* 122-32). Benjy never discovered the illusion. For him there was no difference between the two-dimensional surface of the mirror and the three-dimensional depth of the world: "Caddy and Jason were fighting in the mirror," and Mr. Compson "went into the mirror and fought too. He lifted Caddy up. She fought. . . . Father held her. She kicked at Jason. He rolled into the corner, out of the mirror. . . . They were all out of the mirror" (*S&F* 79).

All of his life Benjy was baffled by space, his great enemy. The reason he had so much difficulty walking lies here. It is no mere coincidence that human beings hold themselves upright as they move about in the world and that among their first acts is the attempt to raise themselves to a vertical position and maintain it. We stand straight and walk erect not wholly because of skeletal and muscular conformation but because we are beings occupying human space. Nor does this existential inherence in space occur only at the beginning of life. It blesses every future movement with human meaning, and with the weakening of our vertical hold, we collapse into an amorphous mass (*PP* 254). Benjy approximated this mass, occupying space not as we occupy it but as an almost shapeless, flaccid object. He sat "loosely, utterly motionless save for his head, which made a continual bobbing sort of movement" (*S&F* 343). Presumably his head also bobbed when he was standing. It is for this reason he had to hold onto the fence while watching the golfers or onto the gate while waiting for Caddy. When Benjy walked, he traveled at the oblique, the vertical hold cock-eyed. At five or six years old, he was still being helped across the small brook running through the Compson property and carried up slight inclines. The corrugated pig lot was an obstacle course, but even when the terrain offered no challenge, he needed someone to hold his hand as he moved along (*S&F* 17,14,23,3). Benjy also navigated poorly when grown. He stumbled, tiffled, and shuffled, moving and bobbing as he tried to maintain his balance, a mosaic of broken movements.

Space is the phenomenological ground which, as I have suggested, keeps us at a distance from everything else in the world, a distance Benjy was unable to maintain. Experiencing a phenomenal "shrinkage of space," he could not hold things off, keep them out there where they belonged (*PP* 286-88); indeed, objects took up their abode in the worst possible place, his own body. After he had drunk some wine, the hog trough in which he was sitting would not stay still, and so he had to hold to the sides. He climbed out of the trough and tried to mount a box, which would not hold still, either. It jumped away from him, hitting the back of his head—trough and box "going around," rooted in his weaving body (*S&F* 24,48,25). He was not much better off when he was sober. His box of trinkets "was full of stars" that were still when he was still; when he moved they "glinted and sparkled" (*S&F* 50). The effect was the same in the famous monument scenes. Benjy, T.P., and Mrs. Compson were riding along in the family surrey, and he noticed the sun glinting on the tops of the wheels, "the bright shapes" that were going smoothly and steadily "on both sides, and when the carriage circled the monument, the shapes "on one side stopped," while those on the other side went more slowly. After the carriage had come to a halt on the square, the shapes stopped, and when the carriage had come to a halt on the square, the shapes stopped, and when the vehicle moved, "the shapes followed on," fixed fast in the body of the disturbed boy (*S&F* 11-13). They were fixed so firmly that when, at a later time, Luster tried to circle the monument from the the opposite side, it was for Benjy perceptual chaos. Phenomenologically it was more. It was an experience so frightening as to be physically painful. The shapes, anchored fast in one side of his body, were being torn out, and Benjy bellowed: "unbelievable crescendo." Then, the appearance of Jason, who jerked Queenie around, and the shapes, the trees, the monument were restored to the right side of Benjy's body where they belonged, all in their "ordered place" (*S&F* 400-01).

That Benjy could not place the shapes in space was bad enough, but of greater significance, phenomenologically, was his difficulty in placing himself in space, that is, in recognizing himself as a figure in the ground of the world. Mirrors can play an important part in establishing this identity. It is not surprising that a child can recognize others in mirrors before he can recognize himself, as Benjy recognized his father and brother and sister, for he had seen them in a way that he had never seen himself—as a whole. Although the normal infant has some introspective knowledge of himself and can see his hands and his feet, he has never seen them as parts of his body. For himself, he is all hands and feet; when he looks into a mirror, he sees much more: a strange body he does not recognize. In an effort to discover who the stranger is, he gazes into the mirror and reaches into space toward the body which he sees; then, discovering that it is beyond reach, he tries another method of identification. He begins exploring the body nearer him. He examines not only the hands and feet but head and chest, and because he can *feel* them at the same time he can see them in the mirror, he discovers they are *his* (*PrP* 127-141). Benjy never made this discovery. As he watched Caddy, Jason, and his father in the mirror, he never saw a fourth figure, and even if he had, he would not have recognized him.

Benjy's failure to recognize himself was his greatest failure, for it deprived him of his sense of belonging in the world. We occupy social and cultural levels because we behave like others, and the basis of our behavior is mimesis. Phenomenologically, our entrance into the cultural world occurs when we perceive that our body is like that of another, when there is one-for-one correspondence between our body and another's, when specifically, we can use our body as others use theirs (*PrP* 117-127). Invisible to himself, almost totally ignorant that his body was like others, Benjy was poorly prepared to imitate anyone else. He was, for instance, unable to dress himself. In itself clothing has no significance, but the aims of dressing are highly significant. It is a way of celebrating our bodies. With little or no perception of his body, Benjy felt no need for celebration. For similar reasons he never learned the connection between soap and water and personal hygiene or between knives, forks, and spoons and table manners (*S&F* 7,337,376).

Benjy's isolation from the social world is even better illustrated in his inability to acquire the ultimate act of social behavior, speech. We are predisposed to speaking in the way we are predisposed to hearing and seeing. The vocal cords are made for speaking as the eyes for looking, the hands for handling, the feet for walking (*PP* 183-86). All that an infant has to do in order to repeat speech sounds his mother is making is to observe her lips and listen, and he will capture them. The only sounds Benjy made were also, unfortunately, the sounds his mother most frequently made: moans, whimpers, sobs (*S&F* 12,52,66). Benjy's speech organs were intact, as were his eyes and his ears, but he could no more raise the figure that is the meaning of a sentence from the ground of linguistic sounds than he could recognize rain from its sound on the roof (*S&F* 82). This inability is the reason for many of his troubles but particularly for his trouble with the little Burgess girl. He was not trying to rape the child, as Jason believed; he was trying to speak to her. As a child Benjy had delighted in waiting at the front gate for Caddy to come home from school, and years after she had left Jefferson, he still waited for her to walk up. Even the sound of the name—one of the few pleasant sounds he ever heard—was enough to start in him a joyful moaning (*S&F* 66). In order to hear it, he would listen for the golfers to shout to their caddies. That he could not say her name had worried Caddy, and after school hours she had tried through repetition to teach him. "What is it. . . . What are you trying to tell Caddy," she would ask (*S&F* 1,37,5). Benjy could never say her name or tell her what he was trying to say, just as he was unable to tell the Burgess child. On the day that the gate had inadvertently been left unfastened, she had come along the street, as Caddy had, and Benjy had run after her as he had run after Caddy. He had no more intention of molesting her than he had in molesting Caddy: "I opened the gate and they stopped, turning. I was trying to say, and I caught her, trying to say, and she screamed and I was trying to say" (*S&F* 63,64).

Perceptual consciousness postulates a field, the result of an active dialectic between the body and the world from which a figure emerges in space "against" a background; figure and ground emerge simultaneously as a whole. For Benjy the emergence continuously failed to take place, for instead of appearing as a whole, the perceptual field was atomized. For the whole, Benjy substituted laborious and confused detail. Where Luster, for example, inferred that the golfers were playing a game, Benjy was incapable of discovering this totality. He looked "through the fence, between the curling flower spaces [and] . . . could see them hitting. . . . They were coming toward where the flag was and I went along the fence. . . . They took the flag out, and they were hitting. Then they put the flag back and then they went to the table, and he hit and the other hit." The perceptual field in chaos, figures without ground, Benjy "watched them going away. . . . They were hitting little, across the pasture" (*S&F* 1-2). Phenomenologically, fragmentation is the first indication of idiocy (*PP* 282), not of clarity, as some critics have maintained,[7] and there were times when his perception was hardly that of an idiot. In his disoriented world, the bowl from which he ate came and went under its own power; flowers disappeared and returned without apparent reason. On these occasions the act of perception became for Benjy a B-grade horror film with seat cushions flying about (*S&F* 30,66,78), and his own hands and voice detached. He reached out toward the fire door, Dilsey yelled at Luster, and "my hand jerked back," while "my voice was going loud" (*S&F* 78).

All of his life Benjy was confused by this fragmented, inarticulate, unarticulated world, but in the dark even this world was unavailable. Nighttime brings radical perceptual changes to all of us, not just to Benjy. At night the world becomes all ground. Figures that emerge in daylight all but disappear in a ground of inky blackness. The world loses its life-giving colors, space no longer holds objects apart (*PP* 183), and Benjy looked at trees "black on the sky," at old Dan "scuffling along, into the moon" (*S&F* 57). One night Miss Quentin crawled out of her window into the tree: "*The shaking went down the tree, then it came out and we watched it go away across the grass*" (*S&F* 90,91). Nighttime is more than the absence of light. It is a time when we lose not only our contact with things and others but contact with ourselves. Night "is pure depth without foreground or background." Depriving us of surfaces and distances, it infiltrates our senses; it engulfs, smothering our identity (*PP* 283). For those who, like Benjy, have little sense of who they are, this destruction is inevitable. In the dark in bed with Caddy, he lost his identity in hers. The last time we hear from him, Dilsey was in the bedroom with them and turned off the light. It "went black, except the door. Then the door went black. Caddy said, 'Hush Maury' putting her hand on me." Infiltrated by the dark, existing only in Caddy's touch, Benjy lost all sense of his own identity. Lying beside her he was unable to bring himself out of the common ground they were sharing. No light, no distance, no surface separated them: "So I stayed hushed. We could hear us. We could hear the dark" (*S&F* 92). Mr. Compson came in to say goodnight, and Benjy regained himself, figure emerging for a few seconds only to give in to the pure ground that is transvestism (*PrP* 135,148): "Father went to the door and looked at us again. The dark came back, and he stood black in the door, and then the door turned black again. Caddy held me and I could hear us all and the darkness. . . . Then the dark began to go in smooth, bright shapes, like it always does, even when Caddy says that I have been asleep" (*S&F* 92).

Sleep provides an even more striking experience of unreality than night provides. At night we have little difficulty holding onto the general setting of daytime, as anyone knows who makes his way about a dark room familiar to him. In fact, night is as natural a phenomenon as day, and thus we are assured of our orientation, even in pitch dark. It is the assurance that the spatiality of objects will in any fixed setting remain constant, whether the objects are visible of invisible. Sleep, however, brings phenomenal changes. Instead of occupying space in the room, objects appearing in our sleep are a part of us. They are fixed in our bodies, not in the world around us. It is for this reason that while we are asleep and dreaming, we are completely immersed in our dreams. Our dreams are we, we are our dreams. Only upon our exit from this subjective world of "inner" space and our entrance into a space alive with realities, the waking world of perceptions, do we realize that we have been dreaming(*PP* 284,303). Benjy was never certain of his entrances and exits: "the smooth, bright shapes" in his dreams were the same "smooth" shapes he saw on the "bright tops of wheels," "*the bright, smooth shapes*" in the fire (*S&F* 92,11,69,79), the shapes that appeared when he was drunk and when Mr. Burgess knocked him cold (*S&F* 25,26,64). For this idiot, unable to separate reality from unreality, the illusory fields of dreamland and drunkenness and unconsciousness were no different from the perceptual fields, and however noble the intentions of the critics in trying to convince us that he did know the difference, whatever their earnest attempts to offer him a helping hand, the poor boy is still stumbling about somewhere in Yoknapatawpha, out there somewhere as confused as ever.

Notes

[1] Joseph Blotner, *Faulkner A Biography* (New York: Random House, 1974) I, 571.

[2] Hyatt Waggoner, *William Faulkner. From Jefferson to the World* (Lexington, KY: U of Kentucky P, 1959) 45, 46. Critics continually make unwarranted use of "mind" in connection with Benjy: Cleanth Brooks, *William Faulkner. The Yoknapatawpha Country* (New Haven, CT: Yale UP 1963), 5; Irving Howe, "The Passing of a World," *Twentieth Century Interpretations of the Sound and the Fury*, ed. Michael H. Cowan (Englewood Cliffs, NJ: Prentice Hall 1968) 36,37; Michael Millgate, "William Faulkner: The Problem of Point of View," *Patterns of Commitment in American Literature*, ed. Marston La France (Toronto: U of Toronto P, 1967) 183.

[3] Irving Howe, *William Faulkner. A Critical Study*, (Chicago: U of Chicago P, 1962) 162.

[4] Joseph Gold, *William Faulkner. A Study in Humanism from Metaphor to Discourse* (Norman: U of Oklahoma P, 1966), 70; Evelyn Scott, "On William Faulkner's *The Sound and the Fury*," *Twentieth Century Interpretations*, 26; Carvel Collins, "Christianity and Freudian Structures," *Twentieth Century Interpretations*, 72; Richard P. Adams, *Faulkner: Myth and Motion* (Princeton, NJ: Princeton UP, 1968), 224.

[5] For more on the field of consciousness, see Aron Gurwitsch; on the phenomenology of color, Kurt Goldstein; on phenomenology and literature, Roman Ingarden. So far as I know, the only existential-phenomenologist Faulkner knew was Jean-Paul Sartre. He said that once, while "drunk" he had "talked with . . . Sartre." The French writer, Faulkner said, "was wrong to do away with God." Sartre, on the other hand, wrote in *The Atlantic Monthly* in 1946 of "the enormous admiration" Faulkner enjoyed in France,

and in 1945 he said, "*Pour les jeunes en France, Faulkner c'est un dieu.*" (Blotner, 1547,1440,1221,1187).

Parenthetically, this god's greatest creation is Benjy, for he more than any other character in Faulkner engages and thus enriches our perceptions—in a word, teaches us to see "with the eye of [the] artist." Of this perceptual act, the artist Robert Irwin, a student of Edmund Husserl whose *Ideas* laid the foundation for present-day existential phenomenology, has said: "There is nothing more real, more interesting, more powerful, more informative, more important, or more beautiful." (Calvin Tomkins, *The New Yorker*, 1985, 147-148). In Benjy, Faulkner, teamed with Merleau-Ponty, unveils this beauty.

[6] John W. Hunt, *William Faulkner: Art in Theological Tension* (Syracuse, NY: Syracuse UP 1965), 90; Irving Howe, *William Faulkner: A Critical Study*, 165; Robert Humphrey, "The Form and Function of Stream of Consciousness in William Faulkner's *The Sound and the Fury*," *University of Kansas Review*, 19 (August 1952), 36.

[7] Ida Fasel, "Spatial Form and Spatial Time," *Western Humanities Review*, 16 (Summer 1962), 231; Michael H. Cowan, "Introduction," *Twentieth Century Interpretations*, 9; Hunt, 86,89; Adams, 115.

Chapter II

FLEM AND HIS ILK

We make our way into the world through our senses. To perceive the world means that we are "attached to it by a natural bond" (*SNS* 53), by "an existential connection" (*PP* 170), and that our rapport is always "accompanied" by feelings (*PI* 39). Percept and affect are inseparable; to perceive something is to feel something. Their structures of perception severely restricted, idiots like Benjy Compson and Ike Snopes were as incapable of an adequately human emotional response to the world as they were of seeing it clearly. Benjy's confused description of the golf course can be matched only by his mistaking a golfer's "caddie" for his Caddy (*S&F* 1); Ike's response to the cow was almost as chaotic: she was a source of love, not of milk and meat (*H* 213). To these retardeds the world was a quagmire of sensations through which they laboriously slogged, but on one occasion Ike gave the impression that this world, for all its imperfections, was preferable to that of at least one other person, his kinsman and "guardian" Flem (*H* 99). When Flem insisted that Ike pronounce his name, the loud cries of indignation (*H* 98) were directed at a man numb to any feelings at all, for others or for himself, and in studying him and his actions we will be studying, according to Karl Jaspers, not an isolated phenomenon but one that, in combining the methods of technology and business to become wealthy, becomes also "man in the modern age" (*MMA*). Owing to "the magnitude of the question of what it may make of man," Jaspers has written, "technology is perhaps the cardinal theme for the comprehension of our present situation" (*OGH* 99). More specifically, he makes clear, the theme is man's ever-increasing dehumanization, and it is concerned not only with the technologist who would turn society into a single general factory where everything is reduced to utilitarian function but with the businessman who runs the factory (*OGH* 98, *E&H* 74). Their close relationship is manifest in certain modes of perception which they share and which, like all perceptions, are disclosed by their bodies.

For an adequate definition of the perceiving body, we should consider it as moving *in concerto* on three levels: as a "physico-chemical" mass, as a biological organism, and as a human entity capable of transcending the restrictions imposed by physics, chemistry, and biology (*SB* 162). All three levels are indispensable, the three bound together in a living unity of action, but sometimes, as with Benjy and Ike, this unity is missing. Adrift somewhere on the biological level, these unfortunates were deprived of the convenience of animal instincts but were unable to take advantage of behavior common to human beings (*MMA* 195). They reacted to the world around them, and that is about all. Perceptual fields devoid of affects, Flem was barely sentient, existentially not much further advanced than a chemical mass. Dead, "soft" flesh (*H* 25) was packed in several layers onto a boneless frame giving the impression of something "bulbous blond omnivorous" (*H* 67). From whatever perspective, back side or front, the thing was "thick" and "shapeless" (*H* 69). The largest aperture in it was "a tight," stingy "seam . . . stained slightly at the corners with tobacco" (*H* 59). The facial skin and hair on the head were dead and colorless (*M* 198), and two "opaque eyes" (*T* 4), "the color of stagnant pond water" (*M* 198) never looked at anyone (*T* 169). A "cold" (*H* 182), monochromatic figure inserted in a monochromatic world, it was a collection of physical and chemical stimuli. Flem gives this impression not only as a benumbed body and "blank" face but, more tellingly, in the relation of the face and the head to the body. They were detachable. "Broad" and "flat," the "face" was an expressionless mask hooked onto a head moored to a trunk (*H* 25). As Flem sat at his desk in Varner's store, it "hung suspended like a balloon above the soiled dog-eared paper." It showed "no sign of life in it, not even breathing, as if the body which belonged to it had learned somehow to use over and over again its own suspirations" (*H* 97). What the body learned is for technology and business the most important of all lessons, that of pure function: Flem's body, like a chemical factory, recycled its own wastes(*MB II*: 50).

To be sentient and human "I *am* my body" only to the extent that it is "irreducible" to "determinate" chemical and physical formulae. I am myself as my body only as it is open to all sensory possibilities (*MB I*: 113-28 esp. 127). In contrast, the functional body is reduced to the possibilities required by the function. It is the body in which abstract properties replace human affects (*MB* 124), and in the business world where the first demand is service, the most important property is "specialization or specification of the self" (*B&H* 172). A clerk, for example, must be a specialist in his field, and so when he approaches us, he becomes that specialist. Like an actor playing a role, he detaches himself from all personal identity; his body is no longer his but a salesperson's. This person's walk is a glide, its voice low and politely inquisitive, solicitous. We ask to see a tie, and our clerk gives a performance, first holding the object up as if it were the royal silk and then deftly and reverently knotting it on a forefinger. The walk, the voice, the display—each gesture mechanical and he a collection of mannerisms, well trained and all business (*B&N* 59).

Flem differed from this clerk in one important respect. He did not play a role. He *was* a function, business personified. Metronomically, he arrived at Varner's store at a set hour early in the morning, he carried out his duties at exactly the same pace each day, and he left at the same hour each evening (*H* 58-60). The essence of efficient service, he won the confidence of country customers, no mean feat. At first "the women . . . came to look at him" (*H* 58); later, "all the countryside," in order to get a close-up, warily entered the store and made "trivial purchases" (*H* 59). Their fears were groundless, for they found not the ogre for which they were looking but a function that served them. The continuously moving jaw added to this impression. Part of an expressionless face, this appendage worked with the well-oiled regularity of a piston in a cylinder and with something of the unvarying routine the owner brought to all his activities, including recreational (*M* 155, *H* 22,68). Flem whittled sticks in the same mechanical manner that he worked and chewed, the slivers "curling with neat deliberation before the moving knife," and he whittled silently (*H* 358).

Nothing irritates customers more than a gabby clerk, for with the breaking of silence, he slips out of his specialty. "I am a human being, an individual," he is saying with his chatter. "Treat me like one" (*B&N* 59-60). But individuals, customers know, are not computerized; they talk and they talk back. Since the sole demand of the customer is for service, he seeks the expert that can render this service, not companionship. Working silently, mechanically, and efficiently as he served customers and looked up accounts, Flem was a clerk and nothing else. The responses of this "apparatus" (*MMA* 37) were generally limited to "Yes and No to direct questions" (*H* 64), and when the answer could not be given in monosyllables, the speech was "matter-of-fact, succinct" (*H* 69). Away from the store he spoke only of business matters (*H* 92), and when he walked past the congregation loafing on "the gallery," he addressed them as a group in a business-like tone, neuturally, "Gentlemen" (*H* 309). In an effort to further an image of quiet and unobtrusive service for all, Flem moved about noiselessly, his feet in sneakers (*H* 167).

His other clothing was also appropriate to his station. Just as the public is offended by the talkative human clerk, it is miffed with the clerk who would express his individuality in his dress. Poorly trained clerks, like the poorly trained waiter at the Café Mably, insist on individuality, and wearing gaudy shirts, sometimes without a "collar" or appearing without a "vest," they forget that service is what they should be offering and not themselves (*N* 98). Jody Varner, whom Flem easily overtook and passed in his bid for control of the store, made this mistake. He habitually wore a "soiled white shirt," baggy and unpressed pants, "a costume at once ceremonial and negligee" (*H* 11). As negligent in business matters as in dress and personal habits, this individualist would often leave the store unattended and depend on the "customers" to wait on "themselves," paying for what they took in a cash box open to all (*H* 28). He was unconcerned when they stole a few cheap items, and when they found him making "mistakes" in his "favor" in their accounts, he would make "a joke of it," leaving them to wonder about the mistakes they did not catch.

Flem, on the other hand, "never made mistakes" (*H* 65), nor was he ever absent from the store, nor did he joke or laugh or make any other effort to be personable. The opposite from the old-fashioned clerk, flesh and blood, he was a forerunner of the modern employee, bland and anonymous, and his clothes reflected anonymity. Never forgetting that service was more important than self-expression, he bought a "new white shirt" (*H* 60), and on his head sat a "cloth cap" which, like the shirt, blended well with the service. It was "gray" (*H* 22). His trousers were of the same neutral shade (*H* 25). As soon as the clerk could afford it, he bought the most important item of his uniform, the one he wore until his death: a small, neat bow tie that topped off the conspicuous inconspicuousness of the functionary (*H* 66). Will Varner inadvertently paid Flem a compliment when, after the first week or so at the store, he did not know his clerk's name. "You there," Will said (*H* 61). Will's daughter looked at this function and ticked off two globous eyes, one globous head, one seam. "Papa," she yelled, "here's the man again" (*H* 167). "In proportion" that "function" had swallowed "up" the man (*B&H* 150), it had become the man, one interesting for his ability to take a conglomeration of physical and chemical properties and use it not only to uproot Jody Varner but also to beat the boss out of "the Old Frenchman place" (*H* 182) and in the process to marry the boss's daughter (*H* 166). What the peasants, Jody, Will, and Eula looked at and did not recognize was the almost perfect coalescence of consciousness and function (*B&N* 58), the first automated entity to appear in the County, a self-made man that made of others the same thing he made of himself (*T* 129).

Our bodies are quickened by a "density" that we feel, and when we perceive others, "by analogy" we "confer on them . . . a [perceptual] density of the same order" (*MB II*: 28-29). Conversely, if our bodies are denied the density, we confer the objectivity that we ourselves exist. For Benjy and Ike the world of idiocy was the real world inhabited by creatures whose sole purpose in living was to annoy them. Existence reduced to function, treating an entity called Flem as something called clerk, Flem saw others as functions too, and on this principle he founded the "Snopes industry" (*T* 129). A businessman and an advocate as well as the embodiment of "the technical life-order" (*MMA* 37), a "function" whose power to limit another came from his power to limit himself (*B&H* 168), Flem established his kinsmen as an assembly line with which he attempted systematically to take over Frenchman's Bend and everything adjacent to it. Just as his success as businessman was dependent upon his own "specialization" (*B&H* 172), with its interrelated properties of automation and anonymity, so the assembly line was dependent upon properties that are closely associated with specialization and with each other, standardization (*E&H* 74) and "predication" (*B&H* 151). Flem's success was also dependent upon beings who, like himself, were existentially separated from their bodies, beings given over to the claims of function (*E&H* 74).

Ordinary Snopeses came in two models, both models offering evidence that "man seems . . . capable of self-oblivion, of losing himself and finding contentment in impersonality," that "we are on the road to . . . functional absorption" (*E&H* 74). Number One Snopes ran to obesity and facial features which were, like Flem's, lost to all animation or, like Eck's, "quiet empty open" (*H* 74). This "face beginning less than an inch below his hairline" (*H* 71) was notable because it was detachable. Just as the balloon floated off Flem's shoulders, so Eck's "empty open face . . . seemed to have been a mere afterthought to the thatching of the skull, like the binding of a rug" (*H* 74). It was as "harmless" and as still as Ike's, and Eck as a blacksmith was on a par with Ike as a servant, shoeing horses the way Ike swept floors, "working steadily but in a dreamlike state in which what actually lived inside him apparently functioned somewhere else, paying no heed to and having no interest in . . . what his hands were doing" (*H* 75). This model featured, besides Eck and Ike, the huge, "bear-shaped" Saint Elmo, an eating machine as voracious and functional as a garbage truck. Like rats and goats, it would ingest anything it could swallow (*H* 363-64).

Number Two Snopes is also notable for a body that could be detached from the chassis. The prototype was the father of Saint Elmo, I. O. Snopes (*H* 364), whose nose, eyes, mouth were "in a constant state" of uncoordinated diarrhetic movement, each feature going its own way as if it had "no relation" to any other, "save that the same skull bore them, the same flesh fed them" (*H* 230). Further evidence of this separation is the look in I. O.'s eyes when he tried to concentrate. Attempting to understand what Ratliff was saying, he watched with an "intentness which . . . seemed actually to be no integral part either of the organs of the process behind them, but seemed rather to be a sort of impermanent fungus-growth on the surface of the eyeballs" (*H* 229). Like the face and the eyes stuck in it, the shaking body was continuously in motion, darting about in every direction at once, each part a stranger to all of the others, violently on the run from one place to another in "furious" dissipation of "energy" that was to no more purpose than Eck's uncoordinated attempts to nail a shoe onto a horse's hoof (*H* 73). Even I. O.'s conversation was disembodied. To see him come unglued is only to listen for a moment as he talked, "Morning, morning. . . . Want that horse shod, hey? Good, good: save the hoof and save all . . .; love me, love my horse, beggars cant be choosers, if wishes . . ." (*H* 72).

Snopes women and children also came in the standard models. Good representatives of Number One were Flem's sisters, who "stood, big, identical, like two young tremendous cows . . .; they did not seem to breathe even." When they spoke, they spoke in unison" like a trained chorus" (*H* 54). I. O.'s first wife was of this strain. Her only acquaintance with activity was I. O. and a "rocking chair" in which she sat at such an "angle" that "her lap" was enclosed "as if she had no movable hinge at the hips at all" (*T* 39). The mother of Lump (another "Snopes encore," who shared with I. O. features that seemed to scurry over his face as if something were chasing them [*H* 225,186]) was a Number Two, "a thin, eager, plain woman who had never had quite enough to eat" (*H* 225). Neither had Mink's ferocious wife Yettie (*H* 275). The children produced by these women were a standard too, as much like their parents as small nuts and bolts are like large nuts and bolts. When Eck and his son hunkered down against a wall, they were "save for the difference in size, identical" (*H* 353), and three or four of I. O.'s facsimiles were so much alike that they were referred to as those "gray-colored chaps" (*T* 39). Two of them were almost indistinguishable, the younger "not looking younger . . . so much as just newer, as the lesser-used axe or machine gun looks newer." Both chaps had "a grayish pasty look to . . . [their] flesh, . . . as if it would not flow blood . . . but instead a pallid fluid like thin oatmeal" (*T* 368). They shared the grayish-pasty looks with Byron's "four things," who arrived in Jefferson under "shipping" tags (*T* 359) and who with their still faces and "black," bowl-cut hair (*T* 360) were as much alike as "four shut pocket knives" (*T* 363).

Whether nuts, bolts, or knives, Snopeses shared with Snopeses the indelible signs of the assembly line: like pieces of machinery or men divorced from all human affects, their faces showed nothing—"depthless" (*H* 186). If the "face is a center of human expression, the transparent envelope of . . . [human] attitudes," and if for these reasons "it seems impossible for us to treat a face or a body . . . like [a function]" rather than as human (*SB* 167), then the Snopeses exemplified, individually and collectively, the existential-phenomenologist's paradox of how a human being can be human and "apparatus" (*MB I*: 119-20, *MB II*: 48-49, *B&H* 168, *MMA* 37). Though "none of them," thin or fat, "seemed to bear any specific kinship to one another" (*T* 40) any more than two automobiles would bear kinship, Snopes' physiognomies (like hoods on cars) all bore a standard blankness (*S* 244). What caused all the members of the assembly line to look alike was what made the four little Indian-Snopeses and Flem's bow tie to look alike; they were "machine-made," "snapped together at the back with a metal fastener," "depthless" (*H* 66). Here was a style wholly functional (*E&H* 74), one that offered Flem an excellent opportunity for consolidating any gains he could make. He had ready-at-hand a never-ending supply of cogs, "interchangeable" as "machine" parts, that neatly interlocked and meshed into the wheelwork he had set up (*E&H* 74). Some of the cogs were smaller than others, some moved more slowly, some wore better, and although different in size, shape, and movement, they were proof that in the business and technological world human "life is not so much motion as an inventless repetition of motion" (*M* 197). Here is found the basis for the common cause Snopeses made against humanity, the bulwark in their "common front to life" (*T* 36).

Lump Snopes, whom Flem chose to take his place at Varner's store (*H* 370), was "exactly like the old one but a little smaller, a little compacter, as if they had both been cut with the same die but in inverse order to appearance, the last first and after the edges of the die were dulled and spread a little" (*H* 183). The assembly did not stop with Lump and the store. After Ab had taken up residence in Frenchman's Bend with Flem, a Snopes took his place on the farm, and a third took over the smithy (*T* 5). "How many more is there? How much longer is this going on?" groaned Jody Varner (*H* 76), and from Jefferson came a similar cry. Gavin Stevens continually criticized the invaders. Haranguing, lashing out until weak and discouraged, he declared that since no one could "defend" the town from them, "let us then give, relinquish Jefferson to Snopeses, banker mayor aldermen church and all, so that, in defending them-selves from Snopeses, Snopeses of necessity must defend and shield us, their vassals and chattels, too" (*T* 44). One of the attractions the town held for Flem was the "automated charac-ter" of the life and the work there (*MMS* 183), and as he scratched and clawed his way from rags to riches (*M* 153), he missed no opportunity to solidify his position. When he became "superintendent of the town power-plant" (*T* 9), he replaced himself in the restaurant with Eck (*T* 31-32), putting into opera-tion "that same sort of osmosis by which . . . they had covered Frenchman's Bend, the chain unbroken, every Snopes . . . moving up one step, leaving that last slot at the bottom open for the next Snopes to appear from nowhere and fill" (*T* 8-9), and during the supposedly fallow years—those between the superintendency of the power plant and the vice-presidency of Merchants and Farmers Bank (*T* 118)—he remained busy "farming Snopeses: the whole rigid hierarchy moving intact upward . . . step [by step]" (*T* 31).

For the movement to be successful, Flem had to know in advance what each step required and have a qualified Snopes for that step (*T* 128); like the smooth functioning of any mecha-nism, the functioning of the assembly depended upon an easy predictability. There can be no exceptions, as I. O. Snopes learned when he tried to usurp Flem's exclusive right to the use of other Snopeses and set up an assembly of his own. For years I. O. had escaped Flem's attention, busying himself with the relatively innocuous occupations of producing Snopeses and teaching school (*H* 183), but when he leased a blacksmith shop and placed his incompetent cousin Eck in charge (*T* 73), Flem looked up long enough to run him out of business. Setting up a smithy of his own, Flem hired an experienced "young farmer" and a month later sold it, "clientele and goodwill and new equipment—to Varner" with Eck serving as "apprentice" (*T* 76). Nothing remained for I. O. except the bustle, the over-weening ambition, the wages of stupidity. He was no longer even a cog, merely expendable.

The "technical life-order" (*MMA* 37), the conglomeration of "mere automata" (*MMS* 183), is dependent on standardization and predication but is even more dependent on rigid control. It depends on the kind of ruthlessness by which Flem reduced I. O. , and the clue to his success can be found in his body. Flem's face, like that of all the Snopeses, retained the quality of nothing, but from it there projected "in startling and sudden paradox, a tiny predatory nose like the bead of a small hawk. It was as though . . . the original designer or craftsman" had "left off" the nose given to the ordinary Snopes "and the unfinished job [had been] taken over by someone of a radically different school" (*H* 59). The new school begins with the assumption that function is more important than the human being, even if the human being is one's own kin, and the new nose signified the ruthlessness needed to carry out the assumption. Montgomery Ward was hinting at this when he confessed that he had come from "a family, a clan, a race, maybe even a species, of pure sons of bitches," but what bothered him was "*THE son of a bitch's son of a bitch.*" Neither he nor any other member of his family ever attained these heights, he complained. "The best we ever do is to be just another Snopes son of a bitch" (*M* 87). Montgomery Ward had no reason to complain. Flem's ruthlessness took him far into son-of-a-bitchery, as Jody, I. O., and others in and around Frenchman's Bend could attest. His finesse in winning the presidency of Merchants and Farmers Bank (*M* 156, 152) gave him undisputed possession.

Flem had "taken hold in the store like he was raised storekeeping" (*H* 56). He took to banking the same way. Just as one's "handwriting on the blackboard resembles [his] handwriting on paper" (*SB* 30), so the function of the banker Flem resembled Flem the clerk. The exalted position entailed a functional reorganization requiring little more than a certain attention to appearances. Disposing of the "cloth cap," selling it "for a dime" (*M* 65), Flem replaced it with "a hat, a new one of the broad black felt kind which country preachers and politicians wore" (*T* 138). His next move in keeping with his new affluence was to acquire a decent house (*T* 223), and then the cachet of the businessman of moderate means, an automobile (*M* 156). In making the acquisitions, Flem had parlayed a body devoid of affects into a valuable asset, functional and ruthless, but, a businessman and a technocrat, he was not above putting it to other uses. In winning the presidency, "*THE son of a bitch's son of a bitch*" (*M* 87) turned "to the techniques of degradation" (*MMS* 19).

The techniques are based upon the theory that "a human being" subjected to certain kinds of "manipulation tends progressively to be reduced to . . . a mere *thing*" (*MMS* 19). The techniques can take various forms. They can be "a whole body of methods . . . put into operation in order to . . . destroy" in a social class or in a race its "self-respect, . . . to transform" the members into human trash, "waste products, conscious of themselves as such." Using these techniques, the Nazi tried "to degrade" the Jew by separating him from any contact with the world he had known and then imposing on him a world in which he became a gibbering idiot who (*MMS* 42), like Ike Snopes repeating his name and then refusing to repeat it, disavowed acts he had once supported and supported acts he had once disavowed (*MMS* 17-18)—techniques that "exploited" in him "every kind of cowardice, . . . excited every kind of jealousy and stimulated . . . every kind of hate" (*MMS* 42). One of the most effective uses of the techniques reverses this approach. It destroys the victim through his strengths, not his weaknesses. This method is a favorite with politicals, as the communist Brunet showed in his attempt to suppress the French priest against whom he was competing for control of a prisoner-of-war camp (*TS* 256). Upon inquiry he learned that the priest spent nearly all his time in the hospital comforting the wounded soldiers and that sometimes the friendly and garrulous man would play cards with several of the wounded officers and the major in charge of the hospital. This information was enough. Ask the wounded soldiers, Brunet ordered his assistants, how they liked "the priest" who was "always hob-nobbing with the officers" (*TS* 259). The line of attack, Brunet explained, would take from the priest his *raison d'etre*: It would isolate him from his men, make them realize that he was not "really one of them" (*TS* 260). A priest in isolation is no longer a priest.

Senator Clarence Egglestone Snopes also made use of this technique. A Number One Snopes, "soft," "thick" Clarence resembled Flem in the bland and empty face (*S* 244) with a nose in which could be seen something of the ruthlessness embod-ied in Flem's, but weaker, the nose of "a squirrel or a rat" (*S* 208), and Clarence's attack on the political structure parallels in a weaker manner Flem's attack on the financial. Both began their careers as proteges of Will Varner (*M* 298). "Old Varner's privately appointed constable" (*M* 297), Snopes brought to the office the impersonal efficiency that clerk Flem had brought to the store (*M* 300). He "manhandled" victims, usually Negroes, with his "blackjack . . . or with the butt of . . . [his] pistol" (*M* 299). His manner was detached, "as if he were using . . . the man's . . . legal vulnerability as testing ground . . . on which to prove . . . how far his official power and legal immunity actu-ally went" (*M* 300). From this high ground he was able, as was Flem in the store, to catch a glimpse of higher. Thus he put aside the blackjack and took up a more potent weapon, human beings. He would, he decided, use men "not merely to expend their inexhaustible numbers like ammunition or consume them like hogs or sheep, but to use, employ them like mules or oxen, with one eye constant for the next furrow tomorrow or next year; using not just their competence . . . but their capacity for passion and greed." A man who could function so coldly and ruthlessly in handling Negroes and reach such coldly elegant conclusions on handling men in general would go far in poli-tics, and under the auspices of Varner, one of the best politicians in the County, it was not long before this Snopes was running "for the state legislature" (*M* 301).

His first act was to appear before his constituency "in a

complete white linen suit with a black Windsor tie" (*M* 296), the politician's politician as Flem was the clerk's clerk. The abstraction he made of himself was so effective that it was years before anyone would oppose Clarence, and then it was no lazy and slothful pushover like Jody Varner but a veteran of World War II with a fine war record. In an effort to eliminate his challenger, Clarence turned to that record. The veteran, whose rank Clarence changed at will—"Captain," "Colonel," "General" (*M* 311), had been commander of "Negro infantry" (*M* 308) and, according to Clarence, had won the Congressional Medal (*M* 313) for saving one of his men in battle (*M* 314). All Clarence had had to do now was suggest that the colonel had brought home from the war a few "new ideas" (*M* 311) which he would take with him into office, new ideas that had to do with consorting "with Negroes" and the breaking "down forever" of "the normal and natural . . . barriers between the white man and the black one" (*M* 312). This technique against the "nigger lover" (*M* 313) was as good as Brunet's against the priest and would have been as successful, except for the intervention of Ratliff and of Devries' two nephews wielding a few "hickory and pin-oak" branches saturated with dog urine (*M* 315-17).

Flem was more successful in his bid against De Spain for control of Merchants and Farmers Bank than Clarence against Devries but then, too, the "techniques of degradation," though effective for politicians, are tailor-make for the businessman. In his "preoccupation with security" (*MMS* 59) in his highly competitive world, he finds that the fight for the next step up must be accompanied by a rearguard action protecting the step he has left. There arises not only the need for another's job but assurance that the other will no longer be a threat. The competitor must be eliminated from competing, and a natural born businessman, Flem showed how it is done when he used his wife to trap De Spain. Several years before Flem and Eula were married, a young school teacher wildly attracted to her, as were most of the males in Yoknapatawpha (*H* 134-35), had envisioned her life with Flem. He saw her married to someone "without glands or desire" to whom she "would be no more a physical factor . . . than the owner's name on the fly-leaf of a book" (*H* 134-35). The "gnome" (*H* 134) would "own her" as he owned any other object and as any other businessman owned his wife, by "the dead power of money, wealth, gewgaws, baubles" (*H* 135). The teacher's vision was dim. In the first place, Flem as businessman *par excellence* had used Eula as a way to wealth, not wealth as a way of holding her, but, more interestingly, he had taken a body without glands, the kind which the teacher had found abhorrent, and once again turned it into a valuable asset. Having no physical desire for Eula (*M* 70), he was not deterred, as the teacher would have been, by human feelings. Impotence made it easy for him to give De Spain, an attractive bachelor, the opportunity to snap her up. Ratliff was noting the expertise of the plan and the cunning with which Flem carried it out when he said that Snopes knew from the beginning of the affair and that "not catching" and exposing the lovers to the community was "like that twenty-dollar gold piece pinned to your undershirt on your first maiden trip to . . . a Memphis whorehouse. He dont need to unpin it yet" (*T* 29). Contrary to Ratliff's theorizing, Flem never did unpin it, and when De Spain and Eula were exposed, it was not their morality that disturbed the community. It was a matter of function.

Chick Mallison, on learning that Flem was to be vice-president of Merchants and Farmers, observed that Jefferson was used to a different "breed" (*T* 137) of banker and cited Colonel Bayard Sartoris, the first president of the bank, who made out bank notes that neither he nor his depositors could "read" (*T* 139), the sort of notes Jody Varner would have written. Back then, a little after the turn of the century, the town had expected in a president what Frenchman's Bend had accepted in a store owner, someone human (*M* 152), but twenty years after that, about the time De Spain became president, the townspeople had changed (*T* 118). Sometime, imperceptibly, during the nearly two decades, Jefferson was moving from a town tied to an agrarian economy to one dominated by commercial and technological interests, a change reflected in the criteria by which the community judged their businessmen, a change which is the theme of Gavin Stevens' history of Mr. Garraway, a grocer (*T* 312).

As long as De Spain was merely vice-president of Merchants and Farmers Bank, few persons in Jefferson had given much thought to the banker's private life (*T* 136-37), but on learning that he was to be president, Garraway, "one of that original small inflexible unreconstructible Puritan group" in Yoknapatawpha, began to think that De Spain was a little too human. He was "the first" to withdraw his funds and "escape the moral contamination" (*T* 312). About a year later, however, he put the funds back, only in the end to withdraw them permanently (*T* 312,314). In commenting on these events, Stevens suggested correctly that Garraway had taken the money out for moral reasons and restored it when he found that he could tolerate what he could not change (*T* 312). But the lawyer was wrong to believe that Will Varner's catching Eula and her lover had caused the grocer to withdraw the funds for a second time (*T* 313). "It was one thing as long as the husband accepted it; it became another when somebody . . . catches them?" Stevens asked the grocer. "They become . . . sinners then, criminals then, lepers then?" Can you give them, Stevens asked in an effort to excuse Eula and De Spain, "nothing for constancy, nothing for fidelity, nothing for . . . eighteen years of devotion?" (*T* 314). To this owner of a small business in the 1920's, it was romantic nonsense to talk of De Spain's moral sins or of his fidelity. To Garraway as well as to Jefferson, the president's personal conduct was not the issue. It was no longer a matter of his being sinful or faithful, in or out of marriage, or a matter of morality at all. De Spain's sin was that he did not function as a businessman functions: he may have remained faithful to Eula, he had not remained faithful to the bank. One or the other—a computer like Flem or a sex machine like Flem's cousin Virgil

(*M* 71-73)—was tolerated by the community, but one who combined business and sex, "that fornicating bank president" (*M* 202), was to modern Jefferson no president at all. De Spain himself accepted the verdict that he was *passé* (*M* 146), an anomaly, and when Garraway cried out, "They must both go— she and De Spain too" (*T* 314), they went (*T* 355, *M* 146). All that was now left for Flem was the easy task of convincing Garra- way and the town of what they already knew, that he, Flem, lived as a banker should live, not for love but for money.

Before we can recognize other entities in the world, or even see them, they have existed for us "in a more intimate sense." This pre-logical consciousness, our perceptions, "is subtended by an 'intentional arc' which projects . . . our human setting" and which unifies our "senses" and sensibilities, our own as well as with those of others (*PP* 136), and thus we may say "almost with certainty" that no one who can perceive has "found it impossible ever to unite himself with another" (*MB II*: 120). We can say with certainty that Flem was so inhuman as never to have united with another person (*T* 152), but we cannot say that he was never united with something. Just as "most of the men" at Doane's Mill "who ran . . . [the machin- ery] existed because of and for it" (*LIA* 4), Flem existed for money (*T* 142).

For the majority of us, those who do not have much of it, money "is less a possession in itself than an instrument for possessing." Money "is evanescent, . . . made to unveil the object, the concrete thing." The value of money lies in this its "transitive being" (*B&N* 589). In order to use it, we must spend it; only as money disappears does it become money. My fasci- nation with money lies in the unbelievable fact that for one thin dime I can, for example, get one hundred fat peanuts. If I have more than a dime, I can get more, endlessly. Or I stop before a haberdasher with five five-dollar bills in my wallet, and I discover that the socks, tie, and shoes I see are mine for the asking. The power of money, which cuts through all manufac- turing difficulties—my inability to knit socks, to tan leather—

renders my wishes "immediately operative" (*B&N* 590). I do not need special skills or to be of any particular race or color or to have any particular creed to spend money and make wishes come true (*ASJ* 126). Even Ike Snopes could have spent the fifty-cent piece, had he not lost it. If one doubts the efficacy of money, he can compare it with other mediums of exchange. A minimum use of money and a maximum use of barter resulted in most of the confusion (and all of the fun) in the business transactions at Frenchman's Bend. Ab Snopes's loss of his wife's "separator money" (*H* 36) and his one "good mule" (*H* 41) in exchange for a pair of broken down mules was such a complicated operation that in the middle of it Ab sought refuge in "a bottle of whiskey" (*H* 45), and before the deal was completed (Ratliff said) it "plumb curdled" him for life (*H* 33). Unlike a horse or a mule, which deteriorates however brilliant the doctoring (*H* 38), or the short-lived "eight White Leghorn hens" (*H* 63) Ratliff took in on a sewing machine, money creates a permanent functional power that overcomes all the contingencies of barter.

Despite manifest advantages, however, there is also a drawback in the spending of money. The number of desirable objects at the disposal of any single human being is limited, and once the limit is reached, money loses its great powers, becoming no longer a means of possessing objects but an object-in-itself (*B&N* 590-91). The history of conspicuous consumption is the history of finding ways to keep money moving. The Morgans, Hills, Harrimans, and "ever other golden advocate of hard quick-thinking vested interest" (*M* 154) hire experts, look to foundations, and seek other means of preserving the creative possibilities of money. Flem was luckier than these golden advocates. Money—"solid, harder than bones and heavy like gravel"—was enough. He gave up tobacco in order to acquire a little more of it. "When he had nothing, he could afford to chew tobacco; when he had a little, he could afford to chew gum; when he found out he could be rich . . ., he couldn't afford to chew anything." But Flem discovered something else about money that was more important than the fact "that the only limit to the amount . . . you could shut your hands on and keep and hold, was just how much money there was, provided you had a good safe place to put that other handful down and fill your fists again" (*M* 66). As the good banker he was, he discovered that the greatest power of money lies in money itself, not in what it will buy. Left alone in a good safe place, it would not produce peanuts and socks, but, a real miracle, it would produce itself: "money . . . , cash dollars, possessed an inherent life of its mutual own like cells" (*T* 267).

With cash, as though money cells had bridged the gap between percept and affect, Flem was one: they were made for each other. Contrary to Stevens' speculation that Flem was a wronged husband seeking revenge (*T* 268-98 esp. 283), Snopes had nothing against De Spain, except that he stood between him and money (*T* 142). All the banker wanted was "simply to move . . . [the bank] still intact out from under De Spain. Because the bank stood for money. A bank was money, and . . . he would never injure money" (*T* 278). Like any other good businessman, all he ever wanted was to be "worth so many dollars" (*MMS* 174), and the Devil himself could not arouse in him any other desire. When Satan laid out "*all the temptations, the gratifications, the satieties,*" in words that "*sounded sweeter than music*" (*H* 174), Flem, invulnerable to anything that did not smell, feel, taste like money (*M* 56), "*just turned his head and spit*" (*H* 174). Affects throttled back to the minimum, he had reduced himself to one thing, a moneymaker, a reduction that is not without its comical aspects and one that makes his death seem as funny as his life.

The comedy of possession lies in our successful efforts to be at one with what we possess, and nowhere do we succeed better than when we become worth so many dollars (*MMA* 174). The Scrooges and the Shylocks, misers and hoarders of all kinds, are fit subjects for comedy because somewhere in their pursuit of the dollar they have somehow metamorphosed into one, a dollar sign impersonating a human being. So had Flem.

Ambulating cash, it wore a "black bow" (*H* 66) that made it a clerk and " a black felt" (*M* 135) that made it a banker; it kept the hat on, indoors and out (*M* 155). Tie and hat after years of wear still looked as new as a freshly minted five cent piece (*T* 354). The coat and trousers draped the body in the temporary fashion of a mannequin. Banking day over, slowly masticating air, the president retired within the bare walls of the mansion, where "table chairs sideboard cabinets chandeliers and all . . . [looked] exactly as . . . [they] had looked in the Memphis interior decorator's warehouse" (*M* 215), to sit in a president's "swivel chair . . . with his feet propped against the side of the fireplace" (*M* 155). The day Mink walked in carrying the old revolver, the funny looking head that had hung suspended over the desk "turned," ballooning "over" a "shoulder;" otherwise, it did not move. Flem was not frozen with fear. Nor was he showing courage or stoicism or any other sign of life. He was still, like the Statue of Liberty on a quarter. "When Mink from about five feet away stopped and raised the . . . weapon," Flem shifted the nerveless body as he would have shifted an object, pushing it "slightly forward in the chair," lowering the "propped feet" to the floor. The revolver misfired, and Flem stopped moving at all, sitting "immobile and even detached," immobility and detachment disclosing for the last time the existential separation of the man from his self (*M* 415). As Mink took aim the second time, it "was chewing faintly" (*M* 416) and watching as it would have watched someone taking target practice. Mink fired and it stopped chewing.

Chapter III

JOE CHRISTMAS, INCOMMUNICADO

Critics have found Joe Christmas to be one of Faulkner's most elusive characters.[1] One has compared him favorably with Sam Fathers,[2] and others with Jesus Christ.[3] Christmas is "magnificent in his isolation."[4] "In *Light in August* Faulkner's image of man and of the universe," writes another, "is not nihilistic, fatalistic, naturalistic; it is dynamic, existential, humanistic."[5] On the other hand, some critics see Christmas' life as that of a "nightmare."[6] "A stage of basic bewilderment and rage such as only the very small child knew."[7] Another maintains that he is "an abstraction seeking to become a human being."[8] He is the "most obsessive . . . character" in "Faulkner's work."[9] Such a diversity of views, as it always will, brings out from the critics a tendency to paste labels rather than to analyze. Christmas is, I suppose, the most "belabelled" of all Faulkner's characters, with the possible exception of the Generalissimo. The mulatto has been called, among other things, "outcast," "Ishmael," "martyr," "scapegoat," "masochistic," "Marginal Man," "modern tragic hero," "Existentialist anti-hero."[10] More useful than labels, it seems to me, is an attempt to discover Christmas's real problem, that is, to discover the phenomenological foundation—"the Transcendental Category"[11]—which underlies his shaky life structure, be it tragic, masochistic, whatever. The place to begin is with the uncontested fact that Christmas was incapable of forming a satisfactory relationship with any other human being. He gives us a classic existential-phenomenological view of a man struggling unsuccessfully to come to terms with other men and, important for this study, his struggle makes clear the original ground where all such struggles take place: pride, shame, and fear.

Whatever direction our emotions ultimately take in our relationships with others—love, hate, indifference—our first emotional contact with them involves, as Sartre tells us in *Being and Nothingness* and other works, pride, shame, and fear. Here we find the phenomenological grounding of all our feelings toward other human beings. Although for the sake of clarity I plan to treat those emotions in three sections, none of the emotions, Sartre makes clear, can finally be separated from the others. Faulkner tells us precisely the same thing in *Light in August*; indeed, this phenomenal fact is the compositional center of the novel. Nowhere else in Faulkner's works is man's affective relationship with his fellow man shown to better advantage than in the life of Joe Christmas. So clearly does the existential-phenomenological pattern emerge that, without pressing too far, we can say that from the time Christmas was five or six years old until he was sixteen or seventeen, his life was dominated by pride, in the following twelve years by shame, and in his thirties he died in fear. Furthermore, this tripartation of emotional difficulties can be traced to two incidents occurring in Joe's early childhood, one involving a black man, the other a white woman.

The first incident was triggered by several white children who, because of Christmas' dark complexion, called him a "nigger." In his short life the child had seen only one Negro, the yardman at the orphanage where he and the other children lived, and, hoping to discover what the shouting was all about, Joe took another look at the man. "How come you are a nigger?" he asked, but before the yardman could reply, Christmas burst out: "I aint a nigger." One good look had convinced the child that he was not nearly so dark as the black man, but this observation presented a problem that had not existed before. If he was not a nigger, what was he? The man answered that, too. You are not a nigger, the man assured him; you are a "little white trash bastard" (*LIA* 336). *White*! Whatever else he might be was at the moment of no importance. He was as white as the children who taunted him, and for years he took great pride in this whiteness.

Pride offers us protection from others, and whatever its ultimate manifestation—intellectual, moral, religious—it is first of all a body phenomenon. The language of pride is before anything else body language (*SG* 121), and no other characters in Faulkner's works speak it so well as Christmas and his foster father, Simon McEachern. Sitting across from McEachern in the reception room of the orphanage, Christmas faced existential pride: Thick flesh the density of iron clad in impregnable black, feet covered with black leather and planted heavily upon the floor, a square hand clutching a black hat. A wiry beard armored a grim face, wiry hair matted a head hard as a cannon ball, cold eyes examined the boy as they would examine a plow. Phenomenally, Christmas' body was the man's in miniature. He sat tight and firm, and when McEachern brought up the question of his parentage, the boy's response was different from his response to the children. He remained "rocklike." Even when McEachern gave the same intonation to *Christmas* as the children had given to *nigger* and insisted that the name would have to be changed, Christmas remained a hard knot, saying to himself with a sigh of resignation: "There was no need to bother about that yet. There was plenty of time" (*LIA* 124-127,143).

The first skirmish between the boy and the man sets forth two of the main characteristics of original pride. First, it is a battle of bodies, and, secondly, great pride cancels out all possibility of reconciliation. Even at this early stage, Christmas was sure of one thing: the battle was to the death: he was resigned to it. This first skirmish also reveals another aspect of pride, "the test." In pride, especially in pride, we exist in so far as we are *engaged* (*B&N* 290-91). Only in the other person and the challenge he presents to us do we come completely alive. In our antagonist who simultaneously draws and repels us, we find our *raison d'être*, as Christmas found in McEachern. The boy's life became a series of ruses by which he would challenge the man who had taken him into his home. At first he annoyed McEachern with his indifferent performance of household chores, but he quickly learned that the best way to bring his foster father to attention was to reject his religion, a religion as rigid as the man and the God inspiring it. For some time McEachern and God had tried unsuccessfully to force their son to memorize the Presbyterian catechism (*LIA* 128-29), and one Sunday morning the three came together in Christmas' bleak room, the man again admonishing in the cold voice that never failed to thrill the boy. Then came a greater thrill, the one for which they both eagerly waited—the trip to the barn. As Christmas and McEachern left the room, they were brothers in pride, twins in "a very kinship of stubbornness. . . , two backs in . . . rigid abnegation of all compromise" (*LIA* 130). Of the two Christmas was perhaps the more prideful; certainly he was the more persistent. He never missed an opportunity to challenge his adversary, and like the truly prideful, if no opportunity presented itself, he created one (*SG* 157). This time he had deliberately neglected bringing the catechism to the barn, and after he had retrieved the book and been ordered to lay it down, he dropped it to the floor. Coldly, but without result, the voice chided, and then the man himself stooped over and picked up the book, giving the boy his first victory. If he was elated, he was too proud to show it (*LIA* 130-31).

Pride gives us a perceptual world of exceptional richness and none richer than Christmas'. Nothing McEachern did escaped him. Eyes became superior magnifying glasses searching the man's every movement for an excuse for confrontation, eardrums were finely tuned sounding boards reverberating to every McEachern nuance, nostrils were set aquiver with the man's odors. The harness strap McEachern was holding "smelled like the man smelled: an odor of clean hard virile living leather" (*LIA* 130). Christmas' conflict with McEachern was not that of the pariah fighting the establishment or that of a mulatto crossing the color line. It was not social or racial in any sense. It was ontological, and now bent over, in existential intimacy, in touch (*PP* 315-18), he would bring clean virile living flesh against clean virile living leather. No wonder, then, he found the strappings "perfectly logical and reasonable and inescapable" (*LIA* 132). Out of his own fleshly pride he made an instrument of such density that it destroyed the instrument brought against it. With each blow Christmas was establishing himself as his own adamantine creation. It was as though he were giving birth to himself, "hard, sufficient, potent, remorseless, strong" (*LIA* 140). Ironically, his strength was the reason for his failure: he became so strong that McEachern could no longer challenge him. The end came abruptly when Christmas was about eighteen. In a quarrel over a calf, he took a blow from McEachern but warned him not to do it again. Not long afterward Christmas realized that the warning had been effective and left for sterner competition.

In accepting adults as the voice of authority, a child accepts their verdicts as he would accept a sentence of imprisonment, living sometimes for years under the interdict and regarding as true that which he never quite succeeds in believing. The older he grows the more he doubts the infallibility of his elders, and after re-examining their opinions, he discovers efficacy in his own ideas (*SG* 46,47). Christmas seems to have made this discovery sometime before the calf incident. McEachern had complained that he was harboring in his home "a blasphemer and an ingrate," and Joe thought of a good way to counter this insult. He asked Mrs. McEachern to inform her husband that he was also harboring "a nigger" (*LIA* 146). A rock-hard black, he had come to believe, was more potent than a rock-hard white. Instead of taking the word of the Negro yardman that he, Christmas, was white, he should have taken the man as a model. Instead of being ashamed that he was a nigger, Christmas believed now that he should have been proud of the fact, and once he had left the McEacherns, he showed this pride. He labored like a Negro, he lived in Negro shacks, and he dressed like a Negro (*LIA* 31,37,27). These actions along with his cigar-brown complexion were enough to bring from white men accusations that he was black, and just as he had once turned *white* into a metaphor of pride, he now used *black* the same way, tricking "white men into calling him a Negro in order to . . . beat them or to be beaten." He would challenge white prostitutes by telling them after intercourse that he was a nigger (*LIA* 196).

Yet this change of roles was more difficult to effect than Christmas had at first imagined. He found that, unlike the children who had called him a Negro and the yardman who had called him white, quite a few people were uncertain as to his race. Some called him "that white nigger," and others said that he did not act like a white man or a Negro (*LIA* 302,306). As he lay in bed with his first white mistress, he asked whether she had noticed the coarseness of his hair or the color of his skin and when she answered that she thought he was a foreigner, he said that there was more to it. He had some Negro blood (*LIA* 170-71). Christmas had evidence in his skin and hair and in the opinions of others that he was black, but *feeling* black—taking *pride* in being black—somehow escaped him. His dilemma is understandable. Pride is a powerful emotion, but it is unstable, a feeling without equilibrium, and the reason for its instability lies in its existential-phenomenological structure. Pride is founded on shame. Without shame there can be no pride; pride is invariably a reaction to shame. In order to be proud of what we are, we must first be ashamed of what we do not wish to be (*B&N* 290). In his conflict with the yardman, Christmas has given validity to this principle. Ashamed of being black, he had blurted out, "I aint a nigger," and for many years he had warded off that shame by passing as white. But now, unable to stabilize his life, to *be* either white or black—proud of being one and ashamed of the other—he lost his pride completely.

Christmas experienced this loss, the existential collapse of pride into shame, in the arms of a black woman with whom he had lived as man and wife. Feeling as close to her as he could ever feel to anyone, he would absorb her into himself, open his body to the body of this black woman. Beside her in their bed, he would "breathe deep and hard . . . deliberately, feeling . . . his white chest arch deeper and deeper . . . , trying to breathe into himself . . . the dark and inscrutable . . . being of Negroes."

Above all he tried to breathe into his body "the dark odor" (*LIA* 197). He looked upon it as life's essence. He lay breathing her odor, letting her make her way into him, and with "each suspiration . . . expel from himself the white blood . . . and being." His effort was great, nostrils white and taut and his whole being writhing and straining to make her odor his own, but the result was not negritude, only "physical outrage" (*LIA* 197). Years earlier Christmas had also suffered physical outrage, this time at the hands of a white woman, who taught him that whatever his color, he was fated to be more ashamed of himself than proud.

The change from pride to shame means a change from phenomenal self-sufficiency to phenomenal dependency (*B&N* 289-90), and existential literature has produced many of these defenseless beings, who make their appearance in both fiction and nonfiction. Jean Genet is one of them. Like Christmas he was an illegitimate child placed in a foster home, his first years there not much different from the first few weeks Christmas spent at the orphanage, a quiet and pleasant time. One day at about the age of ten, however, Jean was caught in the act of stealing a cooking utensil, and the quiet exploded. "*Thief!*" roared a voice (*SG* 26-8), and with this "dizzying word / From the depths of the world" (*SG* 26), the years of shame began. Joe's introduction to shame, more drawn out than Genet's, had begun even as he looked at the Negro yardman. The child had felt a slight buzzing of alarm when the man cursed him, but there was no panic. In fact, he defied the voice, saying, "I aint a nigger." Then the alarm buzzed louder as the voice said, "You little white trash bastard," but again Christmas stood his ground. If that was all he was, he had no reason to be ashamed, for the word *white* easily outweighed the other two. Then the voice and the buzzing started up again. Christmas not only wasn't a nigger, the yardman said, he would never know what he was; only God knew that, and "God wasn't there to say" (*LIA* 336). Taking God's place was Miss Atkins.

When Christmas was in his early twenties, he looked back

over his life, trying somehow to figure out where he had gone wrong. He thought about the children at the orphanage who had tried to shame him, and he thought about the yardman who had given him pride, but above all he thought about the resident dietitian. His trouble with her had begun when he went to her room to eat toothpaste. One day while he was there, she returned unexpectedly with her lover, and as they made love, Christmas remained hidden in the closet. The heat of the small enclosure combined with an overloaded stomach to bring on vomiting (*LIA* 104-06) and to bring in the woman. Dragging the child from his hiding place, she shouted, "You little rat! Spying on me! You little nigger bastard!" (*LIA* 107). A Negro man had called him a white bastard, and a white woman was calling him a Negro bastard, and both were calling him that same name. There were, then, no vague signals of alarm this time; it was a four-alarm fire. Like Genet, whose life is the story of his attempts to relive the shame of the "*fatal instant*" in which he was born a thief (*SG* 10), Christmas was to live all of his mature years, those years during which he had discovered sex and had to carry out its demands, as if his life had lasted only this shameful moment. Vulnerable to women, those beings responsible for bringing bastards into the world, he was in his most despairing moments to exist as though the insides of his body had seeped to the periphery, as if, like bad Camembert, his hard exterior concealed a runny center. Such a moment occurred when, splattered by the dietitian's words, he perceived himself as shameful, a bastard hanging in her hands— "limp, looking with slack-jawed and glassy idiocy." His shame was reified in the body covered with the soft, viscous contents of his own stomach (*LIA* 107).

Phenomenally, viscosity is the body's manifestation of shame as hardness manifests pride. It is a clinging, leech-like softness. There is treachery in its liquidity, for it gives the appearance that it can be possessed, but in possessing it we discover that by a horrifying reversal, it has possessed us (*B&N* 608-10). Sartre's nauseous Roquentin perceived this anomalous quality, "a sort of sweetish sickness," when he picked up a slimy beach pebble. For him the sickness became chronic, making itself felt as he touched, or imagined touching, such messes as excrement, spittle, bleeding flesh (*N* 19,18,134). The flesh and spittle and blood would have been especially shameful if they had been a woman's. Roquentin, Genet, and Christmas perceived a female as an object of shame as well as an object through which they perceived their own shame. For these preternaturally sensitive beings, a woman is the viscous make flesh—soft, yielding, treacherous (*B&N* 609). Viscosity resides in sickly-sweet, feminine colors such as pastels and lavenders (*TR* 116), and especially in pink, a color that, more than any other, caught the eyes of Roquentin (*N* 28,41) and Christmas. Joe had sat in the closet of the orphanage listening to the sounds of sex and watched the viscous "pink worm" of toothpaste crawl onto his finger. He had felt the presence of the "pink-and-white" woman out there having sex and making "his mouth think of something sweet and sticky to eat, and . . . pinkcolored and surreptitious" (*LIA* 105). He was to feel the shame of her presence the first time he attempted sexual intercourse with a white woman.

One of Christmas' young companions had explained to him the facts of menstruation. To Christmas the discharge was disgusting but had deeper significance, for he connected it with viscosity and an overwhelming power to bring about his dissolution. To ward off this shameful event, Christmas deliberately killed a sheep and dipped his hands into the blood. He did not dissolve, but neither did he recover, as he found out several years later when he propositioned Bobbie and she told him that she couldn't, that she was "sick," and in memory he fled back to the blood he had touched, the perceptual price he had "paid for immunity." But the price was not enough. He still had to contend with the source from which the blood had come: he struck Bobbie and ran into a nearby wood seeking safety "among the hard trunks, . . . hardfeeling, hardsmelling." To his shame he found that the trees were female, "each one . . .

cracked and from each crack there issued something liquid . . . and foul." Nature itself, he had discovered through the slimy lens of viscosity, was female, and he reacted to the discovery as he had earlier reacted to the pink dietitian. He vomited (*LIA* 161,163,164,165).

Since the first principle of existential-phenomenological psychoanalysis sets forth the dictum that "man is a totality and not a collection," every action of his life expressing his whole life (*B&N* 568), it is easy to understand that the food Christmas ate was phenomenally as appropriate for him as the food he regurgitated. Before giving us the color, size, shape of an object or the way that it smells or sounds, our senses tell us whether the thing is hard or soft (*SNS* 49-50). Colors first strike us as glaring or soothing, odors as acrid or mild, sounds as harsh or soft (*PP* 304), but the contrasting qualities of hardness and softness are particularly discernible in the food we eat (*B&N* 614). By eating, man gets himself into the world and keeps himself there. He chews and swallows the substance of the world, translating it into himself, "his I-Am" (*IID* 207). We do not, then, eat to satisfy our appetites. We eat in order to explore with tongue and teeth and palate a certain kind of existence, to live a certain kind of I-Am, one that leads us to choose certain kinds of foods and to avoid other kinds. In his long and almost hopeless struggle with shame and *le visqueus*, Roquentin resisted caramels, mayonnaise, and yellow cream (*N* 94,103). For him an appetite for food was tied to sexual appetite, and so in his battle for manhood, he was ashamed to eat a "drum-stick" floating "in brown gravy" (*N* 153).

Christmas, too, had early perceived the connection between eating and sex, but his attitude was not so simple as that of Roquentin. The French youth had connected toothpaste and sexuality when he commented, while glancing around a cafe, that no one was better qualified to sell Swan Toothpaste than a salesman he observed, just as no one was better qualified than another man sitting nearby to put his hand under his girl friend's skirts (*N* 151). Christmas perceived in the pink worm, as he had perceived in menstruation and the sex act itself, something totally shameful, his own dissolution. Bending over a young Negro girl, stretched out and receptive on the ground, the "womanshenegro," he had been "overcome by a terrible haste. There was this thing in him trying to get out, like when he used to think of toothpaste" (*LIA* 137). On occasion, however, he welcomed rather than rejected soft foods. The first time Bobbie served him at the restaurant, she suggested as dessert lemon, coconut, and chocolate pie, and he chose coconut, the sweetest and softest of all. He sat sweating as she placed the pie on a counter sticky with grease. When Christmas entered Miss Burden's kitchen for the first time, he faced a mess of peas and molasses, but such fare was not his only means of subsistence. Almost starving he dreamed of hard Negro food, and when he had the opportunity, he ate ears of hard field corn. He ate "quantities of it, with resultant crises of bleeding flux" (*LIA* 201,292).

There was, then, in Christmas an attraction to softness and an aversion to it. Caught up in a soft world dominated by women, he yearned for the hard man-shaped life that would free him, deliver him especially from Miss Burden. He looked at her, this "hot wet primogenitive Female," with disgust and shame. Under her dress was a "rotten richness" that would "flow into putrefaction at a touch," where he would find himself dissolving, so far gone that he would have to prove to himself that he was still intact (*LIA* 100, 229). On the night he murdered her, he did prove it and in the effort gives us perhaps the clearest illustration in Faulkner of the existential-phenomenological interweaving of shame and pride and of their existential formulation and residence in the body. The muscles, as we have seen, play the key role in pride, for they are visible proof of power, solidity, density (*SG* 121), and, synoptically, one muscle can prove the density of all. Christmas had used his buttocks to prove his mineral existence to McEachern; to prove his existence to himself he used his penis. Moving away from his shack and toward the road in front of Miss Burden's house, he unbuttoned his shirt and ran his hands against his hard chest, and then he removed his clothes and walked to the edge of the road. Naked he stood there watching the miracle of hardness take place, his body growing white in the glare of the head lights of an approaching automobile, and as a woman in it shrieked, he used as epithets words he had once embraced: "White bastards!" he shouted, and for a moment as the car roared away, Christmas had, as with McEachern, attained the clear simplicity of manhood: clean, hard, virile. On a foundation of the shame of being dissolved, he had erected freedom and manliness: "giant penis, the man . . . utterly a sex organ and the organ [the] man" (*LIA* 94, *SG* 121).

It is this tension that gave his life an existential dimension lacking in Genet and Roquentin, victims of pride as they rejected viscosity, or of shame as they accepted it. Christmas was a dual consciousness, not in the duality of the two Frenchmen, but in the mode that his life was divided: the shame and the pride as inseparable as the white blood and the black. The women who attracted Christmas sexually reflected the dualism. The squashy Bobbie had big mannish hands, a hard face, and a small, undeveloped body, features she shared with Joanna Burden. Joanna was "hard . . . and almost manlike," even in the sexual embrace (*LIA* 156,205), so that to have intercourse with her was like having sex with a male and just as frustrating. For many years Christmas was torn between the pride of being white and the shame of being black or the pride of being black and the shame of being white, but all of his life he was torn between the pride of being a man and shame of surrendering to the female. In the end this tension became too great, erupting in the fear that destroyed him.

Of the three modes that make up our original consciousness of the other, fear is the irreducible, the one continuously present to both pride and shame. The moment a human being becomes conscious of another, male or female, he goes on the defensive, faced with the problem of protecting himself (*B&N* 287-88). In pride he will act or in shame be acted upon, but either way the initial action is rooted in fear, fear that if he does not attack, the other will; fear that if he does attack, he will lose. Sartre's Roquentin was afraid of businessmen. They had, he whined, turned him into something in which the spring was broken; almost immobilized by fear, he could not move any part of his body except his eyes. He could turn them, he said, but if he turned his head, it would fall off (*N* 30). Christmas was also afraid of others: McEachern, whom he was afraid not to attack; Miss Atkins, who attacked him; but above all he was afraid of Miss Burden.

There are probably as many personal reasons for murder as there are murderers, but, phenomenologically, the reason underlying all others is fear. Always we murder or wish to murder those of whom we are afraid. Through their deaths we would liberate ourselves from fear, but, paradoxically, exactly the opposite occurs. We are tied tighter to them and to our fright than ever (*SG* 288), as Christmas discovered. His killing of Miss Burden did not bring him the release for which he longed. Instead he found himself more at the mercy of this woman than ever and completely bewildered by this existential-phenomenological fact. Bewilderment is to fear what hardness is to pride, softness to shame, but this elemental force is more. It is an emotional gale that destroys our perceptual world. Roquentin experienced this destruction while dining at a restaurant with a friend. At the start of the meal, Roquentin was at ease, but when his companion sounded increasingly like a businessman, he became at first apprehensive and then afraid and finally bewildered. The glib man spouting bourgeois philosophy became detached from the words he was uttering and then began to float out of his chair. Like a drowning man groping for a straw, Roquentin attempted to hang onto something concrete in his whirling universe, and he arose from the table, to see his friend and other diners frozen in their chairs staring at his hand clutching a dessert knife (*N* 140-48,163-66).

Turning away from his dead mistress, Christmas experienced the same bewilderment. As he ran from the house, he flagged down and climbed into an automobile occupied by a boy and an almost hysterical girl. Sometime later Christmas realized that the boy was speaking to him, begging him to leave the car, but only after he had alighted and a heavy object struck his thigh did the reason for the request come clear. The object "attached to his right hand," was the ancient pistol he had taken from Miss Burden just before he had murdered her. He had not been aware that he held it; he did not know why he held it (*LIA* 247-50). Bewilderment is perception in eruption, the failure of our senses to find anchor in the world. Things float away from us, as did Roquentin's friend, or they insensibly attach themselves to us, like the pistol, but bewilderment involves more than physical disorientation. It is ontological. It is man's overwhelming sense of alienation and abandonment in the world around him, his sense of existing outside of time and space (*B&N* 294,95). Rootless, a "phantom, a spirit, strayed out of its own world and lost" (*LIA* 99), Christmas all of his life had known this abandonment, and as he threw down the old pistol and ran, he was more than ever alone. His flight was not merely desperate, an attempt to lose his pursuers, but plunging ever deeper into terror and loneliness, he lost control even of himself.

Early in life Christmas had experienced this bewilderment that separates man from himself. Sitting in the closet in the orphanage, the fearful child smeared the toothpaste in his mouth, watching himself as if he were watching someone else (*LIA* 106), and some twenty-five years afterward on the night of the murder, he had gone to pieces as he walked the path leading from his cabin to Miss Burden's house. Only his feet seemed to know the direction and he surrendered himself to them, "floating, riding across the dusk, up to the house" (*LIA* 107). Now, as he continued to run from his pursuers, he seemed barely inserted in the world. Space and time were of no account. Successively, he lost the day of the week, then the hours of the day, and then he could not tell day from night. For him "the sun had not set but instead had turned in the sky before reaching the horizon and retraced its way" (*LIA* 291). Time was running but always in the same place, just as he was running in the same place; if he moved time moved, but neither was getting anywhere. One evening, without knowing how he had arrived, Christmas found himself at the kitchen table inside a Negro shack. Even as he sat eating he still ran, "waiting, thinking of nothing in an emptiness, a silence filled with flight" (*LIA*292), and seven days after the murder as he rode with a Negro on a wagon moving toward Jefferson, whence he had started, he was still running, waiting, drifting in a silence filled with flight of the circle in which he ran: "'I have been farther in these seven days than in all the thirty years,' he thinks. 'But I have never got outside that circle. I have never broken out of the ring of what I have already done and cannot ever undo'" (*LIA* 296). The circle was fear, for man the greatest of all fears—the fear of his contingency. At the center of Christmas' difficulty with others lay the fear that he was as useless as they said he was; his murder of Miss Burden was inextricably bound up with contingency and his fear of it.

As nauseating as he had found their affair, Christmas was able to live with it until she announced that she was pregnant (*LIA* 232) and then he could not live with it. The explanation of his aversion to sex and his collapse because of it lies in existential rather than Freudian psychology. Christmas was no sexual cripple victimized by unconscious drives he did not understand (*B&N* 177). Instead he abhorred womansexslime because it served a base and useless purpose; the sex act made life possible, and life, as Miss Atkins, Miss Burden, and other women had told him, was futile, filthy, and fearful. Although he knew that Miss Burden's pregnancy was the result of wishful thinking rather than copulation and that at her age she was, in any case, unlikely to have a child, the very thought of being responsible for another unnecessary bastard, *de trop* in an unnecessary universe, was a burden too heavy for him to bear. After killing her, this incubator of rubbish, he would destroy the germ that had filled the incubator. Christmas' death was as futile as his life, though he imagined it to be otherwise. As he lay mortally wounded, he once more broke into flight, weightless, heading for his last illusion, this one the fanciful benediction that would allow him to establish in death the mark he was unable to make in life. Into the memories of those who had killed him, he believed, he would soar "forever and ever. They are not to lose it. . . . It will be there, musing, quiet, steadfast, not fading and not particularly threatful, but of itself alone serene, of itself alone triumphant" (*LIA* 407). Such was not the case. He was forgotten almost before his body got cold: no one in Yoknapatawpha bothered even to mention his name again.

Notes

[1]This is my second attempt to shed light on him. In "Christmas as Existential Hero," *The University Review*, XXX (June 1964), 270-84, I used Sartre's paradoxical nexus of *etre-en-soi* and *etre-pour-soi* in an effort to lay bare Christmas's paradoxical nature. In my present study, I have used several paragraphs from the earlier one.

[2]Robert M. Slabey, "Joe Christmas, Faulkner's Marginal Man," *Phylon*, 21 (Fall 1960), 276.

[3]Cleanth Brooks, *William Faulkner. The Yoknapatawpha Country* (New Haven: Yale UP, 1963), 379; Walter J. Slatoff, *Quest for Failure: A Study of William Faulkner* (Ithaca: Cornell UP, 1960), 178; Joseph Gold, *William Faulkner: A Study in Humanism from Metaphor to Discourse* (Norman: U of Oklahoma P, 1966), 41; Peter Swiggart, *The Art of Faulkner's Novels* (Austin: U of Texas P, 1962), 43; Michael Millgate, *The Achievement of William Faulkner* (Random House, 1966), 250; Hyatt H. Waggoner, *William Faulkner: From Jefferson to the World*, (Lexington: U of Kentucky P, 1959), 103.

[4]Gordon Price-Stephens, "The British Reception of WIlliam Faulkner—1929-1962, *The Mississippi Quarterly*, XVIII (Summer 1965), 129.

[5]Slabey, 276, 277.

[6]Melvin Blackman, *Faulkner—The Major Years. A Critical Study* (Bloomington: U of Indiana P, 1966), 78.

[7]Glenn Sandstrom, "Identity Diffusion: Joe Christmas and Quentin Compson," *American Quarterly*, 19 (Summer 1967), 211.

[8]Alfred Kazin, "The Stillness of *Light in August*," *William Faulkner: Three Decades of Criticism*, ed. Frederick J. Hoffman and Olga W. Vickery (East Lansing: Michigan State UP, 1960), 252.

[9]Frederick J. Hoffman, *William Faulkner* (New Haven: College and UP,

1961), 70, 69.

[10]Lawrance Thompson, *William Faulkner: An Introduction and Interpretation* (New York: Barnes and Noble, 1963), 67; Brooks, 53; Hoffman, 70, 69; Thompson, 73; Slabey, 266, 267, 269.

[11]Ludwig Binswanger, *Being-in-the-World*, Trans. by Jacob Neddleman (New York: Harper Torchbooks, 1967), 31.

Chapter IV

THE MAGICAL WORLD OF
MINK SNOPES & COMPANY

One of the reasons critics have blown some of Faulkner's characters out of all proportion is Faulkner himself. Although he repeatedly stated that critics should forget about him, his personal life, and his ideas, and concentrate on his works, he tried (also repeatedly) to influence their judgment. A notable attempt occurs in the front pages of *The Mansion* where he writes that for three decades he had been working on the Snopes trilogy and "discrepancies and contradictions" had crept into it. These discrepancies and contradictions, Faulkner explains, are "due to the fact that the author has learned more about the heart and its dilemma than he knew thirty-four years ago and is sure that, having lived with them a long time, he knows the characters in the chronicle better than he did then."

Well, maybe. In the first place, except for Mink Snopes, all the chief characters in the novel remain substantially the same as in the other volumes of the trilogy. There are, however, discrepancies and contradictions in Mink. Faulkner has, without doubt, softened his rendering of this character—a softening which, in turn, has led to a softening of critical attitudes about Mink and the world he and others like him occupied. A good description of this world has been given by a prominent critic who, in commenting on *The Hamlet*, the first novel in the trilogy, writes that the work presents "matter-of-fact detail" but that the detail portrays creatures who are "wraithlike," "without dimension." Thus, the writer continues, *The Hamlet* gives us a "sense of the marvelous and almost supernatural quality of beings and happenings in a remote, entranced world": a county inhabited by troops of elves and goblins, trolls and nymphs and satyrs and other fanciful beings.[1] Certainly the world of Mink and his kind is a magical one, but the source of their magic is found not in the supernatural, as the critic seems to believe, but much closer to home. It is found in the human emotions.

Jean-Paul Sartre's essay, *The Emotions: An Outline of a Theory*, is one of his shortest works and one of his most important. In it Sartre gives us a phenomenology of the emotions that explains what they are, why we bring them into play, and their devastating effect on our behavior. In brief the emotions are body phenomena which we bring to bear on problems that we cannot solve by rational means. The result is the disappearance of the world of perceptual reality—the "pragmatistic world," Sartre calls it—and in its place a magical world of our own creation (*E* 32). Take for example one of our original emotions, fear. I am in my room late at night reading, and suddenly I look up to see a masked intruder pointing a gun at me. No one else is in the house except me, so calling for help is out of the question. There is no trap door through which I can disappear, or, better, make him disappear. All escape routes are cut off, and then I create one: I faint. By eliminating my consciousness of the intruder, I have eliminated him and danger. The perceptual world which I had constituted a moment earlier, the real world of criminals and victims, has disappeared, and taking its place is a world of my devising, one in which there is no place for gunmen. Emotionally, magically, I have escaped to safety (*E* 62-63).

Joe Christmas, when frightened by Miss Atkins, chose a similar means of escape. Instead of taking refuge in fainting, however, he invoked mimesis, an affective intentionality often adopted by weak persons in a passive effort to confer upon their attackers their own passivity (*PI* 98). This phenomenal principle is perhaps at work in the Biblical admonition, "a soft answer turneth away wrath." It is almost certainly the principle underlying Christmas' actions when Miss Atkins loomed in the closet door. There was no place for the child to hide, no place to run, so he tried to escape the only way he could escape: he offered himself as a model for imitation: he went limp in her hands. Phenomenologically, by remaining perfectly still he believed that the enraged woman would remain still too. More often, however, Christmas' fear took an active form. Flight is the failure of mimesis (*E* 63). Once the frightened person realizes that the model he is offering has been rejected, he attempts to flee, and for Christmas the failure was not occasional, as it is for most of us, but his being-in-the-world. Rejected by white people as well as black, rejecting them in turn, he was existentially alienated, a creature incapable of imitating anyone else or forcing anyone to imitate him.

The most significant fact in the examples I have given of the attempts to use the emotions as a route of escape from the world of reality is the futility of the attempt. Fear as well as all other emotions, Sartre tells us, is a subterfuge, a delusionary mode of consciousness aimed at changing difficult situations we cannot change by rational means. "The body . . . changes its relations with the world in order that the world may change its qualities" (*E* 61). It is this existential-phenomenological principle that gives emotional behavior its magical attributes, the illusion that changes in physiognomy can bring about cosmic changes. The easily angered seem to be especially drawn to this kind of phenomenal demonology. They are completely engrossed in the wonderland they create, as Henry Armstid, one of the goblins in the troupe playing Yoknapatawpha County, shows.

Like the emotional Christmas—the very name evokes the magical life—Henry was much traveled in wonderland. Arriving late at the auction of some wild Texas ponies, which was being held at Frenchman's Bend under the auspices of Flem Snopes, the premier business man in the County, Henry was exasperated to learn that one of the ponies had already been given away, and after he had paid five dollars for another, he was even more exasperated to find that he could not claim the animal until after the auction was over. The world of business if full of such conditions—contracts, codicils, commissions, covenants, credits, checks, codes, consignments—which are of inestimable value to the business man. They guide him safely through the barriers of an almost endless variety of difficult situations in his work-a-day world, but they also take time and patience. Henry had neither. Taking matters in his own hands, he cornered the pony and instructed his wife to guard it. He then went to fetch a rope to lead it away. At this point, all was going well for Henry. He had routed the world of business with all its foolish quibbles and qualifications, and he had taught his friends, who had refused to help him catch his pony, that when Henry Armstid wanted something he got it. Unfortunately, Henry's triumph was short-lived. When he returned, the pony was no longer cooperative. It refused the rope, and the more obstinate it became, the angrier Henry became (*H* 335).

Anger is a godsend to those made unhappy by obstinate ponies. Taking the rope, which had proved ineffectual as a lasso, Henry struck his wife and Presto! the difficult world of horse wrangling changed into the easy world of wife wrangling. There she stood, quietly offering herself as a model for Henry to imitate, but, more important, quiet, docile, tractable: the model mare. Anger is one of the most effective and satisfying of all the emotions, for, consistently, the angered succeed in offering their victims a world they are willing to accept. Or to put it another way, the angry man convinces his victim that the magical world he is offering is the real world (*E* 36-37). In this instance, Armstid's belief that capturing his wife was as satisfactory as capturing his pony was matched by Mrs. Armstid's joining him in that belief. In fact, he was so pleased that he had drawn back to strike her again when the Texan, who was Flem's auctioneer, snatched away the rope. Ironically, Henry found himself joining his wife: he froze. Immobile, he would immobilize his foe, and for a minute he did. Then the Texan took hold of Henry's arm and led him and his wife from the lot, as Henry would like to have led the pony. The three of them walked through the gate, the pony remained free, and the difficult world of auctions remained as difficult as ever (*H* 337).

Ab Snopes, another of the wraithlike beings in the troupe

frolicking in *The Hamlet*, shares with Henry a sense of the marvelous and supernatural, but where Henry occupied the enchanted regions of anger, Ab was at home in the witching world of hatred. Anger and hate are different in that anger is a simple kind of enchantment appropriate for simple situations. Hate is complex. First, there is richer body involvement. Good haters show a certain physical kinship, a kinship noted in Cassius and Ab Snopes. Both of them, the Roman and the tenant farmer, looked the part: the old faces, the rock-hard heads, metallic voices, stiff backs (*H* 270). Secondly, hate is an emotion whose aim is nothing so simple as displaced aggression, the conventional psychological term for Henry's rope trick. Hate is the magical means by which we possess an object by destroying it. Ab Snopes gives us several good instances of this magic. The first involves his appropriation of Major De Spain's beautiful French rug, the centerpiece in De Spain's manorhouse. Unhappy that the plantation owner could afford this beautiful object completely out of his reach, Ab deliberately, angrily soiled the piece, and when De Spain insisted he clean it, Ab's anger turned to hate. He not only would soil the rug, he would destroy it. First, he spread the piece on the ground beside a pot of boiling water in which he put lye soap, and then he ordered his daughters to scrub it. Dissatisfied with the effort, he took over. The excuse he gave was that his daughters were not working fast enough (*CS* 13); the phenomenal facts are otherwise. In his hatred Ab wished to destroy the rug and thus deprive the major, but more than this, he would through the destruction make the rug his.

According to Sartre, destruction is a magical means of appropriation—to the man of hate, the favorite means—and in order to make this emotional metabolism clear, Sartre compares it with the metabolic processes of eating, processes that combine the simultaneous annihilation of the object with its appropriation. Phenomenally, Sartre says, the man of hate satisfies his emotional appetite the same way that he satisfies his physical one: he consumes (*B&N* 593-94). And whether it be a ham hock or De Spain's rug, the consumption involves intimate body contact. It is for this reason Ab pushed his daughters aside. Taking up a rock and kneeling beside the rug, he made it his. Magically, the disintegrating fibers found their way through his hands into himself. He absorbed the fine textures, the beautiful design, recreating out of this rug his own, as he indicated when De Spain took him to court and the judge rendered the verdict against him. Asked by the judge whether he had anything to say, Ab kept silent, and well he should have. What difference did it make to him that he had not, as the judge complained, returned the rug to De Spain as it was in its prior condition? The rug was now his. No answer was necessary (CS 13-18).

The premier hater is the pyromaniac, for the ultimate means of destruction is fire (*B&N* 593). Where the lye and the rock did a good job on the rug, there were still here and there a few remnants left, remnants that were not Ab's. If he had burned the rug, everything would have been consumed, nothing left. No wonder, then, this pyromaniacal Snopes loved fire, its very "element" speaking "to some deep mainspring of his . . . being" (CS 7). For him oil and grease for burning a barn were different from the oil and grease on a wagon wheel. In his hands, these substances metamorphosed into combustibles magically invested with vital powers, the phenomenal powers of possession by destruction. And thus carefully, lovingly Ab emptied "the reservoir of the lamp back into the five-gallon kerosene can from which it had been filled," and then he ordered his son Flem to empty a small can of lubricating oil into the larger one and then he spoke to his acolyte, "I'll catch up with you" (CS 20-22). Ab caught up with Flem but not before he had taken phenomenal possession of De Spain's barn. Transported to fairyland he had discovered in the all-consuming flames everything he had ever wished: corn, wheat, cotton, horses—a plantation.

Ab's cousin Mink, another man of hate, also used destruction as a means of possession, and shortly we shall look at his effort. In the meantime, we shall have to pay closer attention to Mink than we have paid to Ab and to Henry Armstid, for his emotions are more complicated than theirs. What made Mink so different from his kinsmen was the emotion that controlled his life, emotion in one of its most subtle, complex, and damaging forms—resentment.

Mink's big emotional problem, the one that led ultimately to the deaths of two men and years of imprisonment for himself, began in late autumn when his cow strayed into Jack Houston's pasture. Not having enough feed to get the animal through the winter, Mink left her there, and when Jack sent word for him to come get her, Mink countered with the lie that he had sold the cow to one of the Goweries. The following spring, when Mink did go to reclaim her, his only thought was that he would have to pay Houston the eight dollars he had supposedly collected from Gowerie, but when he attempted to hand the money over, Houston refused it, offering the same amount and keeping the cow. Mink accepted this news about as willingly as Armstid had accepted the news that he would have to wait for his pony, and he reacted the same way. The world of business too difficult, he would pretend it never existed. He wanted his cow, he wanted it now, and he had reached the top rail of the fence that enclosed the cow lot before he saw Houston's drawn pistol (*M* 9-15). Armstid had found relief in attacking his wife, but Mink was left helpless. Just how helpless was apparent when he resorted to spite, refuge for the weak womanish but not much comfort to a man (*R* 47). Weakly, as he walked away from Houston, he shot his small Parthian arrow, "So long then. In case you do make any eight-dollar stock deals, be sho you dont take no wooden nickels" (*M* 16). Then, as he continued to walk, spite turned to blind rage.

To go blind with rage is like fainting from fear in that it is a magical means of eliminating the enemy. He is no longer there, for he cannot be seen. And so as Mink walked away, Houston, the pistol, the fence disappeared, and as he continued walking, his rage subsided and his sight returned—but not for long. When at last he reached Will Varner, the justice of the peace, and told him what had happened, Will had bad news. Mink could not legally repossess the cow without paying Houston for the cow's keep. This time it was Will who disappeared. Mink went quite blind again, and when Varner reappeared, his voice asking if Mink could pay the required sum, there came over Mink's face the dazed look of someone under a spell, "faint and gentle and almost like smiling" and from his mouth a single sound, 'No'" (*M* 17). To be able to speak gently when there is nothing to speak gently about, to be able to smile when there is nothing to smile about is to perceive a world phenomenally different from a world where words and smiles mean what they say. Mink reveals this world, the world of *resentment*.

Resentment always begins with some other emotion such as spite, anger, hate. If the injured person acts—strikes his wife, as Armstid did—resentment fails to materialize. It can only arise, Max Scheler writes in his existential-phenomenology of *resentment*, if the "emotions are particularly powerful and yet must be suppressed because they are coupled with the feeling that one is unable to act them out" (*R* 48). Powerless to act against the justice of peace, emotions driven inward, Mink masked them: he smiled. Masks are one of the chief weapons of the resentful and take several forms. First, there is the common phenomenon of the resentful, invidious comparisons between himself and the enemy. These comparisons inevitably make use of what Scheler calls "illusory *devaluation*." Unable to compete with Houston, Mink set up subjective standards by which he sought his own superiority by lowering his foe's (*R* 58). This man, Mink told himself, could much better afford to pasture the cow than he could, a man rich enough to raise fine cattle and to keep Negroes but, at the same time, Mink told himself, he, Mink Snopes, was a better man. Though not so rich as Houston, he was independent, a man who paid his own way, while Houston was arrogant, sulky, surly. In actuality, Houston was not the "rich son-of-a-bitch" (*M* 11) Mink called him but another farm boy who, seeking his fortune, first became a time-keeper on a railroad construction gang, then a locomotive fire-man, and, in-between, longshoreman, and construction worker. After some thirteen years, he had come back to Frenchman's Bend to marry his childhood sweetheart and when she died, he returned the installment-plan furniture, fired the Negro cook, and loafed. Several years later, when he began to run a few cattle, his effort was half-hearted at best (*H* 242-248). His modest holdings were of little value to anyone except the de-luded Mink.

Resentment delusion becomes especially damaging when the resentful envisions the resented not only being better off but as being the *cause* of his deprivation. The simple fact that the enemy is flourishing is enough to make him feel deprived (*R* 52). One winter day, cold and hungry, it occurred to Mink that Houston had accumulated the cattle, the Negroes, the horses at his expense. It was Houston's fault that Mink was cold, that he had been deprived of eight dollars he could have spent for Christmas whiskey; it was because of Houston's "wealth that such a condition could obtain" (*R* 51). Even if Houston had made it possible for him to keep the cow and buy the whiskey, there would have been no relief. Mink confessed as much when he said that he did not resent being out-figured by Houston or that Houston was the richer. Neither was it Houston's appear-ance nor any particular action or fault which caused the resent-ment. Mink resented Houston's existence. His trouble with Jack Houston had begun, Mink said, "at the very instant Houston was born" (*M* 7), and the longer the man lived the more pres-sure Mink had to bear until at last he could bear it no longer. Breaking the cover of *resentment*, Mink fled from all semblance of the perceptual world of Yoknapatawpha County into the wildly delusional world of the imagination, the world "of *They, Them, It*" (*M* 6).

The imaginative consciousness is pure affect, emotional necromancy that allows us to exchange the difficult multidimensional worlds of perception and cognition for the easy simplicity of a world without dimension, one outside time and space and thus amenable to whatever we choose to make it (*PI* 188). In describing this world, Sartre could have been taking as his model Mink Snopes' imaginative creation of *They, Them, It,* or, to be completely speculative, it could be that Mink was following directions set forth in Sartre's description. In any event, there is a direct correlation between the existential-phenomenological description and the imaginary creation. For instance, in comparing a perceived object with an imaginary one, Sartre points out that the former presents itself spatially and temporally, like a tree which one can see and touch. The tree was there in the yard last night, it is still there, it will be there tomorrow. The tree imagined lacks the objective spatial and temporal dimensions ruling the precept. Appearing at no particular place at no particular time, the imagined tree takes on the magical aura of *"being absent within its very presence"* (*PI* 104). Mink's *Them* gives off the same aura. Unable to see or touch *Them*, Mink never tells us where *They* are or how much time he spends with *Them*. Imagined, *They* were present only in a phenomenally vague before-after time relation, some place in space.

Denied temporal and spatial dimensions, the image lacks the most important characteristic of the object perceived, a hard-and-fast identity (*PI* 129). We look at the tree with its branches, leaves, trunk and recognize it as an entity different from all other entities. It is unique. Because we never get a sensuous hold on the imagined tree, it does not lend itself to any such individualization (*PI* 129). This failure Sartre calls the *"essential poverty"* of the image (*PI* 189), which, paradoxically, lends it an especially imaginative richness. Unlike the perceived tree, which is "what it is" and "cannot be itself and something else at the same time and in the same relationship" (*PI* 129), the imagined tree can become almost anything we wish it to become: a girl dancing in the wind, a spring bride in white, a witch. Failing to obey the perceptual law of identity, establishing itself unequivocally as what it is, *They*, *Them*, *It* became whatever Mink wished. In a fit of self-pity, he imagined *Them* as "simple fundamental justice" who would allow him to "get his own just and equal licks"; in a mood of braggadocio, he imagined *Them* as a power "testing him to see if he was a man or not" (*M* 5,6).

In addition to, and because of *Their* perceptual poverty, *They* could be kind and helpful but also the exact opposite. In the early stages of his struggle with Houston, Mink had imagined that "*They* would not dare to let him down" in his contest, "else it would be as hard for *Them* to live with themselves afterward as it had finally become for him to live with himself and still keep taking what he had taken from Jack Houston" (*M* 6). As the struggle continued, however, and Mink continued to suffer setbacks, *Their* actions aroused deep suspicions. For one thing, *They* had neglected, as Christ or Justice would not have, to warn him of what would happen if he left his cow in Houston's pasture. Then, too, *They* failed to help him buy the cow back for the eight dollars and to make Varner come across with the cow judgment. Indeed, Mink imagined, *They* were using Varner himself as *Their* tool. From a tentative attempt to see *Them* on his side or at least remaining neutral, Mink came increasingly to use *Them* as an enemy using every means to defeat him. *They* were not Christ or Justice but someone trying "to fling, jolt, surprise him off balance and so ruin him" (*M* 24). There was, Mink concluded, "a pattern to it" (*M* 6), and when Houston pulled the pound-fee deal, using the court to make him pay not only the price of the cow, which was high enough, but that two dollars extra, the pattern came clear. Mink realized that whoever *They* were, *They* would be useless, if not downright dangerous, in his struggle with Houston. Giving up on *Them*, this imaginative accommodation of his impotence, Mink at last acted: Houston's chest came up over the gun-sight and blessed relief. The blast more than eliminated Houston. It gave Mink everything Jack Houston possessed, and thus Mink was highly contemptuous of his cousin Lump Snopes, who had accused him of shooting Houston in order to rob him (*H* 268-69). "Rob him?" Mink could have said. "What do I care about the fifty dollars you say I took off him when I've all his money and barns and cows and niggers, too?" The resentment—that existential cramp, the hard knot in Mink's stomach—had disappeared and with it, *They, Them, It*. Mink would not need *Them* again for fifty years or so, not until he was preparing to shoot Flem. Then *They* would appear in an infinitely more powerful, that is to say, an infinitely more magical guise.

There is no imaginary consciousness as such. There is only the magical "intention": "the incantation destined to produce the . . . thing one desires in a manner that one can take possession of it" (*PI* 81,177). Because Mink's quarrel with Flem was different from his quarrel with Houston, the incantation was different. Reality would play no part in it at all. Mink was mildly envious of Flem, who "with his usual luck" had married that rich Varner girl (*M* 4), but Mink had something even more ephemeral, and therefore more magical, than envy on which to base his quarrel with Flem. It was the imaginary "ancient, immutable laws of simple blood kinship" (*M* 5). After he had murdered Houston and Flem refused to come to his rescue, Mink invoked these laws. Once more he knew that he would need help, and he knew where to find it. Looking past the *Them* who had trifled with him in his struggle with Houston, he turned to the imaginary embodiment of Retributive Justice itself, Old Moster. Here was a Being who clearly understood the all-consuming nature of blood-kinship, a Being who watched vigilantly over His chosen, and when Mink decided on the way to kill Flem for denying any such kinship, he talked with Him and received exactly what he imagined he would receive, confirmation: his ancient pistol would have to shoot. "Old Moster don't play jokes; he jest punishes" (*M* 414). When the weapon misfired, Mink's faith deserted him only long enough to be tested. Then his hands stopped shaking, the magic worked, Snopes' honor was restored.

The magic worked even better as Mink lay hidden in the

cellar of the old house enjoying the fruits of Flem's destruction. Mink again called on Old Moster, inviting Him to join in his good fortune, and as before, the response was all he could hope for. Instead of the Old Man Himself, however, with all those ideas about justice, there appeared someone more like His son, the merciful God "of poor sons-of-bitches." Basking in this mercy and in the warm glow of Flem's murder, Mink waved the wand again. He traded in revenge for mercy, the mansion he had acquired in the killing of Flem for a place much grander, a heavenly place where all the folks were "jumbled up comfortable and easy . . . : the beautiful, the splendid, the proud and the brave, . . . Helen and the bishops, the kings and the unhomed angels . . ." (*M* 435-36). Lying there Mink at last became just like *Them, They, It,* Old Moster—the product of his own imagination, outside time and space for eternity.

Notes

[1]Cleanth Brooks, *William Faulkner, The Yoknapatawpha County* (New Haven: Yale UP 1963), 170,171,172.

Chapter V

COLONEL SUTPEN AND
THE ORIGINAL CHOICE

Over the years Colonel Thomas Sutpen's critics have tried to explain why he failed in his attempt to become a gentleman planter, just as Sutpen himself spent the last years of his life trying to explain the failure. The critics write that he failed because he was "unhuman,"[1] because his "morality was . . . abstract and merely logical," because he failed to "recognize the 'strong work' of love."[2] His failure lay in his inability to "reconcile successfully democratic idealism with aristocratic society."[3] Many critics believe the "'Sutpen's failure,' as Quintin's grandfather observed, 'was innocence.'"[4] All of these reasons for the colonel's failure are interesting and important, but we want something more—a critical method that will lead us away from surface manifestations to the core of his trouble. Sutpen himself gives us a clue to such a method. In trying to track down what went wrong, he came to grips with one of the most widely known existential-phenomenological tools, the *original choice* (*B&N* 570).

In laying the groundwork for modern phenomenology, Edmund Husserl wrote that "it is intentionality which characterizes *consciousness* in the pregnant sense of the term" (*I* 222). In setting forth the doctrine of free choice, Jean-Paul Sartre merely substituted the term *choose* for *intend*. Man chooses—intends—to be conscious in the way that he is conscious (*B&N* 570,573). Although Sartre recognizes sharp and deep conflict among the existential-phenomenologists, he holds that all of them, both Christian and humanist, "have in common . . . the fact that they believe that *existence* comes before *essence*—or, . . . that man first of all exists, encounters himself, surges up in the world—and defines [chooses] himself afterwards" (*EDS* 289,290). Perhaps the most important choice man makes in defining himself—doubtless the one with the most serious consequences for his existence—is the first choice he makes. He decides whether to react emotionally to the phenomenon under scrutiny or to think about it. No matter what the object, man has to choose whether to approach it emotionally or rationally. One way of making clear this choice is to take an example. When I burn my finger, I perceive the pain, but my response to it is my own free choice. I can curse, trying magically to scare the pain away; I can shake my finger, trying magically to rid myself of the offending member. On the other hand, I can think about relieving the pain and head for the medicine cabinet.

Psychic wounds are subject to the same phenomenological principle as physical, and the main difference between Joe Christmas and Mink Snopes and Thomas Sutpen, all of whom sustained such wounds, lies in the phenomenal fact that the colonel was more capable than they of reflecting upon, rather than reacting to, what happened to him. Although it is impossible finally to separate affect and reflection along immutable lines (emotions devoid of thought would be less than human; thought devoid of emotions would exist in a human vacuum [*E* 15, *B&T* 389]), it is fairly easy to show that where Christmas and Mink were greatly confused by the difficult world of which they were a part, Sutpen had some insight into it, and, more importantly for us, his efforts are best understood phenomenologically. They show clearly that man can make a rational choice instead of giving in to a magical one, however alluring, and that this choice can be brought fully into play at an early age (*B&N* 445).

The events leading to Sutpen's crucial decision began a year or so after he and his miserable family had moved from a ramshackle cabin in the Virginia highlands to a hovel in Tidewater. One day in his early teens, Sutpen went on an errand to a large and elegant plantation house. Tidewater etiquette prescribed that poor whites go to the back door of such establishments, but ignorant of this protocol, Sutpen went to the front. A Negro in livery immediately and rudely ordered him to the rear. Even before the black man had finished speaking, Sutpen recalled a dozen similar incidents that had taken place during the two years he and his family had lived in eastern Virginia. The dozen things and the rebuff triggered the first and most important crisis in Sutpen's life: he suddenly found himself having to decide what to do about these incidents. Transfixed, he stood there at the mercy of the other, or, as Sartre would express it, he was "*no longer master of the situation*" (*B&N* 265).

By *situation*, the existential-phenomenologist means all of the internal and external pressures that give shape to our lives. It is the totality of material and psychological conditions which describe the specific character of an era (*E&H* 137). The specific social character of the mountain society in which Sutpen had been raised was light years from that of Tidewater. In the hills there prevailed a rugged, democratic individualism where all men were equal and each respected the equality of others, but in eastern Virginia the rigid class structure of a conservative society was still in force. For several years Sutpen had assumed both societies to be of the same specific character, and when the Negro made him aware of his blunder, he momentarily gave away to his emotions: the words the doorman spoke, whatever they were, had immobilized him as the words of Miss Atkins had immobilized Joe Christmas. But here the parallel ends. Instead of accepting his ignoble condition, going to pieces as Christmas did, Sutpen tried to think about his condition. His first thoughts were of another insolent Negro, this one a coach-man who had sometime earlier shouted his sister out of the road, but in thinking back, Sutpen discovered that what he remembered most vividly was not the insolent driver but the glaring faces of two aristocratic females inside the coach (*AA* 230-31). And now as he stood at the door, what the boy saw was not the black man before him but another aristocratic face, that of the rich man inside the big house. This man

> looked out from whatever invisible place he (the man) hap-
> pened to be at the moment, at the boy outside the barred door

> in his patched garments and splayed bare feet, looking through and beyond the boy, he himself seeing his own father and sisters and brothers as the owner, the rich man (not the nigger) must have been seeing them all the time—as cattle, creatures heavy and without grace, brutely evacuated into a world without hope or purpose for them, who would in turn spawn with brutish and vicious prolixity, double treble and compound, fill space and earth with a race whose future would be a succession of cut-down and patched and made-over garments (*AA* 235).

There, invisible inside the house, was the enemy, Sutpen thought, not the Negro who barred his way.

Standing there, on the threshold of self-encounter and free choice, Sutpen had to solve the kind of problem that faced Ab Snopes in his struggle with Major de Spain. They both "knew that something would have to be done about it," but where Ab knew what had to be done and in a relatively simple, unreflective manner did it, Sutpen was baffled (*AA* 234). Cut off from the old familiar mountain world as well as the present one he was just beginning to understand, the estranged boy again gave in briefly to his emotions. Outraged, he turned from the Negro and walked, almost ran, away. Sutpen's abrupt departure echoed Mink's encounter with Houston when he tried to reclaim the cow. Ears ringing as though a shotgun had gone off too close, Mink knew that he would have to go somewhere to cool off, and so he left (*M* 16). At this point, however, there appears the almost unbridgeable gap between the man of resentment and the reflective man. Continuously in the grip of one mood or another Mink, as we have seen, exchanged the voodoo of spite and resentment against Houston for anger and resentment against Will Varner. Breaking away from such futile attempts to overcome difficulties, Sutpen soon found that he "wasn't even mad," that all he wished to do was "to think, so he was going to where he could be quiet and think." There in a cave, he sat calmly arguing with himself: "*I can shoot him*," but then, Sutpen reflected, "*That wouldn't do no good*" (*AA*

232,233,235). There was a better way, he thought, to beat the man in the big house, and when the moment came to choose that way, the boy made the choice in a moment of reflective exaltation. This experience, which came after he had left the cave and was home in bed, was similar to that which Ab Snopes had undergone in burning the barn and Mink in shooting Houston but was notably different in that it was conceptual rather than visceral.

As Sutpen lay sleepless he gave "the two of them," emotions and reason, a chance to tell him what to do, allowed each to speak "in orderly turn," and then something happened. "All of a sudden it was not thinking, it was something shouting it almost loud enough for his sisters . . . and his father . . . to hear too. . . . It was like . . . an explosion—a bright glare that vanished and left nothing, . . . just a limitless flat plain (*AA* 237-38). Before awakening to the knowledge that through reflection he could reduce mountainous emotional upheavals to sizable reasonable molehills, that, indeed he was free to *choose* his consciousness, Sutpen, like Mink (*M 90*), had believed that life was a matter of luck, "that some people were spawned in one place and some in another, some spawned rich (lucky, he may have called it) and some not, and that . . . the men themselves had little to do with the choosing" (*AA* 222). Now Sutpen knew that he had been wrong. No longer would he be hemmed in by the circumstances of his birth, whining over his lot as poor white trash; above all, he would not be hemmed in by his emotions. Rejecting the magical mode of acquiring property, either by burning a barn or shooting the owner, he could act rationally. First, he would make the money that would buy a house bigger than the man's, then he would keep what he had bought, and, finally, he would turn the house and the land and the slaves over to a son who would continue to build and increase the holdings (*AA* 238).

Long after this moment, decades after, Sutpen again put it very well, this capacity of a man to choose freely the life he wishes to live instead of having his life forced upon him, when he told General Compson that "there was something about a man's destiny (or about the man) that caused the destiny to shape itself to him like his clothes did" (*AA* 245-46). In 1833 or 1834, when Sutpen first talked to the general, the cloth of his destiny fit almost to perfection, for he was on his way to acquiring a large plantation and was well on his way to filling his big-columned house with a family. But by 1859 the cloth had begun to fray badly, and by 1864, when Sutpen talked to the general for a second time (*AA* 270), the cloth was in tatters. The money had disappeared, his wife was dead, his daughter set upon marrying her half-brother, his second son equally set upon killing that brother. Despite Sutpen's careful calculations, the choice he made had brought him to ruins: his "design," as he called it, "house, position, posterity, and all—come down like it had been built out of smoke" (*AA* 267).

One of the reasons Sutpen had sought out the general after the lapse of thirty years was to try to discover why he had failed. Now that the War was about to end, he would come back and rebuild what he had lost, but before he started again and in order to avoid making the same mistake twice, he wished to know what had gone wrong with the first venture (*AA* 271). His approach to the problem was again rational, but, more than that, it was existential. Based on intentionality, existential psychoanalysis postulates that there are no *gratuitous* acts (*CF* 108), that man chooses to act in the way that he acts and, thus, if he wishes to discover why his life has gone wrong, he will have to discover the choice that went wrong. Such an examination, if carried far enough, will lead to the choice of choices, the *original choice* from which all other choices evolve (*B&N* 570). Sutpen's approach and solution to the question show, sometimes clearly, sometimes dimly, that in comparison to this choice all other choices become insignificant. In determining this all-important factor, the transcendental category that homogenizes man's existence, the existential-phenomenologist makes use of a regressive movement that takes him back from the considered act to the "ultimate possible" and then through

means of a "synthetic progression" he returns from this ultimate possible to the considered act. The method of interpretation is strictly *chronological*, not inferential, the goal of inquiry
a precise and concrete choice, not states of consciousness (*B&N*
469). The investigator looks for a decisive choice that has been
made, not for abstract data "buried in the darkness of the
unconscious" (*B&N* 573). Yet because the outline of phenomenal psychoanalysis was first adumbrated by Freud, there is a
similarity between empirical psychoanalysis and phenomenal.

Both psychoanalyses are based on the theory that in each
action of an individual lies the clue to an understanding of all
his actions (we have seen a good instance of this in Christmas'
preference for coconut pie [*LIA* 157]), but the analyses differ in
the method of interpreting the clues (*B&N* 568). Since the
phenomenologists insist that existence comes before essence,
continuously affirming the ontological primacy of phenomena
over consciousness, they start with the phenomenon under
observation and never leave it. Freudian psychology proceeds
on the opposite assumption, insisting that essence precedes
existence. These psychologists assume that the source of all acts
lies primarily in abstract functions such as the libido or the will
to power and then attempt deductively to find experiences that
fit into the hypothesis (*B&N* 570-71). Consequently, they remain
fixed in the shadowy realms of metaphysics and empirical
psychology, speaking of human beings who have an Oedipus
complex or an Electra complex, but they never touch these
phenomena existentially. Even when they succeed in explain-
ing the Oedipal complex to the patient, the patient more often
than not finds it impossible to identify this abstraction with
himself (*B&N* 458,570-72).

To the existential-phenomenologist, then, Freudian psychoanalysis is "existentially irrelevant, psychologically stray-
ing" (*PF & R* 294), the Freudian subconscious is either a mistake or a misnomer, and complexes and libidos are abstractions
without phenomenal meaning (*PP* 171). Where empirical psychoanalysis would probably say that Christmas suffered from

an inferiority complex and would deduce from the hypothesis that the source of his misery could be traced to the cruelties inflicted in his childhood, existentialists would agree that the mulatto did suffer from a consciousness of inferiority but would place the responsibility on Christmas. He had chosen to be ashamed of himself. His "complex" was not forced on him but was a free choice of himself as inferior before others (*B&N* 459). Not wholly unreflective, Christmas as a young man had wondered what was wrong with him and made at least one attempt to find out. Looking back over his life he recalled the early years at the orphanage—the children, the yardman, the dietitian, and the trouble he had had with them, but he was unable to take advantage of this information (*LIA* 102,104). Dupe of his emotions he saw these figures come and go like phantoms in a bad dream and that was all.

Sutpen was rational where Christmas was emotional and thus was able to place the people and events of his life in an understandable order. Looking back he found that he had made two important decisions in connection with the failure of his design: the rejection of his first wife and the repudiation of his son by that wife. He claimed the "second choice" devolved "out of that first one" and the first "was forced" upon him because he married without knowledge of his wife's Negro blood (*AA* 272-74). In undertaking the regressive analysis that leads back to the initial project, the investigator, lay or professional, stops only with the "irreducible" and never believes he has reached the initial project until the projected end appears (*B&N* 457,564). Sutpen did stop before he reached the initial project. Mistaking a "secondary possible" for the "fundamental possible" (*B&N* 470), he was unable to find the one piece that would have made all the other pieces fall into place. The *original choice* did not come with the putting aside of his first wife because of her Negro blood, as he reasoned, but was made seven or eight years earlier when he decided to make himself into a rich man, one like the man who had looked out from inside the big house. This was his original choice, the poisoned spring from whence flowed all other choices. Where Christmas had in unreflective reaction chosen first to be a white man and then a black one, Sutpen had coolly and reflectively chosen to be a white man that he was not. Where Christmas was destroyed, torn apart in pride, shame, and fear, Sutpen destroyed himself in the hell of bad faith, a reflective hell he created out of lying, snobbery, irresponsibility, and cowardice.

In considering these wretched rational phenomena, it is well to bear in mind that all of them are so much a part of each other and of Sutpen's original choice that it is impossible to draw clear lines between them. For example, in distinguishing between lying proper and the lie of bad faith, Sartre maintains that both the liar and the man of bad faith are hiding in themselves a displeasing truth and in their actions presenting as truth a pleasing untruth, but what changes everything is the phenomenal fact that in bad faith, it is not another from whom we are hiding the truth. It is ourselves. Here, the deceived and the deceiver are the same person. We do not learn bad faith, as we learn to lie; we infect ourselves with it (*B&N* 48). Proof of Sutpen's bad faith is found in his original choice: the successful attempt to hide from himself the displeasing truth that he was disreputable white trash and to accept the pleasing untruth that he could remake himself into a respectable gentleman, as respectable as the one looking out from wherever he looked out. First, he had reflected, he would acquire the chief "patent[s] of respectability"—money, land, slaves, a fine house—but he also knew that these were only the outward show, "the shape . . . of that respectability." Only a virtuous woman to preside over these acquisitions would deliver the substance, make his position impregnable; he would find this woman, Sutpen reasoned, in the most respectable establishment in Jefferson, the church. For three years he scrutinized, weighed, and compared daughters and the churches they attended, and then he shrewdly chose one not from a house that would be completely beyond his resources, socially or financially, but from the lesser gentry (*AA* 15,16,41,178).

Rosa Coldfield's opinion of the colonel was biased, but she was correct in the reasons she gave for Sutpen's marrying Ellen and for his indifference to Mr. Coldfield after the marriage. "It was simply because since papa had given him respectability through a wife there was nothing else he could want from papa" (*AA* 28). Sutpen had acquired the respected father-in-law and the virtuous wife and put them (wife and children) in a beautifully appointed house, and yet, despite his efforts, he still remained outside the house, still a dozen miles from Jefferson and respectability. He had been no more successful in blending himself and his possessions into the elegance of plantation society than in blending the wild Haitian Negroes with the tame slaves of Mississippi (*AA* 175,35,36). For all his careful planning he had failed. In bad faith he had chosen himself as respectable only to become respectability's twin, a snob.

An unsavory by-product of man's commitment to respectability is snobbery. This pattern of bad faith is inevitably revealed when man rejects the freedom of an infinite number of social possibilities for those of the particular class he is imitating (*B&N* 626,627). A classic example is Sartre's M. Blévigne, a low-born Frenchman who yearned for the social distinction of *les bourgeoise*. A snob, Blévigne purposefully married someone adjunctive to his business interests, carefully cultivated the social graces of his betters, and commissioned his portrait. In life a squeaky-voiced midget, he appeared in the painting as a tall, well-proportioned, and altogether engaging man (*N* 124-127). Snobbery is different from honest lying, the lie that Mink Snopes told Jack Houston about the sale of the cow (*M* 10), and more destructive. It is a conflict that cannot be resolved by telling the truth, for the snob, as a man of bad faith, already knows in his capacity as deceiver the truth that he is concealing from himself in his capacity as the one deceived (*B&N* 49). Sutpen in his capacity as the one deceived knew that he had no right by blood or education to the aristocratic tradition, and yet in his capacity as the deceiver, he arrogated to himself that right. His portrait could well have hung by that of Blévigne, but instead of a merchant prince, he would appear as the epitome of plantation society, a planter who dabbled at law.

The role of the snob is itself the playing of roles, and Sutpen's came much harder than Blévigne's. To be *un petit bourgeoise*, all that the merchant needed to do was belong to the right clubs, make conversation with the right members, and have a lot of money. Sutpen had to combine the attributes of both planter and lawyer. He had been able to play the first part, convincing at least one person, his prospective father-in-law, Wash Jones, that he was a planter (*AA* 276-84). The role of lawyer was more difficult. He had to look like a lawyer, talk like one, and think like one. When he talked, then, it was as if he were addressing a jury, "head flung up a little," or like an actor playing a judge, he sat his horse, a dais above his audience, "the set of his shoulders forensic, oratorical" (*AA* 240,275). As he sat with General Compson in the general's law offices telling the story of his life, trying to discover why, for all his vigor and alertness, he had failed in his design, he spoke as he had spoken from horseback, overacting to the point that it became increasingly apparent to the general that his visitor had come not for counsel but, like any other actor, in search of an audience. Even when the would-be lawyer realized that the gestures he was making to accompany the story did not ring any truer than the story, it was of little consequence. He was talking to General Compson about someone else, someone he seemed to have known long before, and was "trying to explain the circumstance, to fate itself, the logical steps by which . . . [the person] had arrived at a result absolutely and forever incredible, repeating the clear and simple synopsis of his history . . . as if he were trying to explain it to an intractible . . . child" (*AA* 248,263).

The terms "explain," "logical steps," "simple synopsis" are lawyer's terms, which imply a process of reduction whereby one can put sequences of events, however complex, into a clear and logical order. As Sutpen talked it was evident that where he had perhaps failed in his effort to look and talk like a lawyer, an effort as fake as that of looking like a planter, he had more than succeeded in thinking like a lawyer. Indeed, ironically, his complete devotion to the inductive and deductive processes was a major reason for his sinking even further into the abyss of bad faith. He would apply these processes not only to those areas where they would work well, areas relating to contracts, codicils, and so forth, but also to the one area where the processes would be useless, the life-design of human existence. Sutpen seems never to have learned this lesson, that "his formula and recipe of fact and deduction" when applied to life and the living would not "swim or even float" (*AA* 275). Out of the original reflection on his life had come the knowledge that he was free to choose his own destiny, but he immediately narrowed destiny to what he could reasonably expect, creating the paradox that the more successful he was in establishing this reasonable view of life, the more insupportable his life became. Then, finally, he compounded this error by refusing to accept the responsibility for the life he had chosen.

Evidence of his failure appeared even as he told General Compson how he had left home at fourteen or fifteen for the West Indies and several years later saved his employer's plantation from vandals. As a reward for this act, he was given in marriage the hand of the owner's daughter, and then continuing to talk as if he were an interested spectator recording events involving someone else, Sutpen carefully explained that when he discovered he was married to a Negress, he acted without haste, logically choosing to set her aside, calmly, magnanimously, without reminding her father of the "wasted years . . . which would now leave me behind with my schedule not only the amount of elapsed time which their number represented, but that compensatory amount of time represented by their number which I should now have to spend to advance myself once more to the point I had reached and lost." Instead, Sutpen had coolly told his father-in-law that his daughter's Negro blood "rendered it impossible" for her or the "child [to] be incorporated in my design." Presumably he told his wife nothing. "They deliberately withheld from me," he argued, "the one fact which I have reason to know they were aware would have caused me to decline the entire matter, otherwise they would not have withheld it from me" (*AA* 239-54,264).

Existentially, Sutpen was completely responsible for his marriage, no matter what. All actions, moral or immoral, are controlled by our intentions. We are not born responsible or irresponsible, heroes or villains, nor are we one or the other because of upbringing or education. Intention, not fate or character or some other vague entity, produces the moral and ethical man, the immoral and unethical. We cannot, then, place the cause of our actions beyond our intentions: it is we who choose. In a mood as grim as that of the Hebrew prophets, Sartre writes that "man is responsible for what he is. Thus, the first effect of existential-phenomenology is that it puts every man in possession of himself as he is, and places the entire responsibility for his existence upon his own shoulders" (*EDS* 291). Sutpen's existence was inextricably bound into his wife's, whatever his excuse. His excuse was, in fact, especially reprehensible to the existential-phenomenologist, for Sutpen not only places the blame on his wife but looks upon himself as a victim of circumstances.

One of the sources of the existentialist movement can be traced to Sartre's observation of his countrymen during World War II. He saw France occupied by the Germans and took part in the Resistance. At the center of this movement was the unqualified insistence that a Frenchman could freely choose either one side or the other and that he should be held completely responsible for his choice. He could be either a patriot or a coward. When the War ended, Sartre heard the collaborators give many excuses for their actions, all of them claiming in one way or another that circumstances, not they, were at fault. Sartre denies their excuse: "Since . . . the situation of man . . . [is] one of free choice, without excuse and without help, any man who takes refuge behind the excuse of . . . deterministic doctrine . . . is a self-deceiver" (*EDS* 307). Sartre reserves the innermost

circle of the hell of bad faith for those with deterministic excuses: he calls them cowards. In rejecting his wife and son,
Sutpen joins the French collaborators in that circle.

Mauvaise foi is to the rational man what *ressentiment* is to
the emotional. It is consciousness at its most deceptive, the
"degradation of consciousness in the face of the world" (*E* 77),
and it gave Sutpen's life and the world the unreal quality that
resentment gave Mink's. The phenomenal irony of Sutpen's life
is that this man who spent a lifetime guarding against the
emotions and the magical world they create should have occupied a world just as unreal. It is doubly ironical that Sutpen
himself should never have been aware of its unreality. He told
the story of his life, General Compson noted, as though he were
"telling a story about something a man named Thomas Sutpen
had experienced, which would still have been the same story
if the man had no name at all, if it had been told about . . . no
man" (*AA* 247). It is this insubstantiality that struck Judith,
Clytie, and Miss Rosa when Sutpen returned from the War. "*He
did not seem to sit [on his horse]*," Miss Rosa said, "*but rather
seemed to project himself ahead like a mirage*" (*AA* 159). Miss Rosa,
perhaps more than anyone else saw through this no-man deceiving himself in his impersonation of a man. "He was no
younger son sent out from Virginia"; he arrived from "out of
nowhere" (*AA* 17,16), and when she began in earnest to record
his not-history, she declared emphatically that he was not what
he made himself out to be: "He wasn't a gentleman" (*AA* 14).
Thereafter she used a wide variety of cabalistic terms to describe him—"ogre," "djinn" (*AA* 23), "fiend," "devil" (*AA* 15)—
and searched for perceptual evidence in vain, for "that *speech
sight hearing taste and being which we call human man*" (*AA* 166).
He was "*a walking shadow . . . trying to cling with vain unsubstan-
tial hands to what he hoped would hold him*" (*AA* 171).

Men of bad faith of all eras and climes seem to live the
same unreal existence. Sartre's Aegistheus, the pretentious king
of Argos, sought in vain for life's stays. Like Sutpen, and for
much the same reason, he was unable to define himself: rather

than existing life he chose to play roles. For fifteen years he dressed the part of a king and near the end of his reign he asked bitterly, "What am I but an empty shell" (*TF* 128), and when Orestes came to kill him, he was so weary of his spurious existence that he offered no resistance. "It's too late for me to call for help," he said, "and I am glad it is too late" (*TF* 136). The life and death of Camus' Caligula were just as miserable. He had followed where logic led, "the ruthless logic that crushes out human lives," including his own (*C* 72), and at his death he might have said with Aegistheus, "It's too late." Like Aegistheus, Sutpen had dressed the part and like Caligula followed ruthless logic. At sixty-nine he was still without a son and heir, and on learning that his sixteen-year-old mistress had given birth to a female and not the son he wanted, he became tired of his role. When Sutpen shouted to Wash Jones, the girl's vengeful grandfather, to "stand back," not to "touch" him (*AA* 286) he was repeating for the last time what he had expressed all of his life to everyone, and when Wash did touch him, the colonel at last gave up all pretense, made no resistance. Like the other untouchables, Aegistheus and Caligula, and all other men of bad faith, Sutpen suffered in dying, as in living, from a failure of nerve, the origin of which is found in the choice of himself as something he was not.

Notes

[1] Joseph Gold, *William Faulkner: A Study in Humanism from Metaphor to Discourse* (Norman: U of Oklahoma P, 1966), 30.

[2] John Hunt, *William Faulkner: Art in Theological Tension* (Syracuse: Syracuse UP, 1965), 126, 115.

[3] Peter Swiggart, *The Art of Faulkner's Novels* (Austin: U of Texas P, 1962) 43.

[4] Cleanth Brooks, *William Faulkner: The Yoknapatawpha Country* (New Haven: Yale UP, 1963), 296, 300, 301. Hunt, 122. Swiggart, 14, 156.

Chapter VI

QUENTIN COMPSON AND THE PHENOMENOLOGY OF TIME

Most of the critics commenting on Quentin Compson call attention to his infatuation with time, some of them in passing and some in detail, and nearly all of them finding time to be the "great and powerful enemy" that, in the end, destroyed him.[1] In reaching this conclusion the critics often turn to Henri Bergson's twofold division of time. The first division, we are told, is "pure duration," time in which man can immerse himself in "the stream of becoming." This is time "suffused with *élan vital*," the life-force itself, and, according to the critics, the missing element in Quentin. Instead, he measured his life out in "Bergson's clock-and-calendar time."[2] This is mechanical time, the reference point of which is always the past. Trapped in mechanical time, Quentin was "preoccupied with the past," fixed in it, paralyzed by it.[3] The difficulty with the Bergsonian approach is that it is too simplistic, as Sartre and Merleau-Ponty have pointed out (*B&N* 166-67, *PP* 56-78, *passim* 420-430). Using theories of time first advanced by Edmund Husserl and then Martin Heidegger, the existential-phenomenologists set forth in their holistic description of time a more credible theory than that of Bergson. They are also, as existentialists, more concerned with the effects of their theories on human beings and, by extension, on such fictional beings as Quentin Compson. In turning away from Bergson to the concepts of the existential-phenomenologists, I hope to show, first, that Quentin's life-and-death struggle centered in the future, not the past, and that the struggle was perforce involved with existential freedom and anguish. Finally, I shall point out that Quentin's defeat was not so total as the critics maintain.

For years Sartre carried on a lover's quarrel with Faulkner, most of it revolving around the question of Faulkner and time, especially Faulkner's emphasis on the past. Sartre has written that Faulkner's characters appear to be riding in a carriage and always looking backwards.[4] "You won't recognize in yourself the Faulknerian man," he warns, "a creature deprived of potentiality and explained only by what he was."[5] Sartre goes further. He ties this unfortunate tendency in Faulkner's characters to one of the main precepts of the existential-phenomenologists, human freedom. Reviewing a novel by François Mauriac, Sartre especially discredits those characters whose future actions are fixed in advance by the past, whether it be the past that infects heredity or some outmoded social system or some other deterministic entity. "Do you want your characters to live?" he asks. "See to it that they are free."[6] Although Sartre lists Faulkner along with Hemingway and Dos Passos as having revolutionized the techniques of the novel in France,[7] he also maintains that the very nature of the characters in such a novel as *Sartoris* renders them static:

> This 'nature'—what else can we call it?—which we grasp in terms of its psychological manifestations, does have a psychological existence. It is not even completely subconscious, since it often seems as if the men impelled by it can look back and contemplate it. But, on the other hand, it is fixed and immutable, like an evil spell. Faulkner's heroes bear it within them from the day of their birth. It is as obstinate as stone or rock.[8]

Up to a point Sartre is correct, that is, if we look only at the Colonel Sartorises and General Compsons and the like, those creatures Faulkner has deliberately paralyzed with the venom of the past. Moreover, whether Sartre realized it or not, he is paying Faulkner the high compliment of finding in these characters what Faulkner meant for him and us to find. However, in some of his characters, even in aristocrats, Faulkner evidently wishes us to find something other than paralysis, for he himself maintained that he was always hammering at one thesis: "man is indestructible because of his simple will to freedom."[9]

Contrary to Sartre's belief, Quentin Compson was such a man.[10] Although Quentin did not prove indestructible, he did will to freedom at least once. On June 2, 1910 he attempted to free himself from the past and for the future. Phenomenally, on this day, time was for Quentin not an encumbrance, as critics have maintained, but a mode of freedom.

As children of nature, men are limited physically, as psychological beings they are tied to their emotions, as procurers and gatherers they are saddled with their possessions, but the authority that makes possible all human limitations is time. In an effort to control time and thus cope with the limitations it imposes, man has come up with all sorts of timekeepers— watches, clocks, calendars, logs, journals, histories, ad infinitum. In brief man treats time as if it were an object that can be marked off in segments, each segment existing as a convenience for man and therefore subject to his manipulation (*B&N* 107), as many of Faulkner's characters disclose. When Colonel Sutpen, for example, became displeased with the time he had spent as a boy and a young man, he set aside this time, divorced it from time much more to his liking, the present (*AA* 36). On the other hand, Rosa Coldfield rejected the present for the past (*AA* 134). Gavin Stevens also believed that time could be manipulated. When Temple Drake became pregnant with her first child, she realized, Stevens said, that she could not escape from her dull husband, that she had waited too long. She knew, he continued, that everyone had to pay for his past, which is "something like a promissory note with a trick clause in it": if all goes well, the note "can be manumitted in an orderly manner," he said, but if, as with Temple, something goes wrong, then the past can without warning "foreclose" (*RFN* 162). On the other hand, when Temple's husband, Gowan Stevens, made the same point about the past, Gavin took issue. To Gowan's argument that he was having to pay for his past, in particular the night he and Temple had spent at the Old Frenchman Place, Stevens replied that "there's no such thing as past" (*RFN* 71). Time for Quentin Compson's father was pretty much what it was for Stevens—anything he chose to say that it was. It could be linear, a "gull on an invisible wire attached through space dragged" (*S&F* 129) or like a river, "the fluid cradle of events" (*AA* 66). On yet another occasion, when he handed Quentin the watch that had belonged to his father, he concurred with many of Quentin's literary critics. Time, Mr. Compson said, was the great enemy and warned Quentin that he would do well to forget it, that he not spend all his "breath trying to conquer it" (*S&F* 93).

Like Sutpen, Miss Rosa, and his father, Quentin was compulsively drawn to time, but on the morning of June 2, several weeks after Caddy's marriage, he awakened to a time radically different from theirs, and he immediately expressed that difference. First, he rejected the idea of mechanical time, turning face down the watch given him by his father, and still dissatisfied, he broke the crystal and pulled off the hands (*S&F* 94). Shortly afterward, continuing his attack on mechanical time, he showed the mutilated watch to the jeweler and asked him if any of his watches were correct. The master artisan of sequential time began, "It's twen—" (*S&F* 103), when Quentin, evidently reminded of his own twenty years (*AA* 10), blurted out, "Don't tell me. . . . Just Tell me if any of them are right" (*S&F* 103). Learning that they had not been set, Quentin perceived that the watches were, as his years were, ticking away at a "dozen different hours and each with the same assertive and contradictory assurance" (*S&F* 104). Realizing at last the inauthentic nature of segmented time, the enemy his father had warned him against, Quentin moved off and was to move for the remainder of the day, free in phenomenal time.

Phenomenal time is limitless. It cannot be placed in sequence or poured out like grains of sand or manipulated like hands of a clock. It is like the beat coming from Quentin's watch pocket, like the beat of his heart—steady, life-giving but unrecorded. Instead of moving like a gull in a straight line, out of the past to the present and into the future or like a stream flowing between its banks from back then, until now, to when, it is time as a fountain:

> the water changes while the fountain remains because its
> form is preserved; the form is preserved because each succes-
> sive wave takes over the function of its predecessor: from
> being the thrusting wave in relation to the one in front of it,
> it becomes, in its turn and in relation to another, the wave that
> is pushed; and this is attributable to the fact that, from the
> source to the fountain jet, the waves are not separate; there
> is only one thrust (*PP* 421).

The waves of the past, present, and future are as different as
perception, imagination, and cognition are different; yet these
dimensions can be separated no more successfully than consciousness can be separated. Separating the waves of time is
what separates consciousness: nothingness (*B&N* 147,34). Both
phenomena are a ceaseless, layerless moving outward, for
convenience called time, consciousness, intentionality (*PP* 427).
Quentin Compson expressed the welling-up as all day he
walked the streets of Cambridge: walking, riding, standing,
staring, not staring at anything in particular, not doing anything
in particular, not going any place in particular, finding one
mode of locomotion to be as good as another, one place to go
to or depart from as good as another, one time to leave or return as good as another. He would walk a road, stand on a
bridge, this one or that (*S&F* 114,139,140). He would descend
from one trolley to catch another (*S&F* 109,126), sometimes
alighting and watching boys fishing or swimming (*S&F* 144-
45), and when the boys would ask him where he was going, he
would answer, "Nowhere. Just walking" (*S&F* 147). Now all
day, in phenomenological freedom, free the twelve-hours-
months he would live, he heard chronological time without
listening, saw it without seeing. Once he drew within sight of
a clock in a "cupola," but he never saw the position of the hands
on the clock, only the "round stupid" face (*S&F* 154). All day
he was hearing clocks bonging, the sounds either beginning or

ending. Only once did he hear the hour strike and then he did not hear what hour (*S&F* 97). The chimes were ringing in for him a different time, not heard or seen, but time perceived as movement and movement unceasing. With nothingness between, it was always a "quarter" after (*S&F* 99,78) or a "half" after (*S&F* 101,124) or a "quarter" till (*S&F* 126,128). In the world in phenomenological time where consciousness is presence to all places and all objects and not merely to the privileged, it is presence to human beings in the same mode: that is, in anguish (*B&N* 32,33).

Anguish is the consciousness of a missing center. It is free-floating, like time and space, like Quentin on his last day on earth: freedom itself come to life. Indeed, anguish is the existentially painful realization of our infinite possibilities and our freedom to choose among them. Over and over Sartre insists that human beings, even as they pay lip service to freedom, attempt to escape from it and the accompanying anguish. We attempt to hide anguish from ourselves, Sartre says, by eliminating the contingent in our lives; we fly from an anguished freedom, which by nature postulates the conditional, and toward an easy and inflexible security (*EDS* 295, *B&N* 43). Sutpen was an outstanding example. His flight began the moment he gave up on the endless possibilities of existing a life of his own for the securities of his faked life of a gentleman planter. His relief from anguish was immediate. No longer suffering the torment inherent in freedom's contingency, he embraced the comforting security of the planned existence. Quentin rejected this security. He lived life in the conditional mode, the mode of the future indefinite. Adding to the anguish was the knowledge that no one could help him solve his existential dilemma. Free, he knew that he was alone.

"It is in anguish," Sartre writes, "that man gets the consciousness of his freedom. . . . In anguish I apprehend myself at once as totally free and as not being able to derive the meaning of the world except as coming from myself (*B&N* 29,40). At the heart of anguish, then, lies the knowledge that man is completely alone and can rely on no one but himself. Sartre calls this condition abandonment. "When we speak of abandonment, . . ." he writes, "we only mean to say that God does not exist, and that it is necessary to draw the consequences of his absence right to the end" (*EDS* 294). Actually, Sartre means much more. He not only refuses to look to God for help but he also refuses to seek refuge in such familiar props as empirical psychology, sociology, or history. Furthermore, he denies that any ethical or moral system is of any benefit. Even man himself is powerless to advise another. Man meets his deepest needs alone. Orestes, the anguished hero in the *The Flies*, cries out, "I am alone," and Roquentin, the anguished writer in *Nausea*, groans, "I live alone, entirely alone" (*TF* 162, *N* 14).

Quentin shared their loneliness. Although he roomed with Shreve and listened to him talk and talked to him, phenomenally they are light years apart. One was Southern, the other Northern. Quentin was alienated from his family. He could barely conceal his contempt for his hypochondriac mother and the brassy Jason, he distrusted his father, his jealousy alienated him from Caddy. The only person he could approach with ease was Benjy, who remained inaccessible to him. On occasion he looked in the direction of God and St. Francis, but in neither of them did he place the trust and faith that, say, Sutpen placed in General Compson. Indeed his loneliness was borne in on him in a life-crushing incident revealing that man's actions are invariably motivated by self-interest: their psychological faces always turned inward.

It happened this way. Feeling "noon," (*S&F* 129) Quentin entered a bakery where the only other customer was a little Italian girl, and after defending the child from the owner's accusation of stealing, he bought her a bun and they went to a drugstore for ice cream. On finishing he suggested that she run along home, but she simply stared at him. He walked away, she followed, and frightened he ran (*S&F* 155,156,159,160,165). He ran in a circle and when he stopped he found the child staring at him. Again he set off with the little girl, trying to help her find the way home. This effort was rewarded by a violent attack by her brother Julio who, accompanied by a sheriff, had found Quentin and the child wandering near the river (*S&F* 170,172). After the sheriff had separated them, Quentin began to explain and was warned that anything he might say could be used against him. "Will you come peaceable," the officer asked him, "or do I have to handcuff you?" (*S&F* 170,174). The question struck Quentin with greater force than Julio's blows. Once he had heard Miss Rosa speak of "honor" and "principle" as "*the miragy antics of men*" (*AA* 162), and now he discovered the full import of the assertion. Before his eyes, his own heroic antics evaporated. "Stole his sister . . . Stole his——," and then he "began to laugh." He "tried to stop" but he could not. "I'll h-have to qu-quit. . . . It'll stop in a mu-minute" (*S&F* 174).

Like any other emotion, laughter is a way of escaping difficulties we cannot solve by rational means (see Chapter IV). Quentin had tried very hard to help the child but instead of gratitude, he had received blows. Worse, he was on his way to jail. Worst, he could see that any rational explanation of his antics would have been lost on the two angry men, and, like the immobile Christmas inviting the furious dietitian to join him in immobility, Quentin had invited his persecutors to laugh with him at the absurdity. They refused the invitation, and in a few minutes, Quentin felt "the laughter" running "out" (*S&F* 174). It was not long before it was running back. About the time that his laughing fit was drying up, he was joined by Shreve and other acquaintances, who established his good character and effected his release (*S&F* 175-179). "Now, Quentin," one of them said, "you tell me what all of this foolishness is about" (*S&F* 181). Quentin could and could not tell. What had happened to him had offered, as had the events of Sutpen's life, "thirteen ways of looking at a blackbird," and every one of the ways was as good or as bad as the others: Julio and the sheriff used the foolishness as an excuse for making "six dollars," Spode as an occasion to show off his wit, Shreve as an occasion to sermonize, Missess Holmes and Dangerfield as an excuse to be faintly horrified (*S&F* 180-181). Whatever meaning Quentin gave the foolishness would have been of no more value than theirs. More urgently, there was no reason for his giving any meaning at all to it: equivalence itself in suspense, he "began to laugh again. I could feel it in my throat. . . . I couldn't stop it and then I knew that if I tried to stop it I'd be crying" (*S&F* 182-183).

Hysteria is this uncertainty, caught somewhere between laughing and crying (*PP* 379). Hysteria is like resentment in that it is driven inward. The damage the hysterical person does is to himself, not others; thus it is easy for us "to treat him as a dissembler," maintaining that he is feigning the laughter and tears, and to a degree we are right. "The victim of hysteria [does] not feel what he feels, and feel[s] what he does not feel" (*PP* 379). As abductor of the child, Quentin felt guiltless, unable to feel his guilt, feeling what he did not feel. Unable to give himself wholly to guiltlessness or to guiltiness, to laughter or to tears—unable to feel what he felt and feeling what he did not feel—there was "left . . . at his core," as at the core of all hysterics, "a zone of tranquillity" (*PP* 379). The core is like the eye of a cyclone, a dead silence; it is also the aim and end of hysteria. When we see someone hysterical, struggling to tell us what is wrong but unable to express himself, we think that he is too upset to speak. This is what he wishes us to believe, but the truth lies elsewhere. Quentin did not go into hysterics "*because*" he could not say "*anything*"; he became hysterical "*in order not to say anything*" (*E* 31). Indeed, what was there for him to say about his foolishness? Why should he explain it? How could he explain it? Values in suspense, his explanation would have been no better or worse than the person who had asked the question, and so laughing-crying, he was mute. Even when the hysteria disappeared, the dead silence remained, in fact deepened as, at the end of the day, he returned to his room and once again lay on the bed he had occupied for five months (*S&F* 183). But still there was no peace: the chimes struck the half hour and then three quarters (*S&F* 214,219) and, as throughout the day, "the chimes" in suspense, "saying Quarter to what? All

97

right. Quarter to what?" This time the question led him to the final silence and, for a third time, to the same ending: existence somewhere "between silence and nothingness" (*S&F* 212).

The simplest explanation of death is like the simplest explanation of time or values or hysterics: we can call it something else. Sartre has explained it as the end of life, proclaiming, "Death . . . 'transforms life into destiny'" (*B&N* 540). Harry Wilbourne and Gavin Stevens equated death with sleep, "the little death called sleeping" (*WP* 282, *T* 317). Mr. Compson, in his letter to Quentin on the death of Miss Rosa, spoke dogmatically of its *"irrevocable and unplumable finality"* (*AA* 173). Miss Rosa herself stood by Bon's grave and delivered him up to that finality: *"He was absent, and he was; he returned, and he was not; three women put something into the earth and covered it, and he had never been"* (*AA* 153). In this concept of death, the deceased is given over to those who outlive him. He is an object that can never become a subject (*B&N* 297): Sartre's actor Kean expressed the condition when he said that "there's nothing more naked than a corpse" (*K* 225). Only the memory of the deceased, say those who hold with Kean, can prevent his "life from shriveling up" and falling "into oblivion" (*B&N* 541). Sometimes these memories make him prey for the living, as Bon was for Miss Rosa and Sartre's Garvin for those he had betrayed. "I'm locked out," Garvin said; "they're passing judgment on my life without troubling about me, and they're right, because I'm dead. Dead and done with" (*NE* 40).

At other times the deceased can remain in purgatory (*B&N*544). No one's point of view of Sutpen can be taken as final, General Compson's, Mr. Compson's, Shreve's. Often the dead become objects of indifference to those who knew them, like Quentin himself: only Roskus and a few others seem to have remembered him at all (*S&F* 245,249,374, *M* 322). At other times the deceased will (also like Sutpen) forestall this backhanded blow from life by having ready a monument or some other form of memorial. Sutpen's daughter tried to pass on her existence through Bon's letters (*AA* 126-127). Still other simplistic views of death show that such efforts are unnecessary, that we have no choice, that it is we who are immobilized by the dead. "A man will talk about how he'd like to escape from living folks," said Byron Bunch. "But it's the dead that do him the damage. It's the dead men that lay quiet in one place and dont try to hold him, that he cant escape from (*LIA* 65). Old man Falls and Bayard Sartoris respectfully remained under the spell of Colonel Sartoris long after his death. The old man coming in from the county poorhouse fetched "like an odor . . . the spirit of the dead man into that room where the dead man's son sat." The Colonel "was a far more palpable presence than either of the two old men" (*Sart* 1). Sartre's Von Gerlach was making the same point when he said that for him death was "merely the continuation of life without me" (*CA* 25), in this continuation he would go on exercising a tyrant's control of his family. Perhaps the best expression of the dead capturing the living is made by Gabriel Marcel's Andre and Mireille Verdet. Acting the role usually reserved for the possessive mother-in-law, Andre's aunt had taken charge of his household, and when he and his wife attempted to recover it, she threatened to take her life. If she were to kill herself, they reasoned, their life together would become "unbearable." Her death, they believed, would make her "invincible" (*VC* 276-282,21).

Such views were anathema to Marcel. Man in death, he writes, resembles man in life; the uniqueness of life and death is the same. Whatever man is in life, he is in death: "it is death that will open the door to all we have lived on earth" (*CF* 141-143,173). It is for this reason that Quentin's day is so painful for him and for us. His possibilities for living were, in anguish, correlated with his possibilities of dying. His anguish in being-toward-death is the existential-phenomenological correlative of his being-toward-life: "murmuring bones and the deep water, . . . and after a long time" (*S&F* 98) the bones suspended in and indistinguishable from the water, moving in the stream in death as he was moving in life. The last glimpse we have of him, as he leaves his room to make real what he has imagined,

he again reveals his anguish, being-toward-death as the ontological analogue to being-toward-life.

We can reduce thoughts of suicide to the same over-sim-
plified contexts to which we can reduce thoughts of death in
general (*B&N* 137). We can, for example, narrow our options to
whether life is or is not worth living. Baudelaire was working
on this option when he wrote, "I am going to kill myself . . .
because I am useless to other people" (*B* 29). So were Eula
Varner Snopes, Joe Christmas, and Colonel Sutpen when they
chose to remove themselves from a world that would not accept them (*T* 340, *LIA* 404,406, *AA* 285,286). Although neither
of the males actually pulled the trigger or wielded the scythe,
both welcomed death with open arms. Mr. Compson also gave
support to this approach. He believed that we need a reason for
committing suicide, and when Quentin spoke to him of his attraction to Caddy, his father said that disappointment in love
was no reason (*S&F* 221).

To Quentin this logic was, as usual, too easy. Suicide was
not a matter of killing himself or not killing himself over Caddy,
not a matter of incestual love, whether returned or rejected. Nor
was it a matter of usefulness or uselessness in the eyes of others. The poet James Mossman was expressing Quentin on suicide when he left a note reading, "I cannot bear it any more, but
I don't know what it is."[11] What neither of the young men could
bear was the anguish of not knowing "what it is": "Quarter to
what?" (*S&F* 212). Christmas, Sutpen, and Baudelaire had
struck the hour, something or nothing, and Harry Wilbourne
saw the existential-phenomenological ding-dong in the dying
eyes of Charlotte. They were "open full upon him. . . . Then he
saw it begin: the I. It was like . . . a fish . . . [rising] in water—
a dot, a minnow, and still increasing, in a second there would
be no more pool but all sentience." Something. Then "the fish
became the minnow again and then the dot; in another second
the eyes would empty again and blank" (*WP* 262). Nothing.

Quentin was neither something nor nothing: he was
neither *I* nor Not-I: he was *i*.

The "null relation" (*B&N* 88), the anguished in-between has been adumbrated in the plastic arts especially in the i-men of Giacometti, these beings that refuse to congeal into something or nothing (*Sit* 177-192, esp. 180-181, 184). His beings are neither finished nor unfinished but in the act of finishing unfinishing (*EA* 48-51). Caught between being and nothingness, they are the embodiment of uncertainty. The elongated bodies with long, stringy limbs are, on the one hand, all tensile strength, tough as the metal that molds them; the heads, faces, and hands are flesh as hard as bone and bone as soft as flesh. Life here does not rise like a fish or sink like a minnow; the source of existence wells up from the anguish of becoming. Life is created in the image of anguish, of nothingness, and of human reality, a quarter till, elapsed and yet-elapsing. Quentin could have been Giacometti's model: all day caught up in the ontological tension, he was, like the model, on the verge of breaking into life or sinking into death, existing somewhere in-between. This is the reason he kept secret his thoughts of killing himself.

Karl Jaspers, like Marcel, believes that life and death are irrefutably linked; both phenomena can evince man's priceless possession, his freedom. To illustrate the point, Jaspers takes a man who finds himself living in a world existentially different from the world others live in, who finds that every attempt to realize his goals has failed, who finds himself doomed to "watch his own sinking." If this man, Jaspers continues,

> proceeds to take his life without defiance, calmly and naturally, having put his affairs in order, it may be as if he were offering himself as a sacrifice. Suicide becomes the last freedom left in his life. It . . . hurts no living person . . . commits no betrayal. It marks the limit of the capacity of realization, and no one is the loser (*KJP: II* 269).

The man Jaspers has in mind could have been Quentin Compson: life in a different world . . . life without defiance, . . .

commits no betrayal, . . . puts his affairs in order, . . . the last freedom left in life, . . . watch his own sinking. *Watch his own sinking*: to watch Quentin that day in June is to have the sensation of watching him watch himself as he was going down in a sea of his own creation. All day long we are with this drowning man who sees his life passing before his eyes. We watch his bones floating in the Charles; we listen to him deliver his funeral oration: "*Non fui. Sum. Fui. Nom Sum.* Somewhere I heard bells once. Mississippi or Massachusetts. I was. I am not" (*S&F* 216).

All day caught up in the existential-phenomenological ding-dong, he was trembling on the verge of breaking into life or sinking into death, and as he was preparing to leave his room in Cambridge for the last time, he gives us one more glimpse of this i-man. Once more he heard without listening to the last note of the college clock sounding. It stopped vibrating, and he snapped on the light, put on his coat, and got out a fresh handkerchief. Taking great pains, the pains of one under grave tension, he brushed his teeth, carefully squeezing the brush and putting it into his traveling bag. That morning, when Quentin was getting dressed, Shreve teased him about all the primping. "Is it a wedding or a wake? he asked" (*S&F* 100). Quentin was pleased. If Shreve could not guess what it is, no one can, even Quentin himself, and he cannot guess now. He can be going to a wedding or a wake or both. Free to choose, he can be going to neither. All awaits confirmation in the future he is making for himself.

Notes

[1] Frederick J. Hoffman. *William Faulkner* (New Haven: College and UP, 1961), 55; Peter Swiggart, *The Art of Faulkner's Novels* (Austin: U of Texas P, 1960), 94.

[2] Ida Fusel, "Spatial Form and Spatial Time," *Western Humanities Review,* 16 (Summer 1962), 227,229.

[3] John W. Hunt. *William Faulkner, Art in Theological Tension* (Syracuse: Syracuse UP, 1965), 58; Michael Millgate, *The Achievement of William Faulkner*

(New York: Random House, 1966), 96; Vernon T. Hornback, "The Uses of Time in Faulkner's *The Sound and the Fury*," *Papers on English Language and Literature* I (Winter 1965), 51; James D. Hutchinson, "TIme: The Fourth Dimension in Faulkner," *South Dakota Review*, 6 (Autumn 1968) 92.

4 Jean-Paul Sartre, "On 'The Sound and the Fury,'" *Literary and Philosophical Essays*, trans. Annette Michelson (New York: Collier, 1955), 82.

5 Jean-Paul Sartre, "Time in Faulkner: *The Sound and the Fury*," *William Faulkner: Two Decades of Criticism*, ed. Frederick J. Hoffman and Olga W. Vickery (East Lansing Michigan State UP, 1954), 187.

6 Jean-Paul Sartre, "Francois Mauriac and Freedom," *Literary and Philosophical Essays*, trans. Annette Michelson (New York: Collier, 1955), 7.

7 Jean-Paul Sartre, "American Novelists in French Eyes," *Atlantic Monthly*, CLXXVIII (August 1946), 117.

8 Jean-Paul Sartre, "William Faulkner's 'Sartoris,'" *Literary and Philosophical Essays*, trans. Annette Michelson (New York: Collier, 1955), 77.

9 "William Faulkner," *Writers at Work*, ed. Malcolm Cowley (New York: Penguin, 1958), 126.

10 Jean-Paul Sartre, "Time in Faulkner: *The Sound and the Fury*," William Faulkner: Three Decades of Criticism, ed. Frederick J. Hoffman and Olga W. Vickery (East Lansing: Michigan State UP, 1960), 230.

11 "September Report on Atlantic Monthly Books," *The Atlantic*, CCVIII (Sept. 1971), 105.

Chapter VII

THE ROMANTIC WOMAN:
CADDY, TEMPLE, AND CHARLOTTE

Of all the women Faulkner has given us, Caddy Compson, Temple Drake, and Charlotte Rittenmeyer have received the most attention from the critics. The reception of these women has been mixed. Although several critics have denounced them as depraved, immoral, nymphomaniacal,[1] others have found them worthy of praise—Caddy's loving treatment of Benjy, Temple's suffering over the murder of her child, Charlotte's bravery in the face of a disastrous love affair.[2] Furthermore, critics write sympathetically that these women should not be judged too harshly for their weaknesses. They are caught up in a "primal force"[3] over which they have no control, a force alluded to as the "reality principle,"[4] the "force-of-life."[5] It is, the critics write, "both villain and hero," a "trap which every woman possesses and is possessed by."[6] These comments are interesting and somewhat enlightening, but like much criticism of Faulkner's characters, they are weakened by generalities and gentility. It is surely no secret that the force alluded to is sexual and that sex gives the romantic female an inordinate amount of trouble. In the treatment of these women, Faulkner and Sartre, on whom I depend for most of my information, both use explicit description: some of it x-rated. Indeed, Faulkner plus Sartre plus the romantic women equal combustion. I shall go as far as possible and without losing credibility try to control it. Once more, what critics need for a valid description of the romantic woman is less generality and more existential-phenomenological fact: what they need is an existential-phenomenology of female sexuality.

Jean-Paul Sartre, the existential-phenomenologist most interested in the subject, accepts Freud's observation that the romantic female's unique genitalia offer the key to understanding her sexuality, but he differs radically from the conclusion Freud drew from that observation. Rather than considering the female sexual organ as deprivation, the sign of the romantic female's inferiority to the male, as Freud does, Sartre suggests that this organ is her greatest strength. He likens it to the most powerful "organ," the human consciousness. Human consciousness, Sartre writes, is a "hole of being" perpetually seeking fulfillment in something other than itself (*B&N* 79,614,617). Our first consciousness of ourselves, he says, is our discovery of our phenomenological emptiness: there are holes in us. First there is the discovery of the hole which we later learn is in our face, then the hole in the backside, and if we are the romantic female a third discovery awaits which, existentially, outweighs all other discoveries (*B&N* 612-614).

It is this discovery that structures the romantic consciousness, a revelation that is a perfect instance of physical fact yielding existential-phenomenological meaning. Like a tunnel open at both ends, sex is for the romantic a flesh-lined emptiness which she possesses and is possessed by (*B&N* 613). Empty, "in the form of a hole" (*B&N* 614), even as a child she shows great interest in holes of all kinds: an interest indicative of a pre-sexual being which she spends a lifetime articulating (*B&N* 612). Rosa Coldfield put it very well when she realized that in the adolescent romantic female there exists a "*caesarean lack,*" an "*itching discontent*" (*AA* 145), and the nubile Dewey Dell Bundren was obsessed with it: "I cannot help it. It will be that I had to do it all the time and I cannot help it" (*AILD* 26). Whether these romantics are twelve or twenty, forty or eighty, they are aware of this lack they must fill, and if Faulkner and Sartre are correct, there is only one sure way to fill it: men. Phenomenally, for this female, sexual desire is, before anything else, a yearning for fulfillment, a yearning to complete the emptiness that she feels. The greater the consciousness of emptiness, the greater the desire. Leni von Gerlach, Sartre's incestuous heroine, was so aware of the emptiness that even her brother was fair game. Leni, who probably had a lot of Caddy

Compson in her, said of her brother; "I win. I wanted to have him, and I have him" (*CA* 70). Although Caddy's victory was not so complete as Leni's, both played the game the same way. They would use the male as the means of their own fulfillment, a fulfillment that doubtless began for them where it usually begins for the romantic female, with a caress.

Men caress, women are caressed, and it is so for phenomenological reasons best known to the impassioned woman. In the caress she feels the stroking hands, the pressing lips, but most of all, she feels *herself*. No longer empty she is tangible. She is filled, as Sartre suggests, with her own flesh, the incarnation of the emptiness she was (*B&N* 612). The cavernous Belle Mitchell forced Horace Benbow to place "his hand against her silk thigh" (*Sart* 193), and Caddy Compson forced Quentin. As they lay beside the Compson brook, she took his hand and laid it flat against her chest, and when he shifted slightly, she moved his hand to her throat. Her heart hammered, and it hammered harder when she persuaded Quentin to caress her with a name (*S&F* 189).

Sex is touch. There is no way sexuality can be perceived without somehow involving the tactile. Even words, especially those calling forth tactile imagery, have a sexual physiognomy. A word like *warm* can have sexual meaning, creating in the body sensations of warmth, but the words that carry it headlong into the act are words that describe it explicitly (*PP* 235). These are words that caress. When Horace Benbow left Miss Reba's, he passed two lovers standing face to face, "the man speaking in a low tone unprintable epithet after epithet in a caressing whisper," the woman in "voluptuous ecstasy" (*S* 265). This verbal flesh was flesh which the exasperated Linda Snopes Kohl tried to procure from Gavin Stevens when she asked him to " " her. This invitation was pure sex, for Linda phenomenal fornication (*M* 238 *SG* 336). For Caddy the name Dalton Ames embodied the phenomenon. All she needed to fill the emptiness was to hear *Dalton*, and the six-letter word became what the four-letter word became for Linda, sounds-made-flesh. Caddy ordered Quentin to say the name, and when he did her body grew still, receptive—the filling surge; "Dalton Ames, Dalton Ames" (*S&F* 203).

Like consciousness itself moving from relatively simple perceptual structures to the more complex imagination and cognition, the progress the caress-consciousness is from simplicity to complexity. A good instance of this movement is found in the visual caress (*B&N* 390). For the male the bare leg is interesting, but it is much more interesting encased in hose, as the romantic female knows. First her victim is invited to explore the relatively simple and unbroken pattern of the silken calf and a bit of the covered thigh, but as his eye travels up and slows down as it meets a more complicated area, the change of texture where the top and body of the hose meet, he becomes increasingly excited. Skittering back and forth at the boundary, running quickly over the sheer hose and slowing down as the top begins, he has great difficulty in leaving the intersection. And then, combining great reluctance and unseemly haste, he moves on to the cliff where even the top ends and with breathtaking suddenness falls off to be swallowed up in the quicksand of female flesh. Jody Varner took this plunge. For weeks he had been aroused by his rapidly developing sister, and one afternoon on the way home from school he looked around at her astraddle the horse they were riding and succumbed to "the bare section of thigh between dress and stocking-top looking . . . gigantically and profoundly naked" (*H* 114).

While some romantic women, the female exhibitionist in particular, find caresses of this kind satisfactory, many of them react as Jody's sister did, with considerable if not total indifference. They have good reason. Males who look upon flesh look from a distance and thus are not much fun. They give themselves without giving themselves; they are over there, out of reach. Those who caress with hands are not greatly satisfactory. Merely by lifting the hand they escape, and the female sinks back into her emptiness (*B&N* 390). Viscous surfaces afford the caresser no such freedom (*B&N* 579-83). That is why Sartre's romantic Parisian chanteuse, impatient with her lover who lay beside her with his hand on her thigh, took his hand and placed it on her genitalia (*AR* 35,37). It is this three-dimensional touch, touch possessed even as it is possessed, utterly yielding yet absolutely clinging, that assures the chanteuse of her wholeness (*PP* 315-17, *B&N* 610). For her this, the pure caress, is the real affirmation of the romantic female consciousness, the affirmation of her fleshly existence through the capture of the male's (*B&N* 396). It was this captivity that drove Christmas to despair; the very thought of being captured drove Quentin out of his wits. Reluctantly he had put his hand on her breast, and under duress he had repeated Dalton's name. He refused absolutely to touch Caddy anywhere else, imagining "liquid putrefaction like drowned things floating flabbily filled" (*S&F* 159).

Quentin had every right to fear Caddy, for in the highly sexed romantic female the search for completeness is continuous: she is emptiness personified (*B&N* 610-614). Her sexual desire and her consciousness are synonymous, her desire correlating phenomenally with her reason for existing, that is, to fill her emptiness. Such women are not seduced by the male's "dash and swagger" or by men at all. They are seduced by themselves, seduced, as Faulkner said of Eula Snopes, by an emptiness "whose only ease was in creating a situation containing a recipient for gratitude, then supplying the gratitude" (*T* 272). Obsessed with their incompleteness, romantics are continually exciting it, turning it off, varying the means of assuaging it (*B&N* 385). Caddy did it *"like nigger women do in the pasture the ditches the dark woods hot hidden furious,"* and any "pimpled-faced infant" could "whistle her out like a puppy" (*S&F* 113-114).

For Caddy there had been "too many," she told Quentin, and still there were never enough (*S&F* 184). She described the itching emptiness as "something terrible in me sometimes at night I could see it grinning at me" (*S&F* 128). "My God," asked another of these romantics, "Why do I do it? What is the matter with me?" (*CS* 209). The matter was her heightened consciousness of her emptiness. To fill it her best bet would be the sadist: he is to the romantic what crack cocaine is to the drug addict. It is the sadist whom these women love, hate, and fear the most, for it is he who would touch her flesh which he cannot resist, filling her with himself, and yet refuse to be caught up in the flesh in which he finds himself. He robs her of her completeness at the same time he is completing her. Sartre's Electra, attached as she was to her brother, looked beyond him to her ideal, "a big, strong man a born fighter with bloodshot eyes. . . . He scares me . . . and I love him" (*TF* 87). The some-time prostitute Ruby LaMarr said that "a real man" was enough to make a girl "crawl in dirt and mire" just to hear him call her "whore" (*S* 69), and Temple Drake found her hero in Popeye.

For the romantic woman all true passion is spiced with pain. To be filled with fear of pain generated by her lover is to add a dimension to this female's attraction to him, as Temple shows in her conquest of Popeye. She looked at the Memphis gangster, and all she saw was cruelty and hardness. He wore a "stiff hat," his suit fit tight against his hard body, he was "all angles." He smelled "black," the hands hooking onto "small arms light and rigid as aluminum" (*S* 5,6,282). In turn, Popeye was drawn to this woman precisely to the degree that he was repulsed by her. He has an intense aversion to what awaits him yet he cannot resist it. He wants action but wants it across the grain, thus he makes repulsive that which attracts him in order not to be attracted by it (*B&N* 401). Where conventional lovers welcome the female's attempt to cover herself, hoping as it were that she will somehow veil what she eventually must expose to him, Popeye insists on exposure. Temple was as expert as he was in playing this game, as the notorious corn cob episode shows. After her defilement, which occurred at the Old French-man Place, and on the road to Memphis, Temple made the first move: "'It's still running,' she whimpered. 'I can feel it.'" Excited by her humiliation, he gripped her by the back of her neck, she stopped whimpering, and they pulled up next to a filling station. There she continued to excite him, first by refusing to leave the car and then, as soon as he had gone inside, making a half-hearted attempt to escape. He found her crouched behind a trash barrel; she refused to move. The supreme moment for the sadist comes when his victim is completely shamed, confessing that she is as repulsive as he says she is, and now Temple confessed: she lifted her skirt, "Look." Furious with himself for acting on her command—the game lost—he seized her and the game started up again (*S* 165-168).

Eight years after leaving Memphis, Temple was married and having an affair. When Nancy Manigoe, her maid, learned that her mistress was planning to take her infant daughter and leave with her lover, Nancy killed the child. Gavin Stevens, the lawyer defending the Negress, believed that Temple should share Nancy's guilt, that, in fact, it was Temple, not Nancy, who was guilty. Only through painful re-examination of her past and of the murder of her child could she overcome the injustice done Nancy and come to terms with her conscience. At the same time she would have to plead with the governor of Mississippi to commute the death sentence that had been passed on Nancy (*RFN* 49-58). Nothing could have given Temple more pleasure than to recall those wretched, pain-filled, fun-and-games days. She would, she promised, "make it good and painful" (*S* 124). Standing before the governor, this romantic told how she had suffered, this girl of seventeen more a fool than a virgin. How painful it was, she bragged, to be held prisoner in that Memphis whorehouse where there was nothing to do except parade around in her fine furs and flashy underwear (*S* 130,141,143). More painful, she went on, was leaving the house and marrying a man who could not understand how much she had suffered. To suffer as she had suffered, Temple explained to the governor and Stevens, meant "not suffering for or about anything," but "just suffering, like somebody unconscious" (*S* 133) and to make the point clear she stopped talking and turned to illustration. In true suffering, words are not enough. It must be seen: others must *know* that the suffering *is* suffering (*B&N* 91) and so with Temple. Silently she knelt with face buried in hands and remained motionless until Stevens touched her arm as if to help her to her feet. At first she refused to budge, and when she did, she arose blindly, gesturing like "a little girl about to cry" (*RFN* 194). Later, as she reviewed the tableau, she said proudly, "Don't you see? That's just suffering. Not for anything: just suffering" (*RFN* 211). Temple had a right to be proud. Her recitation of painful events gave her a certain amount of satisfaction, but only when she threw herself on her knees was she completely satisfied.

In drama suffering finds its true being. That Faulkner wrote *Requiem for a Nun* as a vehicle for the actress, Ruth Ford, is interesting, for suffering is pure theatre. Like acting it is wholly self-conscious. Where, for example, an angry woman is conscious only of the object that caused her anger, swept up completely in her effort to destroy it, the suffering woman is conscious only of herself and her audience. She knows that she is suffering in the same way the actress knows she is acting (*B&N* 92). Indeed, the two are one: suffering-acting, all style and no substance. For this reason Temple could tell Stevens (actress conferring with director) when he ordered her to suffer that she would think it over, decide whether she would take that road to redemption (*RFN* 93-95), and then, decision made, she gave the strong impression that she was more interested in an appreciative audience than in being redeemed. Sartre comments on this phenomenon through his hero Roquentin who says of a lovelorn charwoman that her strength to suffer came not from some inner resource but from him and others around her. Without these sympathetic witnesses, her histrionics would have died aborning (*N* 40-41). Temple displayed her ribbons, dramatizing herself and finding fulfillment as a suffering virgin, a suffering whore, a suffering housewife, and when she decided she had enough of suffering, that is, when her audience had disappeared, she brought her act to an end. Her final gesture in the play is made to an audience of one: taking out her compact she looks into the mirror and applauds

herself. It had been a fine performance, suffering well done—
not once but thrice: Act I, On the Road from the Old Frenchman
Place to Memphis. Act II, At Miss Reba's brothel in Memphis.
Act III, In the office of the Governor of Mississippi.

The difference between Caddy Compson, Temple Drake,
and Charlotte Rittenmeyer is that Charlotte believed (at least
in the beginning) that romantic women and men can coexist,
that neither has to win or lose, subdue or be subdued. Charlotte
did not wish to enslave Harry Wilbourne or be enslaved by
him. She strove for a stable relationship between two equals;
she wished to love freely and to be loved freely, as she reveals
the first time the two met. They were at a party in New Orleans
when she saw him looking at a painting and asked over his
shoulder, "What do you think about it, mister?" (*WP* 34). Her
approach would seem to be that of an ordinary pickup, and yet
throughout the exchange that followed, there ran a thread
missing from that game. As they talked she asked him to come
to her house for dinner, and free and in the ascendant he countered with, "Don't you have engagements yourself?" She gave
him his triumph. "'There are some people coming. . . . But they
won't bother you.' She looked at him. 'All right, if you don't
want a lot of people, I'll put them off. The night after tomorrow?
At seven?'" Victory was his, but she went further. She asked
whether he wanted her to come after him in her car, and continuing to enjoy complete confidence, he declined. Freely, she
delivered herself over to him completely, "I can, you know,"
and he accepted, "I know it. . . . I know it" (*WP* 36,37).

Free love exists only between equals (*B&N* 367), a balance
which Charlotte worked hard to maintain, but in one instance,
as she and Harry talked, she made too much effort to impress
him. She had set herself up as a rare combination—an art critic,
a woman of means, a talented painter (*WP* 35)—but alarmed
at the impression her claims had made, she immediately gave
up her advantage. She confessed that she had lied to him, that
she worked in clay, not oils, and then for proof she held out her
hand. "Feel," she said, drawing his fingers over her hand, "the

broad, blunt, strong, supple-fingered hand, . . . the skin at the base and lower joints of the fingers not callused exactly but smoothly hardened. . . . 'That's what I make: something you can touch'" (*WP* 36). Free love embodies this touch. Unlike Belle Mitchell's hand, warm, prehensile, exploitive, Charlotte's hand on Harry's was cool, supple, smooth, the essence of the freedom she extended to him while preserving her own.

"In the theatre as in love," observed Sartre's actor-lover, Kean, "there is only one law: improve, or slip back" (*K* 177), and Charlotte carefully tried to obey this law, preserving Harry's freedom as well as her own. At their first meeting, even though she was highly sexual, Charlotte had gone against her nature, playing down sex as a means of capturing Harry, and instead had led him away from her body into the world of art and lofty regions of sentiment, striving to fill her aching emptiness with his admiration, esteem, and respect. After several more meetings, even when sexual love did make its appearance, she was still able to keep herself and Harry on an even keel. In fact, she handled expertly one of the most sensitive areas of sexual love, the male's ignorance of it. She and Harry had registered at a New Orleans hotel, but once in the room, he stood staring at her, at a loss as what to do or say. Caddy on a somewhat similar occasion had shamed Quentin for his innocence (*S&F* 113) and Temple shamed Popeye for his impotence (*S* 278), but Charlotte did not shame Harry. Carefully, this romantic woman protected his freedom to be ignorant as well as her freedom to know. She placed the blame not on them but on the situation, pleading, not here—"Not like this. Jesus, not like this" (*WP* 41).

More to her liking was a roomette on the train she and Harry had taken out of New Orleans for Chicago. As they sat beside each other on coach seats, Charlotte had begun to suspect that their courtship had been several tones too high. Her charity and his admiration, their mutual declarations of esteem were not enough. Neither was Harry's freedom: briskly she ordered him to get a drawing room, and once in it, she instructed him to lock the door. At the same time, she was taking off her dress; then the romantic woman unknotted his tie (*WP* 53-54). From the first meeting there had been hints that Charlotte's interest in Harry went beyond his freedom. Although she encouraged him to express his thoughts and frequently gave in to him, creating the impression that he was in control, free to act as he chose, he seems always to have acted as she would like for him to act. Instead of acting on his own behalf, he seemed always to be acting on hers. So mesmerized was he that on one occasion he looked into her eyes and appeared to be drowning, a phenomenon familiar to many male lovers. Joe Christmas found himself drowning in Miss Burden and out of fear killed her. Quentin feared the same fate: his memories of Caddy are full of running to escape it. Unlike Joe and Quentin, Harry put up no resistance. He became Charlotte's—every romantic female's—dream, a lover who yielded, consented, acclaimed the one who filled the emptiness. He was her true servant, the center around which she built her empty life. Through him Charlotte discovered what it was to be privileged, rare and precious, in command and indispensable. He gave this romantic woman the faith to be herself, stuffing her with importance, filling her to the brim with attention. Had he not abandoned his career in medicine for her? This woman on the edge of thirty no longer felt on the edge at all. How good he made her feel, even to be, especially to be, an adultress. It was so fine of him to have eyes to look at her, a mouth to speak her praise and kiss her, to lavish himself tirelessly on her. No longer superfluous, through the magic of unconditional surrender, she found in him her fulfillment—her "existence justified" (*B&N* 371).

Harry loved the chains that bound him. Once settled in Chicago he proclaimed that nothing could beat them (*WP* 77), and he might have been right, if there had been no one else in the world except him and his beloved romantic. Of all worlds theirs is the most thrilling, but it is also the most fragile, so magical that the moment another enters, the world disappears (*B&N* 377). To escape this disaster lovers insist on being alone with each other. Quentin was speaking of this necessity when he urged Caddy to flee with him: he would take her to hell itself where there would be "nobody else . . . but her and me." They would dwell in *"the clean flame"* (*S&F* 97,144). In search of that flame, Harry and Charlotte had left New Orleans for Chicago, where they found that it did not burn either. Too many people knew them, but, ironically, through the kindness of one of these people, a newspaper reporter who had been a friend of Charlotte's brother, they found what they were searching for, a cabin beside a lake miles from Chicago.

Here at last was the solitude which lovers cherish, "the solitude," Harry said, "wavering slow while you lie and look at it" (*WP* 92). He and Charlotte gave themselves over to this solitude. An adored object in the abyss of her emptiness, requiring neither food nor sleep, he existed in a "drowsy and foetus-like state, passive and almost insentient in the womb of solitude and peace" (*WP* 123). Unhappily, this paradise could not cope with cold weather, and with the onset of winter, Charlotte and Harry were forced to return to Chicago. Their return proved disastrous.

At the lake all that Harry and Charlotte possessed was each other; the phenomenal balance—the romantic need for him, his supplying that need—was perfect. In the city the balance was upset. Taking his place was money and the ever increasing desire for more of it. When Harry's short stories and Charlotte's puppets began to sell, never had they had so much and been so miserable, especially Harry. Longing for his rightful homeland, the center of her existence, he continually complained of his ejection from it. The only time they were together, he said, was on a street car or in restaurants or bars. They did not sleep together anymore; they took turns watching each other sleep (*WP* 117). Charlotte was almost as unhappy as Harry. If what she had now was what she wanted, why had she left her husband? she asked. Her hunger was not of the gut, she said; it was an emptiness which only Harry could fill. "Hold me! Hold me hard!" (*WP* 78,109). This entreaty finds an echo in Caddy's pleading for Quentin to speak her lover's name, in Temple's begging Red to press against her (*S* 289), but it was especially poignant coming from Charlotte. The harder she and Harry tried to hold each other, the further they slipped from each other's grasp. They left Chicago, fleeing into the wilds of Utah, and, finally, to a beach cottage on the Gulf Coast: they had gone, as Faulkner himself expressed it, "to infinite labor and risk to escape from the world"[8] but if there had been no one or nothing in the world except themselves, they would still have remained apart. Romantic love itself betrayed them.

Charlotte and Harry believed that love is the ultimate expression of togetherness, two people giving wholly of themselves to each other, while in actuality love is precisely the opposite. It is the essence of selfishness. To love another has nothing to do with giving or sacrifice or any other noble sentiment. Instead, it is the wish in the lover to be loved, and if the wish comes true, all that he has accomplished is to set up a similar wish in the beloved (*B&N* 375-76, *HV* 58-59). Between lover and beloved there exists an unbridgeable gap, for love is, as it must be, centripetal, a series of infinite references in which neither lover comes remotely close to the other: "Each one wants the other to love him but does not take into account the fact that to love is to want to be loved and thus by wanting the other to love him, he only wants the other to want to be loved in turn" (*B&N* 376). For this reason love is, of all the feelings expressing togetherness, the most deceiving. Even as she says she loves him, she lies: she does not love him: *she merely wishes to be loved*. Love is built on such deceptions and the greater the love, the greater the deception. Of all human relationships romantic love is the least satisfying. It is a lie bearing its own destruction, the ultimate lie which Roquentin was rejecting when he said of his girl friend, "Take her in my arms what good would it do? I can do nothing for her; she is as solitary as I" (*N* 203).

Neither could Charlotte nor Harry do anything for the other. They had lived the romantic lover's lie for three years, moving restlessly from pillar to post until, in the end, they were back where they had started. They had gone in circles just as their love had gone, getting nowhere. Ill from the abortion Harry had bungled, Charlotte had the greatest need for his love, and he wished greatly to give it to her, but love, as it always will, failed them both. He was as powerless to give it as she was to accept. This realization, not the abortion, killed her. Like all lovers lonely beyond the powers of expression, all day long she sat in a chair on the beach, just sat, a "complete immobile abstraction from which even pain and terror were absent," and when Harry approached her she remained an abstraction, as if there were nothing between them and had never been. There was "no sign from her, no movement" (*WP* 3). Nothing moved except her eyes, which stared out "with profound and illimitable hatred" (*WP* 8).

Hate is our first line of defense against the hell of romantic love, the defense that serves best and lasts longest. Unable to fill the emptiness with love, that which in itself is all emptiness, romantic women fill themselves with hatred. In hate the female finds the impregnable armor. Or to put the matter more precisely: the reason that we hate is to protect ourselves from the wish to be loved (*B&N* 410-12). The reason that Rosa Coldfield hated Sutpen was to protect herself from the handsome man. Miss Burden hated Christmas for the same reason, but more in love than either of them, Charlotte discovered that she needed more protection than hate could offer, and with an assist from hallucination, she got it.

Like all other consciousnesses, hallucination is intentional and like all other emotional consciousnesses it attempts to shelter us from the unbearable world of human reality (*PP* 341-42). But hallucination differs from the other emotions in that the pragmatistic world is rejected completely. Henry Armstid was never so angry that he did not know that he was at an auction; Christmas was not so frightened that he did not recognize Miss Atkins. Both of these men had for a time lost their grip on reality, creating magical bypasses around a hostile world, but neither had lost his grip on the existential temporal-spatial coordinates that kept him oriented in that world. As Charlotte lay dying in the beach cottage, she lost her grip, the coordinates disappeared, she cut loose from all time-space moorings. Magically, she found herself in New Orleans with her husband, whom she begged to save her lover. No longer suffering the excruciating pains of septicemia but self-possessed and optimistic she was, in her hallucination, confident that she could convince her husband that Wilbourne was not at fault for what had happened. "It wasn't him, you see. . . . I ratted off on him like I did you. It was the other one" (*WP* 17). Hallucination resembles the imagination in that the images lack individuation, but unlike the imagination these images are free floating; that is, once formed they move in directions beyond our control. This is one reason that hallucination is so terrible, as Charlotte discovered. The Rittenmeyer standing before her now was much less tractable than the one she had known earlier in her life. He refused absolutely to believe her. Thrust once more on herself, knowing that Wilbourne, the "bungling bastard" (*WP* 17), would not beat the charge of infanticide, she fell back on the great romantic female imperative, the phenomenal fact that had borne her through life and that now sustained her in dying. She no longer need look to Rittenmeyer for help. She would win the jury the same way she had won the man she was pleading for and the way she had won herself. She played her best card, her phenomenal emptiness: "I'll plead my ass," she said, triumphant (*WP* 17).

These three women who lived in the labyrinth called romantic love are held together, individually and collectively, by the phenomenal emptiness that they were. Every romantic attempts in her own way to fill that emptiness—Caddy in the caress, Temple in suffering, Charlotte in a combination of the two and hallucination. These three modes are the original modes through which romantic women seek fulfillment, and in their search lean, as in Faulkner's women, more heavily on one mode than they do on the others, and all of them, if

Faulkner and the existential-phenomenologists are right, provide the same conclusion: the single-mindedness with which they pursue their objective and the shattering results of that pursuit.

Notes

[1] Kenneth Richardson, *Force and Faith in the Novels of William Faulkner* (The Hague: Mouton, 1967), 79; Harry Mordean Campbell and Ruel F. Foster, *William Faulkner: A Critical Appraisal* (Norman: U of Oklahoma P, 1951) 45.

[2] William Van O'Connor, *The Tangled Fire of William Faulkner* (Minneapolis: Gardian P, 1954), 157; Michael Millgate, *The Achievement of William Faulkner* (New York: Random House, 1956), 174.

[3] James Gray Watson, *The Snopes Dilemma: Faulkner's Trilogy* (Coral Gables: U of Miami P, 1968), 226. Richardson, *op. cit.* 80.

[4] Irving Howe, *William Faulkner. A Critical Study*, 2nd. Revised and Expanded (New York: Vintage, 1962), 144.

[5] David M. Miller, "William Faulkner's Women," *Modern Fiction Studies*, 13 (Spring 1967), 8.

[6] Miller, 16,14,10.

[7] Joseph Blotner, *Faulkner. A Biography* (New York: Random House, 1974) II, 1689.

[8] Frederick L. Gwynn and Joseph L. Blotner, *Faulkner in the University*, (Charlottesville: UP of Virginia, 1959), 178.

Chapter VIII

LUCAS BEAUCHAMP:
EYE OF THE STORM

Although Lucas Beauchamp is the central figure in one of Faulkner's novels and plays a large part in another, critics have shown relatively little interest in him. Routinely they note his patience, courage, independence. Even though Lucas is guilty at times of overweening pride, he is also a man of dignity and integrity. He is an ever private person who keeps his own counsel. When he is asked for his opinion, he gives it succinctly—and finally. He never complains, he never explains. He asks no odds and he gives none, even to a twelve year old boy. His favorite pastime is getting in the last word. In short, he is rather larger than life but not large enough for the mythologists. He is too well adjusted for the psychologists and offers little or nothing to the symbolists. He is, on the other hand, just right for the Sartrean existential-phenomenological hero: self-made he makes his own world, one in which he is continuously affirming himself at the expense of others. Unlike Joe Christmas, a mulatto who gave in unconditionally to the world, accepting himself for what the white world of Yoknapatawpha said that he was, Lucas rejected the labels the county placed upon him and the cage into which they tried to force him. He fought the county to a standstill, he whipped it, and he whipped it with the most powerful weapon in the existential arsenal, the Existential *Look*, which I wish to examine in some detail.

Existentialism is *par excellence* the philosophy of ambiguity. It centers in the paradoxical nexus of *être-en-soi* and *être-pour-soi*. According to Sartre in-itself refers to the static world of objects. These objects, he explained, are "there in the midst of the world, impenetrable and dense, like this tree or this stone" (*B&N* 91). They exist as what they are and can never exist as what they are not: they can never change. Conversely, being for-itself, Sartre maintains, postulates infinite possibilities. It means to become, to do, whereas in-itself means to be, to have. As much as these two modes of being differ, however, they exist as integral parts of each other (*B&N* lxv, lxvi). Sartre writes that "the for-itself without the in-itself is a kind of abstraction; it could not exist any more than a color could exist without form or sound without pitch and without timbre" (*B&N* 621). Yet and at the same time, the modes exist separately: they cannot be synthesized. Such a synthesis would postulate a being that could "exist only as a perpetually evanescent relation" (for-itself) and at the same time as a "substantial being" (in-itself) (*B&N* 13), one manifestation of which we have seen in the romantic female sexual consciousness. Those women spend their lives attempting to escape their feeling of emptiness, a consciousness that presupposes yet another mode of being, *être-pour-autrui*. In order to fill the nothingness that they are, they make use of the male. Adding complexity to this already complex situation, the male himself is caught up in the same phenomenal net.

Bound outward forever, a nothingness intending to be that which it can never be, human consciousness can never realize itself by itself; its identity must come from others. Man, Sartre states, "cannot be anything . . . unless others recognize him as such. I cannot obtain any truth whatsoever about myself, except through the meditation of another. The other is indispensable to my existence, and equally so to any knowledge I can have of myself" (*EDS* 303). At the center of this knowledge lies a conflict whereby every man attempts, through means of what Sartre terms the *Look* or the *Stare* or the *Gaze*, to assimilate the freedom of the other (*B&N* 262-64). The loser is thereby stripped of his human qualities. He becomes merely an object, the prized possession of another. Roquentin, one of Sartre's spokesmen, comments on such entities: "You use them, put them back in place, you live among them: they are useful, nothing more" (*N* 19).

A major difference between Sartre's fiction and Faulkner's is that the French writer nearly always treats, as he does in the

Roads to Freedom series, the inner conflict man undergoes in his battle for freedom, while Faulkner is mainly concerned with the conflict as it exists between man and other man. He discovered this primordial conflict intuitively and reveals it in characters that live; Sartre has been able to explain brilliantly the conflict in his philosophical works but to render it only indifferently in his plays and novels. "I . . . just . . . write about people," Faulkner declared "not ideas."[1] What makes these people fascinating is that they are continuously fighting the Battle of Others, as this study has shown. So far we have seen human beings in an unremitting struggle to preserve their own freedom while trying to usurp that of others, and much of the irony in Faulkner's works results from the obtuseness of characters who lose their freedom without being aware that they have lost it. Colonel Sutpen is an excellent example. From the time he wilted under the *Stare* of the Negro major-domo in Tidewater Virginia until he died at the hands of Wash Jones in Mississippi, he existed merely as the pawn of others. To his undying discredit and to the grim amusement of the reader, he never realized that he was a pawn.

Many another character in Faulkner loses his freedom through the *Stare*. Harry Wilbourne drowned in Charlotte Rittenmeyer's "yellow stare," in that "unwinking yellow stare" depriving him of "volition and will" (*WP* 34,80), and Christmas shriveled under the murderous *Gaze* of his grandfather *"watching me all the time"* (*LIA* 121). Jody Varner cowered before Ab Snopes, "a pair of eyes of cold opaque gray" (*H* 9). Eyes do not have to be seen by the victim in order to be effective. Miss Rosa rode up to Sutpen's Hundred feeling Clytie in there "somewhere watching us" (*AA* 366). Eyes can be potent even when sightless. Temple Drake was more frightened of Lee Goodwin's father than she was of Lee or Popeye, this old man with the "cataracted eyes . . . like two clots of phlegm (*S* 12). Eyes are not the only part of the anatomy that can trigger the *Look*. Flem's "tiny predatory" nose frightened most of Frenchman's Bend and half of Jefferson (*H* 59). The *Look* can reside in a tone. Jody

Varner was scared of Ab's "inflectionless," "lifeless voice" (*H* 9), laughter in a restaurant rocked Christmas (*LIA* 156), and Sutpen was torn by the "terrible laughing" of Negroes (*AA* 234). The sneering mouth of Bayard Sartoris, III, was the *Look* that stalled Simon (*Sart* 116); the Yankee soldier's teeth gleamed derisively at young Bayard and Ringo (*U* 160). Parts of the anatomy, sounds—any of the myriad gestures of the human body—can be incorporated into the *Look*. In fact, Sartre maintains and Faulkner obviously agrees, man's ability to affirm himself as man lies in the "ensemble of the phenomenon which we call the *look*. Each look makes us prove concretely . . . that we exist for all living men" (*B&N* 281).

Faulkner never tires of showing us men using the *Look* as proof of their existence, as I have tried to make clear, but the *beau ideal* is Lucas Beauchamp. Lucas's face was "pigmented like a Negro's but with a nose high in the bridge and even hooked a little and what looked out through it or from behind it not black nor white either, not arrogant at all and not even scornful: just intolerant inflexible and composed" (*IID* 11). It was this *Look* that served first to intimidate and then defeat the white trash of the Yoknapatawpha community. Wearing a worn, black broadcloth suit and fine old beaver hat, Lucas appeared one Saturday afternoon at a crossroads store. His supremely confident manner or the fact that "perhaps just nothing was enough" caused a white man to get to his feet, saying:

> "You goddamn biggity stiffnecked stinking burrheaded Edmonds sonofabitch:" and Lucas . . . turned his head quite slowly and looked at the white man a moment and then said: "I aint a Edmonds. I don't belong to these new folks. I belongs to the old lot. I'm a McCaslin."
> "Keep on walking around here with that look on your face and what you'll be is crowbait," the white man said. For another moment or at least a half one Lucas looked at the white man with a calm speculative detachment, . . . and said: "Yes, I heard that idea before. And I notices that the folks that brings it up aint even Edmondses." (*IID* 15)

The white man was forcibly restrained from killing Lucas, who "didn't move, quite calm, not even scornful, not even contemptuous, not even very alert, . . . just watching while the proprietor's son and his companion held the foaming and cursing white man." When Lucas did leave, he went without haste or, as Sartre would express it, as "*master of the situation*" (*B&N* 265).

By *situation*, Sartre means all of the external and internal pressures that give shape to a man's life: it is the totality of material and even psychological conditions that describe the specific character of an era (*EH* 137). The specific social and political character of Lucas Beauchamp's South was the rigid class structure of feudalism. By all rights, he should have been locked in a fierce struggle with the Gowries and the like to see who would occupy the bottom rung. The trash was, it turned out, not worthy of Lucas's mettle. Neither was his own white kinsman. Shortly after Lucas's white cousin, Zack Edmonds, became a widower, he brought Lucas's young black wife into his house ostensibly to nurse his young son. Lucas suspected the real reason and went after her. At first Edmonds refused to give up the woman, but then he "looked up again at the impassive, the impenetrable face under the broad, old-fashioned hat. . . . 'I'm going to be the man in this house,' Lucas said. It was not stubborn. It was quiet: final. His stare was as steady as Edmond's was, and immeasurably colder" (*GDM* 121). Lucas took his wife home.

In the same way, Lucas beat the aristocratic Chick Mallison and Chick's uncle, Gavin Stevens. Much of *Intruder in the Dust* is devoted to the attempt on the part of Lucas and Chick, each to dominate the other: the compositional center of the novel is an account of the ruses each used in an effort to prove the other an object and himself a human being. The first clash between the two occurred when Chick was only a child. Out hunting one autumn Chick fell into a creek and was rescued by Lucas, who took him to his cabin, dried his clothes, and gave him a meal (*IID* 7-11). Refusing to be beholden to a Negro, Chick offered Lucas money for the food:

"What's that for?" the man said, not even moving, not even tilting his face downward to look at what was on his palm: for another eternity and only the hot dead moveless blood until at least he could bear the shame: and watched his palm turn over not flinging the coins but spurning them downward ringing onto the bare floor, . . . and then his voice:
"Pick it up!"
And still nothing, the man didn't move, hands clasped behind him, looking at nothing; only the rush of the hot dead heavy blood out of which the voice spoke, addressing nobody: "Pick up his money." (*IID* 13)

The money was retrieved by several boys who were with Chick, but it might as well have been picked up by Chick himself. In the ensuing year he learned the impossibility of doing what "every white man in that whole section . . . had been thinking . . . for years: *We got to make him be a nigger first. He's got to admit he's a nigger. Then maybe we will accept him as he seems to intend to be accepted*" (*IID* 14). Chick also learned that his own being had been completely assimilated by the other: that "Lucas had beat him" (*IID* 16).

Phenomenally, the Look is the power of one human being to force another human being to accept the world he has created for him. To be *seen-by-the-other* is to live as if we were an object in a world the *Look* has created. It is to be phenomenally conscious of our vulnerability (*B&N* 257). This vulnerability weighed heavily on Chick; it was a burden he could not escape:

. . . the man, the Negro, the room [he thought sometime after the creek incident], the moment, the day itself—had annealed vanished into the round hard symbol of the coin and he would seem to see himself lying watching regretless and even peaceful as day by day the coin swelled to its gigantic maximum, to hang fixed at last forever in the black vault of his anguish like the last dead and waneless moon and himself, his own puny shadow gesticulant and tiny against it in frantic and vain eclipse: frantic and vain yet indefatigable too because he would never stop, he could never give up now

126

who had debased not merely his manhood but his whole race too. (*IID* 16)

Existing as an object in the domain of *en-soi*, Chick failed completely in trying to win back his freedom. His first attempt was to send Lucas's wife a new dress. Four long months passed with no counterattack, and Chick began once more to breathe freely, as if he were again on his own terrain. The coin—that incessant reminder of his shame and humiliation and thing-ness—"still hung in the black vault but . . . the vault itself was not so black with the disc paling and he could even sleep under it as even the insomniac dozes under his waning and glareless moon" (*IID* 17). Then came the pail of homemade sorghum molasses. Even before Chick's mother told the boy where it had come from, he knew the answer:

> They were right back where they had started; it was all to do over again. . . . Then he realized that he couldn't even start over again because to take the can of molasses back and fling it into Lucas's front door would only be the coins again for Lucas again to command somebody to pick up and return. . . . Whatever would or could set him free was beyond not merely his reach but even his ken; he could only wait for it if it came and do without it if it didn't. (*IID* 17-18)

Chick's main hope for freedom lay in Lucas's forgetting him, and thus when the old Negro passed by one day on the square apparently without recognizing him, the boy was greatly relieved: "*He didn't even know me. He hasn't even bothered to forget me*: thinking in a sort of peace even: *It's over.* That was all because he was free, the man who for three years had obsessed his life waking and sleeping too had walked out of it" (*IID* 19).

But Chick was wrong: Lucas had not forgotten him. When the boy stood outside the jail as Lucas was being dragged in to be charged with murder, the Negro turned, looked straight at Chick, and said, "You, young man. . . . Tell your uncle I wants to see him" (*IID*11). Chick complied but in vain. His uncle, Lucas's lawyer, refused for the moment to help the intransigent old black man, and thus came the opportunity for which Chick had been praying. Lucas sent for him. As he walked to the jail cell, he imagined that Lucas would remind him of that plate of greens and bacon, but better, '*Maybe he'll . . . tell me I'm all he's got, all that's left and that will be enough*" (*IID* 46). That would have been enough, almost any showing of deference would have been, but the old man never told him that. Refusing to complain, explain, or apologize he used Chick once more for his own convenience, forced the boy to accept his own terms: Dig up the corpse of the murdered man, he ordered. "This was all Lucas was going to tell him and he knew it was all; he thought in a kind of raging fury: Believe? Believe what? because Lucas was not even asking him to believe anything; he was not even asking a favor, making no last desperate plea to his humanity and pity" (*IID* 49). For the third time, then, the boy had tried to win back his freedom, escape from the cage in which Lucas had placed him and failed; now he admitted his failure, even to himself: "*He's not only beat me, he never for one second had any doubt of it*" (*IID* 49). Lucas never had any doubt that he could beat Lawyer Stevens, either.

The lives of Stevens and Chick intertwined in that way peculiar to a doted-upon nephew and an adored uncle, and sometimes Lucas found that he had to take both of them on together. This situation is not unusual in the Battle of Others; as often as not, *être-pour-autrui* involves a Third. Indeed, with lovers the Third assumes primary importance, for it is the Third that upsets the emotional balance between the two. Described phenomenally, this situation is one in which two persons are in relative rapport, a Third *Looks* at them, and one of the two persons deserts the other, joining the Third (*B&N* 415). When Harry Wilbourne and Charlotte Rittenmeyer were jobless in Chicago, Harry contentedly submerged in her yellow stare, Charlotte's reporter friend suggested that in order to economize the lovers move out of the city to a cabin owned by himself and one of his friends. Suddenly, to his dismay, Harry discovered that Charlotte was no longer looking at him or even speaking to him. Ignored, left high and dry, he felt utterly alone while his beloved basked in the warm *Look* of the Third (*WP* 88-89).

Another situation involving the Third is that in which someone is under the *Look* of another, and the Third appears, joins the victor, and both *Look* at the captive (*B&N* 415). Mink Snopes suffered this coalition. Rebuffed by Jack Houston when he tried to reclaim the cow, Snopes petitioned Will Varner for a restraining order, which Varner denied. "When you pay Houston eighteen dollars and seventy-five cents, you can have your cow," Varner said. Mink did not have the money, and turning to Houston, Varner continued, "Then he'll have to work it out." Houston suggested digging postholes, and Mink, under the combined weight of four eyes, began digging (*M* 16,17). Shortly afterward, Mink had his revenge on both Houston and Varner. Realizing that bad blood between Mink and Houston might lead to bloodshed, Will intervened, ordering Mink to stop digging holes and go home. This is a situation in which the captive has a choice either of allying himself with the Third and with him Gazing at the other or of rejecting the alliance (*B&N* 416). Mink refused to join Varner, asking, "Have you heard any complaint from me?" and when Varner replied in the negative, Mink told him to mind his own business and he would mind his (*M* 19). With this gambit, which creates a situation the resentful dream about, Mink became an object for Houston who was an object for Varner who was an object for Mink.

Still another combination occurs when the oppressor has his victim under control and the Third *Looks* at the oppressor, who is unable to return the *Look*, thus giving the Third domination over both (*B&N* 417). This is the situation between Gavin, Chick, and Lucas. Chick's life had been a continual effort to please his uncle; the boy gave in to the benevolent despotism of his hero—until Lucas appeared. Then, against his will, he found himself moving away from his uncle and toward the old Negro. A fine instance of these rites of passage, phenomenal style, occurs in the final scene of *Intruder in the Dust*. In complete accord with the existentialist in dissent, Lucas throughout the novel is not only "solitary . . . intractable, apparently . . . without friends even of his own race but proud of it" (*IID* 18). As he said, "I pays my own way" (*IID* 44). He therefore insisted on paying Stevens for representing him. Once Lucas was in Stevens' office, the lawyer tried to dismiss the affair but at the old Negro's insistence set the bill at two dollars. In making up the amount Lucas included fifty pennies he had saved. "I was aiming to take them to the bank," he told Stevens, "but you can save me the trip. You want to count um?" Startled at this impudence, Stevens ordered Lucas to do the counting. Chick watched the transaction in silence, his way of saying, "Goodbye, again." It was as though he were watching the same scene he had watched for years: the airy, condescending white man, whom he loved, being bested by the black man to whom he was irresistibly drawn, and now he watched Lucas count the money, wipe his hands with his handkerchief, and stand "again intractable and calm and not looking at either. . . . 'Now what,' his uncle said. 'My receipt,' Lucas said" (*IID* 158). The receipt Lucas forced from Stevens was the same kind that he had forced from the silent, compliant Chick, from his white cousin, and from the white trash—their recognition of him as a human being capable of claiming his freedom while usurping theirs—and he did so with great flair. He *Looked* the part.

Notes

[1] Frederick L. Gwynn and Joseph L. Blotner, eds., *Faulkner in the University: Class Conferences at the University of Virginia* (Charlottesville: UP of Virginia, 1959), 10.

Chapter IX

YOUNG IKE MCCASLIN:
TRAVELS IN TERRA INCOGNITA

The young Ike McCaslin seems to fit neatly into any number of critical approaches—symbolic, religious, historical, political, sociological, mythological—but whatever the approach, critics seem to miss whatever it is that Faulkner had in mind when he created Ike. Francis Lee Utley suggests that the failure lies in "the temptation" to reduce Ike's life-story "to the religious, the social, the local" and asserts that he will treat the story "in breadth without reduction."[1] What he gives us are the same well-worn themes of initiation, repudiation, redemption. If we are to avoid reductionism in our effort to understand Ike, we will have to begin by turning away from much the critics have written about him and turn to Faulkner himself and to several of the existential-phenomenologists, especially to perhaps the greatest of them all, Karl Jaspers. Both the novelist and the existential-phenomenologist agree that man can, and more often than not does, choose to live at the ground level, but they also believe that he can scale the heights. Jaspers sets forth this belief in his description of man as the Encompassing, and Faulkner in the Nobel Prize Speech was expressing the same belief when he said that man, because he has a soul, will not only endure but he will prevail. Young Ike McCaslin is Faulkner's creative embodiment of the belief and Jaspers' *beau ideal* of the existential hero.

Man as the Encompassing exists on three interrelated levels: empirical existence, consciousness-as-such, and Spirit. On the first level of the Encompassing, man lives almost exclusively a life of the senses, of the body and perceptions. He recognizes others and is recognized in turn much as animals recognize other animals. Sometimes he lives alone, sometimes he runs with the pack, but always he is a member of a species con-

fined to a blind reliance on nature, self-repeating, non-historical. Men limiting themselves to empirical existence are barely
human. They are men in name only, as in Jaspers' *Reason and
Existenz* (55,87). In the second mode of the Encompassing, consciousness-as-such, men come down from the trees and out of
their holes. Here thought has its origins, for at this level occur
the mechanical operations of the human mind, inductive and
deductive thinking. This consciousness distinguishes, defines,
classifies, seeks causes. It strives for judgmental awareness
(*R&E* 123). Nearly all of Faulkner's characters confine themselves to the first and second levels of the Encompassing.

In *Geist*, the Third Mode, we are given over neither to empirical existence nor to the life of the mind but to a movement
leading us to an all-embracing reality. No longer can we look
to mechanisms and categories for an understanding of man; the
Third Mode leads us beyond all categories. It is the mode that
brings all three modes into existential totality, a process which,
as we see in Jaspers' *Way to Wisdom*, is never completed (58).
In the Third Mode, "out of a continuously actual and continuously fragmenting whole," Jaspers writes, man creates again
and again from the fragments his "own possible reality" (*R&E*
57). Attempting to explain this elusive mode, Jaspers suggests
that one source to which we can turn for clarification is the
works of creative artists (*KJP*: I xxi). Whatever else Faulkner
makes of Ike McCaslin, he gives us a human being existing in
the Third Mode. The three great crises in Ike's life—his encounter with Old Ben, his discovery of Negro blood in his family,
and rejection of his inheritance—clearly describe the existential-phenomenological possibility that man can move beyond
the limitations of perception and cognition to the all-pervad-
ing experience of *Geist*. In creating these crises Faulkner also
breathes life into two other notions Jaspers associates with the
Encompassing: man in human history and man in communication with other men. Let us see, then, how these aspects of
existential-phenomenology which lie at the heart of Jaspers'
philosophy and psychology, interrelate with Faulkner's render-

ing of Ike McCaslin in such a way as to give us Young Ike with nothing left over or, to express it as the existential-phenomenologist would express it, man in the fullness of his possibilities.

The first crisis in Ike's life began with his first hunt and his long commitment to the wilderness. In the big bottom of the Tallahatchie, a year younger than Chick Mallison when Chick began the demeaning struggle with Lucas Beauchamp and a year or two older than Joe Christmas when Joe began the degrading life as a "nigger," Ike lived an empirical existence. He was entranced by the smells of the woods and the camp fire, the sounds of the wilderness in the night, the taste of the coarse outdoor food, the feel of the coarse outdoor blankets, the sight of the impenetrable forest greenness. Everything striking his senses was fixed by a new intensity, but there was more to living the life of a hunter than living the life of the senses, however conflagrant. He had to learn, be taught how to hunt—where to look for game, how to stalk it, the mechanical operations of holding and loading and pointing a gun—and he learned from Sam Fathers. When the boy pulled the trigger on his first buck, pulling it "quick and slow," as Sam had instructed, the buck dropped (*GDM* 163-174). Perception and reason, the first and second modes of the Encompassing, had brought Ike to the dreamed-of threshold of the hunter but only to the threshold. To breathe the rarefied air of the hunter, "the best of all breathing" (*GDM* 233), he had to enter another realm. Sam led him into this realm. Under the old man's instruction Ike cut the buck's throat, and dipping his hands into the blood, Sam wiped them across the boy's face, making him forever at "one with the wilderness which had accepted him" (*GDM* 178).

Ike never forgot this moment of joy, humility, and pride, but however he expressed this consciousness, whatever the realm he occupied, it was not that of the Third Mode. Of all modes of the Encompassing, *Geist* is the least amenable to ritual, no matter how inspired. It cannot be perceived or learned, it cannot be made official, it abjures rites of all kinds. Above all, it is life-giving, not death-dealing. The counterpart of anguish, the mode leading to self-destruction, *Geist* is the preserver (*R&E*, 57-59). Ike had moved to the edge of this *terra incognita* when the buck appeared, looking as if "all of light were condensed in him" (*GDM* 163), but when he pulled the trigger, he shot out the light. Nothing that Sam Fathers or anyone else could do nor all the mimetic magic in the world could restore it. Only Ike himself, on his own, could experience the Third Mode of the Encompassing.

It came about when Ike was ten years old. Ever since he could remember, he had heard of an enormous bear which few hunters had ever seen, much less been able to bring down, and on a hunt that took place about a year after he had shot the buck, Ike decided to go after the fabulous creature. On the third day, Ike consulted Sam, who told him he was looking in the right place but in the wrong way. "It's the gun. . . . You will have to choose" (*GDM* 206). If it had been just hunter's meat, meat on the table, or merely the joy and pride in the kill or even the greater excitement of rites of the kill, Ike would have hunted Old Ben the same way he had hunted the deer. But the bear would open possibilities beyond those of a great hunter, a crack shot like Walter Ewell, whose bullet always found the mark, and beyond those of the ideal hunter, Sam Fathers, whose rifle never missed but who never fired it (*GDM* 164,176). Hints of these possibilities had come earlier with Ike's realization that Old Ben was close by, that the bear was looking at him, but now on the fourth day, the boy left camp without the gun. He would reach out to Ben across the last greatest gap separating human beings from all other beings: he would call off the ancient war between man and animal. This leap for the Third Mode would break down the unnatural border between the upright kind and all other kinds, but the leap fell short. Ike had exchanged the gun for a stick to ward off snakes and beat down underbrush; the offering was not enough. He clung to particulars, refused to yield himself to the whole: he was still in bondage to needles and pivots, to coils and springs, to letters and numerals on dials and mechanisms (*GDM* 203-09).

The Third Mode is the mode of infinite possibilities, a mode that accommodates the possibilities not only of the human but of all the other species. To see Old Ben, Ike would have to see him on the bear's terms, and so the boy hung the watch and compass on a bush, placed the stick beside them, and continued the search. Casting aside all human advantages over the bear he would live as the bear lived—but not quite (*GDM* 208). To live in the Third Mode, Jaspers writes, means always to remain oriented to consciousness-as-such; indeed, he maintains in *Reason and Existenz* that the generating power of this mode is man's power to reason (57). Faulkner, in his creative rendering of the Third Mode, makes the same point. There was one advantage over Old Ben that Ike could not leave behind and still remain human: "that thin clear quenchless lucidity which alone differed him from this bear and from all . . . other bears" (*GDM* 207). Ike could not relinquish the second mode of the Encompassing. It was as constitutive to him as instinct, the built-in compass and watch, was to the old bear, and when after several hours of fruitless searching for the animal, Ike discovered that he was lost, he relied on reason to lead him out, just as the bear would have relied on instinct. He went to the woodsmanship he had learned from Sam. After several casts across his back track had failed, he still did not panic but sat down on a log to think what to do next. All conditions met, that is, existentially stripped to existence-as-man as the bear was stripped to existence-as-animal, both of them at last existentially equal, he looked up to see "the crooked print, the warped indentation in the wet ground. . . . " Even as he looked up he saw the next one, and, moving, not hurrying, running, but merely keeping pace with them as they appeared before him" (*GDM* 208-09).

There is something timeless about the Third Mode. Past, present, and future give out to eternity, like the bear's tracks—the "fusing the reconstructing [of] all totalities in a present which is never finished yet always fulfilled" (*R&E* 57), time elapsed and yet-relapsing, keeping pace with its own modality. For Ike, who arose from the log and followed, it was as though mode and tracks "were being shaped out of thin air," their own creation and, suddenly, he looked up to find himself back where he had come from, back at the bush on which he had hung the watch and compass. It was as if Old Ben in leading Ike had *known* that the boy was lost, as if Ike had *instinctively* followed Ben's tracks. But it was neither. It was both instinct and reason, empirical existence and consciousness-as-such, all moving in the harmony that is in the Third Mode. Then Ike saw the bear itself. Like his own perception of the animal, Old Ben "did not emerge, appear: it was just there. . . . Then it moved. It crossed the glade without haste. . . . Then it was gone." And the bear left as he had come, as consciousness leaves: "It didn't walk into the woods. It faded . . . into the wilderness, . . ." into the quintessential moment in Ike's young life (*GDM* 209). Out of the continuously fragmenting whole had emerged the whole itself. The bear and the wilderness became a part of him as his own life was a part of him, and he was no more afraid of them than he was afraid of himself.

To live as a man, Ike believed, was to live without fear (*GDM* 204), but the difficulty with fear, as he and others in the county discovered, is the difficulty with every other consciousness: it keeps coming back for more. Out of fear Mink Snopes killed Houston, and then, when he had caught up with Flem, the trembling old man was afraid the pistol would misfire (*H* 249, *M* 415). The frightened Joe Christmas ran from Miss Atkins only to meet Miss Burden (*LIA* 109,202). Jody Varner fled from one Snopes to be harassed by another (*H*1-28); Gavin Stevens ran from Manfred de Spain, who ran from Flem Snopes (*T* 56-57,86-99). Everyone in the county seems to have been in flight, but there was one threat from which none of them was free, Snopeses and Stevenses alike. "And do you know what that is?" Shreve McCannon had asked Quentin Compson. Quentin knew. It had brought the house of Sutpen down, and, if Shreve's deduction was valid, it would eventually bring down the

South, the United States, and the entire Western Hemisphere (*AA* 378). Some five or six years after Ike had seen Old Ben, he was faced with the fear. Here was the bear of bears, bigger than Old Ben, and Ike met it in the McCaslin chronicles.

"No reality," Jaspers writes, "is more central to our consciousnesses than history" (*WW* 96), and in treating this matter so crucial to our existence, Jaspers turns once more to the Encompassing. In *Philosophy*, he suggests that most history comes to us on the second level, what he calls pseudohistory. In this approach the historian searches for a thesis that will give meaning to the past, a thesis that "enables" him "only to exist in longings and romantic visualizations" (*II* 121). A good example of history written on the second level appears in *Requiem for a Nun*. In the prefaces to Acts I and II, we learn that everyone in the county is at the mercy of the planters who are at the mercy of cotton. Nearly always the historian—at least the Southern historian—writing on this level prefers the past to the present, and so in the history of Yoknapatawpha County, Gavin Stevens' main concern is to preserve the way of life associated with the Sartorises, Compsons, Habershams, "cognomens long and splendid in the annals of Yoknapatawpha" from attacks by the nameless "new people in town" (*T* 271, *R* 249) and, above all, from those whose names would not bear mentioning at all, Snopeses. But whether Stevens gives us epigones of the past or dross of the present, he gives us history in stasis. All of it seems to be dead and done with. If we wish to see Yoknapatawpha County brought to life, we must turn to a different kind of history, history in the Third Mode of the Encompassing.

History at this level, what Jaspers calls "historicity" (*KJP II* 104), makes no attempt to set forth a thesis, especially a thesis that uses the past to condemn the present. Historicity becomes aware of the present by knowing the past, not the romantic past closed off and separated from the present, as Stevens conceived it, but a past that remains open to possibilities. It is past that "is not absolutely past but remains as though sheltered in eternal being," past which, as historicity, becomes "transcendent possibility" (*KJP II* 123). This transformation is effected through assimilation. Assimilation, Jaspers maintains, occurs when past and present come together in such a way as to illuminate, not conflict with each other. What assimilation values, then, is not a break in history, a separation of past and present, but the continuity of history. Furthermore, assimilation is realized not in abstract theory but in self-awareness (*KJP* 121-123). Or, as Jaspers writes in *Man in the Modern Age*, "Assimilation occurs only through a rebirth . . . by means of which the past is transformed thanks to the entry into a spiritual region wherein I become myself in virtue of my own originality" (*KJP* 132). Young Ike McCaslin experienced this transformation, the assimilation of his past, and in the experience came to grips with the greatest of all fears of the Southern white man, miscegenation.

Occasionally, those times he was not in the woods or dreaming of being there, Ike would glance at the plantation records his father and uncle had kept, thinking that some day he would spend a dull evening or two going over them, a past "fixed immutably, finished, unalterable, harmless" (*GDM* 268), but at the age of sixteen, he discovered a radically different past. The old books were not merely plantation history, "that chronicle which was a whole land in miniature," but *his* history (*GDM* 293). As a child, before he could read, Ike had listened to the stories of the old days that "would cease to be old . . . and would become a part of the boy's present, not only as if they had happened yesterday but as if they were still happening, the men who walked through them actually walking . . . and casting an actual shadow" (*GDM* 171). Now he read the chronicles as he had listened to the stories, perceiving men actually walking, casting actual shadows. He would create from these ragtag and bob-ends not the past of another, like Quentin Compson creating Sutpen's, but his own past. As he read, the chronicles came alive, "took substance and even a sort of shadowy life . . . all there, not only the general and condoned injustice . . . but the specific tragedy" (*GDM* 265-66).

Nothing is easier when going over the past than to look at it romantically, gazing as Stevens did at the Old Lot; nothing is much harder than to keep gazing as it begins to crumble. Harder still is to know from the beginning that it is going to crumble. Hardest is to discover that the sight is worse than you had imagined it would be. The record of the McCaslin slaves— of Thucydides and his wife Eunice, Eunice's daughter, Thomasina. Thomasina's son Turl—was not new to Ike, but now, for the first time, he read with apprehension the entry his father had made on the drowning of Eunice, and the sardonic question his father had asked: "*Who in hell ever heard of a nigger drownding him self*" (*GDM* 267). For Ike's father, who pursued the question no further, it was a matter of "nigger" history. For Ike it was a matter of *his* history. And he had to pursue it. He pursued it the same way he had pursued the bear. First he recognized that he was in a new and alien country, the *terra incognita* where a nigger could lay claim to the same human feelings as a white man, and after wandering for a while lost in this country, he made a cast across his backtrack, to the time where it intersected with that of his grandfather, Eunice, and Eunice's daughter. When this tactic failed to bring results, Ike made a cast in the opposite direction and much wider, this time to an intersection with Thomasina and her son, Turl (*GDM* 269). It worked. Ike knew where he was now, but he would not accept it. In an effort to find some excuse for his grandfather who fathered the mulatto child and thus ease the burden of his past, Ike wandered on, accepting the illusion that Thomasina had come into his family channeled by love, "*Some sort of love*," and if not love, then at least the result of loneliness, a lonely old man and an attractive young girl. Then the wandering and the illusions ceased. Ike began to think instead of rationalizing, and the unbearable reason for Eunice's suicide came clear: "The old frail pages seemed to turn of their own accord even while he thought [Copulating with] *His own daughter*. No No Not even him" (*GDM* 270).

History in the Third Mode is like pages turning, moving,

keeping pace with its own modality, here the mode and the pages of history turning of their own accord, with a life of their own, moving out of the distant past assimilated into the present: Turl was Carothers' and Thomasina's son, Carothers' and Eunice's grandson, Ike's great-uncle. Like the bear, Turl had not emerged, appeared: he was just there, dimensionless, looking at Ike. Then Turl in the pages of the Chronicles, like Old Ben in the Big Woods, moved and was gone, he and "the yellowed pages in their fading and implacable succession," like the bear fading. The pages would never again hold fear for Ike, any more than Ben held fear for him. "He would never need look at the ledgers again," just as he would never need look at the bear again. "That was all" (*GDM* 271). But that was not all.

In *Philosophy*, Jaspers has written that the "leap from fear to serenity is the most tremendous one man can make" (*KJP III* 206), and Faulkner has said that to be a man means teaching oneself "that the basest of all things is to be afraid" (*NPS*). We have seen Ike teaching himself the baseness of physical and of racial fear, but the way he learned these lessons leaves something to be desired. In both instances the lesson took place in private, removed from the world of living men. Ike was the only sentient human being present, and the questions he answered were only the questions he himself had asked. Although questions and answers of this kind are important in that they encourage us to believe what we already know—Ike's knowledge of his kinship with Old Ben and Turl—they are like taking an examination we ourselves have made out, the questions answered even in the act of questioning. If man is finally to test himself and his beliefs, Jaspers says in *Philosophy and the World*, he cannot remain in solitude: "man can only come to himself with his fellow man" (100), not with bears or his own past, however noble the one or vital the other. Only in communicating with other men will he find himself, a communication carried on primarily through speech.

On the first and second levels of the Encompassing, speech is sometimes given over to irrationally attacking the other, Mink

Snopes snarling and growling, or to hiding what we have to say in a cocoon of banality. Gavin Stevens is rational enough but unintelligible. Only in the Third Mode do we *communicate* with the other. Man in this mode does not forget his aggressions or his weakness for rationalizing, but he does not surrender to them. He knows that he is made not only for conflict but also for communication, knows that he is free only in so far as the other is freed. As Jaspers writes in *Philosophy*, "It is a struggle in which both combatants dare to show themselves without reserve and to allow themselves to be thrown into question" (*KJP II* 60). Thus instead of confronting others, attempting by countless ruses to subdue them, he tries in countless ways to reach out to them" (*KJP* 59-60). "As soon as man uses language to establish a living relation with himself and with his fellows," writes Merleau-Ponty, "language is no longer an instrument, *no longer a means; it is a manifestation, a revelation of intimate being and of the psychic link which unites us to the world and our fellow man*" (*PP* 196). Ike McCaslin, with an assist from his cousin, Cass Edmonds, reveals how this is effected and, what is more, does so in three important areas, the very fabric out of which Yoknapatawpha was woven: the land, religion, and race.

The dialogue took place in the old commissary on the McCaslin plantation, which Ike as Carothers McCaslin's only white grandson stood to inherit. Cass, who was sixteen years older than Ike as well as Ike's guardian, was in nominal control of the property; and only once, when Ike insisted on taking part in the death watch over Sam Fathers, did the boy question his guardian's authority. This contretemps, which involved a few days off from school, was easily resolved (*GDM* 249-50), but now, with Ike's coming of age, he would again question Cass, in this instance about the inheritance of the plantation. Ike wished to reject it and his reasoning, as we shall see, was such that Cass, who was second in line, would have no claim to it either. Given these conditions, we would normally have expected a confrontation between idealistic youth and greedy middle age, but we get something much different. Confrontation becomes commu-

141

nication: language in the Third Mode.

As authority for rejecting his inheritance, Ike went to the Bible, arguing that the land was God's, turned over to man to be held in "suzerainty . . . in His name." Trouble had arisen, Ike continued, when men used His earth for their own selfish purposes. One of these men was Ikkemotubbe. The Indian had no right to the land and thus his selling it to Ike's grandfather was fraudulent. How rash this red man who believed he could convey for any sum any fragment of God's wilderness, how fatuous of Carothers to believe he could buy it (*GDM* 256,257)! Ike then could not repudiate his inheritance, as Cass had accused him of doing, for it had never been his to repudiate. Naturally, Cass was not convinced, for if it was not Ike's to inherit, neither was it his. The McCaslin plantation, Cass maintained, was a fact both as land and as purchase. Carothers not only had bought it but had developed it into a valuable property; Ike's attempt to relinquish it had proved there was something to relinquish (*GDM* 257-58). As Cass talked he became increasingly convinced of the absurdity of Ike's position and of the validity of his own, and yet he sought to protect this young man whom he raised. He would shift the blame for Ike's refusal from Ike's shoulders onto those of the God who had advised him. "He—this Arbiter, this Architect, this Umpire—condoned [Carothers' actions]—or did He? looked down and saw—or did He? Or at least did nothing: saw and could not, or did not see . . . or perhaps He would not see—perverse, impotent, or blind: which?" (*GDM* 258).

The certainty of men communicating with each other resides in an unreserved openness that takes nothing for granted, which questions everything (*KJP II* 60). The contest, however, is different from, say, that of Colonel Sartoris in *The Unvanquished* subtly cutting up Redmond (258-60). For men in communication the struggle is "a loving struggle" (*KJP II* 59) in which questions asked lead not to death, physical or psychological, but to mutual enlightenment. Cass's question was no exception. As Cass had tried to deliver Ike from the absurdity of relinquishing the plantation, Ike delivered Cass from blasphemy. For the rope to pull his cousin out, not bind him, Ike used the time-honored argument justifying the ways of God to man: free will and foreknowledge. God did not condone nor was He impotent, Ike told Cass. He was as God is, man's greatest friend, for He gave him his freedom, allowed him to work out his problems, yet knowing what the results would be— failure first in Eden and then in Canaan. But loving man as He did, Ike continued, God did not forsake him. He discovered to him the American South, the New Eden, the best hope of the world—even as He knew what man would make of the discovery (*GDM* 258-59). This time, though, man went too far, even for God. Into this Eden man brought slaves to do what he himself should have been doing. The ungrateful creature took one of His own beings and bought and sold him as if he were an object (*GDM* 282-83).

The truth of speech is sounds for sounds have lexical meaning, the basic thought unit of which is the word. Combinations of words into appropriate syntactical patterns give semantical meaning. One of the sharpest points of conflict among linguists is whether lexical meaning or semantical is more important (*B&N* 514-515). For those caught up in the sounds of their own voices, it is always the word. Rather than words integrated into sentences to produce meaning, the word itself becomes the meaning. This suggests in turn that sentences become sentences in name only, as moonlight is light in name only. They do not illuminate but cast the kind of weird glow that began to shimmer on Ike's use of the Bible to denounce slavery:

> Maybe He saw that only by voiding the land for a time of Ikkemotubbe's blood and substituting for it another blood, could He accomplish His purpose. Maybe He knew already what the other blood would be, maybe it was more than justice that only the white man's blood was available and capable to raise the white man's curse. . . . Maybe He chose

> Grandfather out of all of them. . . . Maybe He knew that
> Grandfather himself would not serve His purpose . . .; maybe
> He saw already in Grandfather the need . . . . (*GDM* 259)

Maybe. Maybe. Maybe: If Ike could rescue Cass from blasphemy, Cass could save Ike from this feverish emotionalism by reminding him of the facts. The Book itself had relegated the black man to servitude: "The sons of Ham," Cass murmured (*GDM* 260). Cass had questioned God's authority, and now he questioned the authority of the Bible, striking at the heart of that authority, its inconsistency. No emotional appeal could deliver Ike from that indisputable fact, so he turned to something that would deliver him, to that which had delivered him in the wilderness and in the chronicles. He reasoned that the Bible was like everything else good in the world, a joint effort of God and man. At times, Ike argued, it was difficult to tell where God's words left off and man's began. It was difficult to decide whether the Book was revealing divine thoughts about man or human thoughts about God, but it was not difficult to tell where He stood on race. Or if it was hard to tell, all Cass need do was to look at the War. God would free the Negro if He had to kill every white man in the county, in the South, and in all of the other counties and sections (*GDM* 284-85).

It was their polarity on the black man that offered the severest test to make sounds make sense. No longer was their subject the land, Populism as an acceptable alternative to Feudalism. Nor was their subject religion, the advantages of Fundamentalism over Rationalism. What good, they were asking, is a human being if he happened to be black? For Ike the War was proof that blood and violence were not the solution to the question: after four years of war, the Negro was as much a slave as he had ever been (*GDM* 289). For Cass the War was proof that the Negro had not been worth trying to save in the first place; thousands of white Southerners had died in the freeing of creatures not worth freeing. And so when Ike proclaimed that Negroes were better than white men, Cass said that they were also more promiscuous, violent, unstable. When Ike proclaimed endurance as one of the mistreated black man's virtues, Cass answered, "So have mules." When Ike said the black man has pity, forbearance, fidelity, Cass countered, "So have dogs" (*GDM* 294-95).

Ordinarily in the county this word used to denigrate either black or white would have been almost as effective as *Yankee*, and by all rights it should have ended Ike's and Cass's attempts to characterize the Negro. Instead, it brought the cousins together in a mutual understanding of the black man. For Ike the hunter who spent so much time with dogs, the word was synonymous with *courage: "Maybe that's what courage is,"* he had said of the young hound that had been brave enough to attack Old Ben (*GDM* 239). Ike had also attributed this absolute to the nameless little fyce that had also attacked the bear, and now with the generosity possible only for men in communication, he looked for concurrence in Cass and found it. As he told Cass about the attack, about this dog "not humble because it was already too near the ground to genuflect, and not proud because it would not have been close enough for anyone to discern what was casting that shadow, . . . so that all it could be was brave" (*GDM* 296), Ike was looking at Cass, and "it was in McCaslin's eyes too, he had only to look at McCaslin's eyes and it was there" (*GDM* 295). In Cass's eyes, without either Ike or Cass saying so, in the twilight as they sat with each other in the commissary, the dog, the black man, and courage were as one. So were both men as one. Both understood each other and the legacy, each in his own way, each to his own. They gave proof that men in communication can be true without knowing The Truth and both win. Cass got the plantation, Ike his freedom from it—almost.

Communication in the Third Mode has much in common with Gabriel Marcel's "philosophy of intersubjectivity" (*MB I* 223), but where Jaspers comes on strong, setting forth his views of communication at length and in great detail, Marcel is strictly low-key. His description focuses on the preposition "with." Like the little fyce, unpretentious, barely casting a shadow, this connective is also powerful in that it is used almost exclusively to express human relationships. To be "with," Marcel maintains, is to come "together at the ontological level, that is qua [human] beings" (*MB I* 219). A chair stands beside, behind, in front of but not with another chair. Often human beings relate to each other the way chairs relate to each other. Lucas Beauchamp was expressing this object-relationship when he stood before his kinsman, Ike McCaslin, in Ike's kitchen saying, "Whar's the rest of that money Old Carothers left? I wants it. All of it" (*GDM* 282).

The strongest ties between human beings, Marcel believes, are blood ties. In his terms blood ties are with-ties. Ike had learned this when he was sixteen: Carothers, Eunice, Thomasina, Turl were with him then, and now Turl's son joins them. The legacy, Ike told Lucas, was not his "to give or withhold either. It was your father's. . . . Even if grandpa hadn't left money for Tomey's Turl. . . ." (*GDM* 108). Lucas had been waiting twenty-one years to hear this. Like the word *dog* bridging the chasm between Ike and Cass, two cousins at odds over the black man, *grandpa* bridged the chasm between the black grandson and the white one. Ike was looking at grandpa's curved nose and piercing eyes, and without saying so, Lucas knew what Ike was looking at. Both were McCaslins, both belonged to the Old Lot, they were at one with each other. And so they left Ike's home to walk side by side, the white one who had relinquished his inheritance because of mistreatment of the black, on the way to the bank where together they stood while the white man showed the black man how to make out his check, and together they stood as the black man drew out the money, counted it twice, and returned it to the teller. Long afterward the county remembered the two walking, standing, counting, and was privileged to look upon, the county historian wrote, a "minor" event in the annals of the place. What the county looked upon and did not see was communication at a level where a white man and a black man cannot raise the question of equality without answering the question of brotherhood, black and white together and free at last.

Notes

[1] Utley, Francis Lee "Pride and Humility: The Cultural Roots of Ike McCaslin." *Bear, Man, and God: Seven Approaches to William Faulkner's "The Bear"* (New York: Random House, 1964), 234.

Chapter X

THE BUNDRENS AND
THE MYSTERY OF THE FAMILY

In treating the characters in *As I Lay Dying*, critics, more often then not, revile Addie. They write that she "is alienated from her family," materialist, manipulative, "responsible for the hatred and pain within the Bundren family."[1] "Even in death," one critic writes, "she dominates and corrodes the family."[2] The members of this family receiving most attention from the critics are Darl and Vardaman. Dewey Dell and Anse are hardly mentioned (one critic calls Anse a "human buzzard"[3]), and Cash is seldom given serious consideration. Jewel, we are told, "is too reckless and impulsive" to make much of a contribution.[4] Darl is labeled "detached" and "amoral,"[5] but he is also seen as an "idealist," and an "enchanted knight."[6] "Only Darl," says a critic, "was concerned to get his mother's body decently buried as quickly as possible."[7] The verdict on Vardaman is also mixed. He is "close to idiocy," all the bother over his mother and that fish.[8] Some critics, on the other hand, attempt to make sense out of his obsession: the fish is "a child's way of conceiving death," the "chopping up of the fish is ritual magic to prevent . . . [Addie's] death," the eating of the fish by the other members of her family means to Vardaman that "she will be able to breathe, or live."[9] Several critics turn to phenomenology to explain the characters. One examines them through the three modes of consciousness, "sensation, reason, and intuition" and comes to the conclusion that Cash is the hero of the story, the one Bundren who "ultimately achieves maturity and understanding by integrating these modes into one distinctly human response."[10] Another, also using this approach, concentrates on Darl, who is an excellent example of "pure consciousness," one containing "images of the mystery of existence."[11]

Throughout these comments, whether the critics are writing about the mother and / or the other members of the family, there is present, implicitly or explicitly, the ever profound relationship between the dead and the living. Addie's "consciousness and her memory of the Bundren past, . . ." writes a critic, "make the narrative passages of her family what they are."[12] She "is dead," writes another, "and yet is given a voice in the novel."[13] Indeed it is this voice that provides the compositional center of *As I Lay Dying*, and we wish to hear it as clearly as her family heard it. Gabriel Marcel was tuning in on such a voice when he wrote that ". . . a certain holiness . . . is the most precious thing the West has known, a certain attitude of reverence for existence, . . . the mystery of death and the mystery of birth, . . . this sense of holiness, this fundamental reverence for life and for death . . . the poetry in us . . . " (*HV* 75). Immediately we are struck with the beauty of the passage, but more than that we are surprised and delighted at the weight Marcel gives to death in our existence. He equates it with life.

Of all modern philosophers the existential-phenomenologists are most concerned with death. Their concerns lead in two directions. The first is that of Martin Heidegger and those who emphasize the existential necessity of each of us facing the fact that he will die. Only when a human being comes to grips with this profound fact, Heidegger tells us, will she be ready to live. Heidegger also tells us that few, if any of us, do come to grips with the fact; instead we spend a life-time avoiding it (*B&T* 279-311). A second group of existential-phenomenologists, represented chiefly by Marcel and Karl Jaspers, are not so much concerned with our facing death or understanding what it is like to die as in how an existential-phenomenological relationship can exist between the living and the dead. Marcel calls this relationship "one of the most important . . . with which the existential philosopher has to deal" (*HV* 148), and he poses two interrelated questions concerning it: "What attitude can and should we adopt to this being who is at once present and gone forever?" If our attitude is, as Marcel believes it should be, one of an "active and even militant fidelity," how can the attitude be realized (*CF* 149)? The answer to the questions, the answer Marcel gives to all deep and abiding relationships is existential communication. Jaspers agrees with Marcel. The "total will-to-communicate, once it is on its way," Jaspers writes, "can not surrender itself. It has a confidence in itself and in possibilities in the world which may be deceived again and again, but it can doubt only in its limited expression, never its own principles" (*R&E* 101). Marcel sets forth this belief in his philosophy of Intersubjectivity and Jaspers in his view of man as the Encompassing. In this study I plan to use interchangeably these philosophies to throw light on Faulkner's great faith in communication as revealed in *As I Lay Dying*. Specifically, let us see how the three levels of the Encompassing in addition to Marcel's notions on Intersubjectivity give us insights into the existential crisis in the lives of the Bundrens, the death of the mother.

To review Jaspers' concept as it was developed in Chapter IX, man as the Encompassing exists on three interrelated levels: empirical existence, consciousness-as-such, and Spirit. On the first level of the Encompassing, man lives almost exclusively a life of the senses, that of the body and perceptions. He recognizes others and is recognized in turn much as animals recognize other animals. Sometimes he lives alone, sometimes he runs with the pack, but always he is a member of a species confined to a blind reliance on nature, self-repeating, non-historical. Persons limiting themselves to empirical existence are barely human. They are humans in name only (*R&E* 55,87). In the second mode of the Encompassing, consciousness-as-such, man comes down from the trees and out of his holes. Here thought has its origins, for at this level occur the mechanical operations of the human brain, inductive and deductive thinking. This consciousness distinguishes, defines, classifies, seeks causes. It strives for judgmental awareness (*R&E* 11,123 *WW* 87). Nearly all of Faulkner's characters are confined to the first and second levels of the Encompassing.

In *Geist*, the Third Mode, we are given over neither to empirical existence nor to the life of the mind but to a movement leading us to an all-embracing reality. It is the mode that brings all three modes into existential totality, a process never completed (*WW* 58). In the Third Mode, "out of a continuously actual and continuously fragmenting whole," Jaspers writes, man creates again from the fragments his "own possible reality" (*R&E* 57). Attempting to explain this elusive mode, Jaspers suggests that one area to which we can turn for clarification is the works of the creative artist (*KJP: I* xxxi). Whatever else Faulkner gives us in the Bundren family, he gives us one of them existing in the Third Mode.

In the first mode of the Encompassing the relationship between the living and the dead is that of empirical existence—the relationship between Addie and her son, Cash. He saw his mother as an object. The dying woman would need a coffin soon, so he would make one to her measurement and make it straight, "tight as a drum and neat as a sewing basket" (*AILD* 83), and when Addie breathed her last, Cash looked into her room for a moment, noted that she had died, and went back to work. When the coffin was finished and Addie placed in it for the trip to Jefferson, Cash complained that it was off center on the wagon. During the journey he frequently wiped away splotches of mud on the coffin, and when at Tull's washed-out bridge, it slipped off the wagon into the swollen river, he tried to save it, even though he could not swim (*AILD* 49,102,147). He had put too much work into that box to lose it now. But he thought that this loss was easier to bear than losing his tools. Regaining his senses after being pulled from the water, he did not ask what had happened to the coffin or to Addie lying in it; all that interested him was what had happened to his saw, his adze, his hammer (*AILD* 155,172).

Where Cash treated his mother as an object that was worth less than the coffin in which she lay, worth much less than the tools he used to make it, her husband treated her as an abstraction. Anse had been pleased that Cash was taking great pains with the coffin, but apprehensive of the gathering rain storm, he urged his son to work faster, even at the expense of craftsmanship (*AILD* 49,50). Anse had given Addie his word that he would bury her in Jefferson and better to bury her there in a half-finished box than not at all. "I promised my word," he said; "she's counting on it" (*AILD* 17,18). What Addie had counted on from Anse was a decent burial; what she got from him was a burial on the second level of the Encompassing. Promises nearly always seek this level. For instance, my friend is seriously ill in the hospital, and I promise to see him every day. For a week I keep my promise, and then I begin to falter. I notice that he is a little weary of my daily visits, my work begins to pile up, I myself am not too well—in short, the compassion I felt earlier has begun to evaporate or, possibly, has disappeared altogether. In any event, it can no longer compete with my other interests, but what now of my promise? If I continue my visits, acting one way and feeling another, I am being deceitful; if I do not continue, I break my promise. One alternative is as distasteful as the other. Attempting to solve the dilemma, I formulate a third alternative. I treat the promise as an ethical-conceptual rather than a human bond, treat it as an obligation I have imposed on myself. The promise becomes for me what Anse's promise to Addie became, a matter of principle. My affirmation is now unconditional, but it is also empty in the way that Anse's was. He and I have replaced a human relationship with a contractual one; we are not bound to human beings but to our word (*B&H* 41-45). Anse makes this relationship abundantly clear. It was his "given promise," he insisted. He told Vernon Tull three times that he had "promised her," told Samson three times that he had given "her my promise," all the while the irascible, contentious woman, with whom in life he had fought and to whom he had made love, in death became a concept (*AILD* 34,84,119,108,109).

In treating Addie as an object and as an abstraction, Cash and Anse had made the same grievous error: they equated consciousness with sentience, believing that with the cessation of breath consciousness ceases. As intentionality consciousness defies any such effort at objective definition. We cannot speak of consciousness as if it were a thing; it cannot be defined ostensively as something appearing at a precise instant in time and then coming to an end at a precise instant. All that we can say is that it appears and disappears; we cannot say that just because it has disappeared, it has ceased to exist. As Marcel writes, "there can be no question of treating the absolute cessation of consciousness as a fact" and thus no question of proving that consciousness stops when the lungs or the heart or the brain stops (*HV* 148). Consciousness is a boundless horizon that cannot be fixed, the existentiality that manifests itself most clearly in the Third Mode of the Encompassing.

On this level of existence, human beings accept the all-encompassing nature of consciousness: they remain open to it whether manifested in the living or in those no longer alive. Just because the other being is a silent being, there is no reason to believe that he is a non-being (*HV* 148). Jewel was trying to say something like this as he led the funeral procession from the house toward New Hope. Addie had requested that the family sit together on the wagon carrying her body (*AILD* 94), but Jewel, the apple of her eye, demurred. He would have his mother sit up and take notice of him in death as she had in life, would have her see her Jewel on his horse coming "up the land fast, . . . the mud flying beneath the flicking drive of the hooves. Then he slows a little, light and erect in the saddle, the horse mincing through the mud" (*AILD* 101). Jewel waits until the wagon passes, waits to see if his mother is looking, and then he comes on again. The horse, the "pussel-gutted bastard," the "sweet son of a bitch" (*AILD* 13) dances up, "arch-necked, reined back to a swift singlefoot," as the rider "sits lightly, poised, upright, wooden-faced in the saddle, the broken hat raked at a swaggering angle" (*AILD* 102). The queen is dead, long live the queen.

But the Encompassing as the Third Mode transforms performance, the magical antics of an actor performing as much for his own amusement as for others'. Abjuring egotism this Mode arises from the ontological need for communication(*CF* 241,242). The living and the dead are bound together in such a way that the line between the one who gives and the one who receives disappears. In this Mode, "we receive in giving, or to put it still better, giving is already a way of receiving" (*HV* 146). To say that the dead can give nothing to the living is to say that we have nothing to receive from them. To say this is to deny, as Faulkner tells us in *Go Down, Moses*, what Sam Fathers gave Ike McCaslin. Taking Sam's word that consciousness can move beyond anything he had ever known, Ike in the Big Woods witnessed "his own birth" (*GDM* 195), and two years after he and Boon had buried Sam, Ike stood beside the grave conscious that his spiritual father was alive as long as the wilderness lived: "There was no death," he meditated, "not Lion and not Sam: not held fast in earth but free in earth and not in earth but of earth, myriad yet undiffused of every myriad part, leaf and twig and particle, air and sun and rain and dew and night, acorn oak and leaf and acorn again, dark and dawn and dark and dawn again in their immutable progression" (*GDM*328-29). It is to this wilderness that Darl Bundren would deliver Addie.

As Cash worked on the box that would hold Addie, Jewel had expressed his profane dismay, listening to his brother "hammering and sawing on that god-damn box" and then imagining himself and Addie high on a hill where she would be safe with him (*AILD* 14,15). More reflective than Jewel, Darl had consoled himself with the thought that Cash was a good carpenter, that Addie could not want a better coffin, that it would give her "confidence and comfort" (*AILD* 4,5). Once the coffin was finished, however, Darl could hardly bear the thought of Addie in it. He reached out to her as Ike had reached out to Sam. First, he euphemized, calling the coffin "a strange room" (*AILD* 76) with Addie asleep in it, and then as he and his brothers were lifting the coffin, it was as though the occupant had awakened, as though, Darl reflected, "within it her pole-thin body clings furiously . . . to a sort of modesty" (*AILD* 91).

It clung also to life, giving "buoyancy to the planks." Sensing this change, this quickening in the dead weight of the dead, Darl perceived that the pallbearers moved more "carefully, . . . balancing it as though it were something infinitely precious." It slid "down the air like a sled" (*AILD* 92). Darl's end was weightless so that he did not have even to touch it, Addie for him no longer a being held fast in the box but free in it and of it, moving volitionally, and when at last the movement stopped, coming to rest on the wagon bed, Darl was not discouraged (*AILD* 93). A few hours later he would see to it that Addie was free and moving again.

To Darl the flooded Yoknapatawpha was not a barrier but an opportunity, and when at Tull's washed-out bridge, the box slipped off the wagon into the water, he slipped in after it, not to save Addie from the stream but to give her to it. The infinitely precious body would be free, if he had his way, in and of the free-flowing "thick dark current," it running and talking "in a murmur become ceaseless and myriad." To Darl the yellow surface of the river was "dimpled monstrously into fading swirls traveling along the surface," "silent," "profoundly significant, as though just beneath the surface something huge and alive waked for a moment of lazy alertness out of and into light slumber again." The sleeping and waking Addie would be at one with the stream as Sam Fathers with the earth, be in and of the dimples and swirls of the clucks and murmurs, of the gouts of foam, of the plaintive sound, a musing sound, of and under the ceaseless surface (*AILD* 134,135). When Addie would not stay under, despite Darl's "strong and steady [hand] holding her under" (*AILD* 144), Darl was still not discouraged. He would try once more, this time to leave her free in and of and as air.

The Third Mode does not deny the efficacy of communication in silence, the communication between Ike McCaslin and the dead Sam Fathers or between Darl and Addie, but to leave communication here would mean postulating a closed system. Human communication, if it is not to be destroyed at its very center, must remain open to every manifestation, even the voices of those no longer living (*HV* 152). On the first and second levels of the Encompassing, these voices reputedly come through in seances, table rappings, and so forth. The Third Mode dismisses mechanical contrivances of all descriptions. On this level, Marcel writes, the notion of subjective or of objective transmission is unthinkable; the communion in which presences of the living and dead "become manifest to each other" does not "belong to the same realm of being" as the transmission of purely objective and of purely subjective messages (*HV* 255).

Darl shows us the realm to which they do belong as he listened to Addie as she lay beneath the branches of the apple tree at Gillespie's place. The moonlight awakened the sleeping woman, as had the movement of the tipped coffin, and when she spoke, she spoke as the water had spoken. "She talks in little trickling bursts of secret and murmurous bubbling," Darl said (*AILD* 202), and she talked to "God, . . . calling Him to help her." She was too modest to take off her clothes while others were looking, Darl believed, and so she wanted God "to hide her away from the sight of man" while she was disrobing (*AILD* 204). But Darl was too impatient to wait for God. He would preserve her privacy, free her from the box, and give her life everlasting. Darl's vision of freeing Addie at the washed-out bridge was like that of the Grier boy, whose brother Pete had drowned in the Pacific during World War II. The boy believed that since no one could say exactly where Pete "stopped being *is*," where he became "*was*," Pete was still alive, "still *is* everywhere about the earth" (*CS* 104). Darl would deliver Addie to a freedom beyond this: she would be alive everywhere *above* earth. For this reason he set fire to the barn to which the coffin had been moved (*AILD* 205). Addie's remains would be for Darl what Sam Father's were for Ike McCaslin. They would be as the breeze carrying them, free in ". . . air and sun and rain and dew and night, . . ." eternal (*GDM* 128).

The living and the dead are equally open to existential-phenomenological description; in the first mode an object embedded in empirical existence, in the second, reduced to a concept, in the Third transcendent, and any mode existing at the expense of the other two is equally unsatisfactory (*HV* 146-151). Darl came close to assigning Addie to the second mode. He did not make of her the abstraction Anse had made, but he often treated her impersonally. It was sometimes difficult for him to identify the person in the box as his mother. Often he rejected her: "I cannot love my mother because I have no mother," he said (*AILD* 89), but more often, she was somebody called Addie Bundren—"Addie Bundren is going to die," "Addie Bundren is going to die" (*AILD* 39), "Addie Bundren could not want a better . . . box to lie in" (*AILD* 4-5). "Addie Bundren will not be," "Addie Bundren must be" (*AILD* 76)—Addie Bundren free-floating and anonymous in the stream and in the air. Vardaman's attempt to keep Addie alive was also dependent upon the life-saving properties of air and water, but it depended too upon all three modes of the Encompassing, not one or two. Indeed, his awareness of his mother in death is an almost perfect progression in modes of communication from the first to the Third.

In the first mode Vardaman gave Addie up for dead, treating her as an object, and then attempted to avenge her death in the first mode, magically. Addie's doctor had been at bedside when she died; therefore, Vardaman believed, he had killed her and he would pay for it. Out of sight and hearing of the huge fat man, the boy tried to curse him out of existence, and when the incantation proved ineffective, he turned to other magical means. Vardaman could not drive "the fat son of a bitch" from the premises, but he could drive off his team of horses. "You kilt my maw!" the angry boy shouted as he substituted the animals for the doctor, driving them down the road, and as they-Peabody fled, the magic worked: the tears dried up, the anger subsided, and the pragmatic world gradually returned. Vardaman saw Cash, heard the cow lowing, heard other sounds that drowned out his quarrel with Peabody and led him away from the futility of avenging his mother's death to a profound understanding of it. (*AILD* 53-55).

Just before his mother died, Vardaman had caught a large fish. His first thought was to show his prize to her, but when he reached the house, company was there. Adding to his misery, Anse ordered him to clean the fish; he refused. But instead of reacting as he had to Peabody, attempting to curse him out of existence, Vardaman sought the quiet of the barn. It was there, when he heard Dewey Dell calling him for supper and chopping wood to cook the fish, that he made the existential-phenomenological connection between the fish and his mother (*AILD* 29,30,55). The experience must have been something like that of young Sutpen when he made the connection between himself and the man in the big house. All of a sudden it was not thinking, it was something shouting it almost loud enough for his sister and his father and his brothers to hear. It was like an explosion, a bright light (*AA* 238). Before Vardaman had caught the fish, he reasoned, Addie had been alive. She was not dead then—"Hit hadn't happened then"—and now if he could retrieve his fish, take it away from Dewey Dell and show his mother, she would see it. She would be alive. Another thought struck him, depressing: Dewey Dell would not turn the fish over to him: "Cooked and et. Cooked and et" (*AILD* 55) and his mother disappearing with it. Then a brighter thought. If he could not prevent her from leaving him, he would bring her back.

Marcel maintains that death is like life in that we do not know what either phenomenon "is veiling, what it is protecting, nor what it is preparing." The treason against both life and death is to believe that these phenomena are veiling, protecting, preparing nothing. The final treason is to separate the phenomena as if there were nothing between them (*HV* 148). One of Doom's slaves refused to commit treason. In dying, the slave believed, "man leaped past life into where death was; he dashed into death and did not die, because when death took a man, it took him just this side of the end of living" (CS 330). Vardaman took this phenomenology further than the slave. He believed that once a woman has crossed the border, she can return. At least he believed that his mother could return: all he had to do in order to bring her back was to prove that the "*not-fish*" had existed (*AILD* 52), that it *was* and then his mother would be *is*. For proof he would go to Vernon Tull. Vernon had seen the fish. "You mind that ere fish," Vardaman had cried out when he reached Tull's house. "You was there. You seen it laying there" (*AILD* 66-67). Tull never denied that the fish had been lying there, which was assurance enough for the boy, and he returned home to find his mother lying on the bed where he had left her. This was his mother before the fat man had come, as alive as when the not-fish was a fish. Vardaman's first concern, then, was to give her more air. He opened the window of the stuffy room, and when someone closed it, he opened it again. Then the window was nailed shut and Cash nailed Addie inside the air-tight box, but the situation was not irretrievable. The boy waited until everyone had gone to bed and bored holes in the coffin. Even when Cash plugged the holes, there was still hope (*AILD* 69,70).

Our ignorance of the "exact state" of existence of the dead, Marcel writes, is not surprising if we consider our ignorance of the "exact state" of the living (*HV* 149). If in life the adulterous Addie could appear to be a loyal wife, as her husband believed (*AILD* 18), it is no surprise that in death she could appear as a fish, as Vardaman believed; if in life she had been an ever private woman, in death she could certainly return to the ultimate privacy, the depths from which she had arisen. Eons ago from out of the depths, Addie had come up for her brief moment of atmospheric oxygen, which had proved to be too much for her, so now she would go back for it dissolved, moving about in her original homeland and the marvelous reconciliation of life and death—the not-difference, as Vardaman could have expressed it, between her life and her death. Thus when Cash plugged up the holes Vardaman had bored in the top of the box, the boy did not worry. His mother no longer needed air. She needed a place to swim, and she found it at Tull's washed-out bridge, found it in the flooding Yoknapatawpha where Vardaman, anxious to see her again in the flesh, urged Darl to catch her. "He came up to see and I hollering catch her Darl catch her." Addie had been moving too fast for so small a boy to catch, and now she went too fast for a man, "I hollering catch her Darl . . . because in the water she could go faster than a man." Darl was the finest "grabbler" there was, but, Vardaman knew, Addie was the best fish "in the water . . . faster than a man or woman," and when Darl climbed up the bank without her, Vardaman wanted to know where his mother was. "Where is ma, Darl? . . . You knew she is a fish but you let her get away" (*AILD* 143,144).

If being open as the Encompassing brings large rewards, the effort is continuously in danger of failing. The danger lies mainly in the constitution of the Third Mode. In this Mode, objects and concepts no longer furnish benchmarks, and sometimes we move so far beyond the tangible and the solid that our being-in-the-world becomes detached being, like Darl on the way to the insane asylum at Jackson (*AILD* 228). More often the danger comes from the opposite direction. We refuse to let go, even for a moment, the empirical and conceptual workaday world of the first two modes, the safe harbor of Cash and Anse, and even if we do venture beyond, we have continuously to battle the undertow of these two modes pulling at the Third. Vardaman gives us a good instance of the battle and what it means to lose it. As he stood by the coffin, which had finally been retrieved from the river, and saw Cash vomiting on it, he was not overly concerned: "He is sick on the box. But my mother is a fish" (*AILD* 185). And when Dewey Dell asked skeptically how Addie got out of the box and into the river, Vardaman had an easy answer: "*She got out through the holes I bored*" (*AILD* 187). There was, however, something about Addie harder to explain than going through holes: What was that stench?

The nose is the most effective of the sensory organs in detecting corporeal death, for it is the final arbiter. We gaze at a corpse and it looks as if it could speak to us; we run our fingers through the hair and the living, growing strands feel warm. We smell the decaying body and there is no longer doubt. We can avoid looking and touching if we choose, but even though we pinch our nostrils shut, the odor is still there. It is everywhere (*PP* 223 *H* 289). As the funeral procession moved toward Whiteleaf, Cash had said that in a couple of days the corpse would be stinking, and he was right. Samson and Armstid, the Bundren's neighbors, could smell it, and after Addie had been dead eight days, women in Mottson scattered about the street holding handkerchiefs to their noses (*AILD* 103,108,178,193), but none of this had any effect on Vardaman. Samson and the others were outraged by the stranger in the box, not by his mother. "*My mother is not in the box. My mother does not smell like that. My mother is a fish*" (*AILD* 187). Then on the ninth night, the undertow pulling hard, Addie returned to the box. She went back in as she had come out, except that the modes of the Encompassing were in reverse, running backward Third to second to first, like a movie reel reversed and spinning fast as if Vardaman had realized his mistake and could not correct it quickly enough. Earlier in the journey, after the procession had forded the river, Vardaman had told Dewey Dell that his mother had escaped into the water through the holes he had bored in the top of the coffin (*AILD* 187), and now as Addie rested under Gillespie's apple tree, Vardaman thought she could see him sitting beside her in the moonlight. Then another thought struck him: how could she look at him through the wooden sides: "How can she see through the wood, Darl?" he wished to know, the Third Mode giving away to the second. His mother "cant see out there," Vardaman reasoned, "because the holes are in the top" (*AILD* 205). Then the second level gave away to the first. She could not have seen him, he knew now, no matter where the holes had been bored. She could not have seen him whether they had been plugged or not. She could not have seen anyone. She was no longer a fish: she was in that box where Cash had nailed her: "I can smell her," Vardaman told Dewey Dell. "Can you smell her, too?" (*AILD* 206).

The reason that he wrote, Faulkner once said, "the reason for it all" was to say "No to death,"[14] and nowhere in his works does he say "no" more clearly than through three of Addie's sons. The communicative bond between them and their mother—this militant fidelity toward the one gone—did not last forever, but the fact that it took place at all is remarkable as well as inspiring. If the bond can manifest itself in the by-blow of an adulterous love affair, in a man who spent his life teetering on the edge of insanity and finally going over, and in a child it can manifest itself in any one of us.

Notes

[1] Melvin Backman, *Faulkner. The Major Years. A Critical Study* (Bloomington: Indiana UP, 1966), 56; James M. Mellard, "Faulkner's Philosophical Novel: Ontological Themes in *As I Lay Dying*, *The Personalist*, 48 (Autumn 1967), 511; Kenneth E. Richardson, *Force and Faith in the Novels of William Faulkner* (The Hague: Mouton, 1967), 75,76.

[2] Peter Swiggart, *The Art of Faulkner's Novels* (Austin: U of Texas P, 1962), 116.

[3] Cleanth Brooks, *William Faulkner. The Yoknapatawpha Country* (New Haven: Yale UP, 1963), 155.

[4] Swiggart, *op. cit.*, 112.

[5] Brooks, *op. cit.*, 398. Swiggart, *op. cit.*, 114.

[6] Mellard, *op. cit.*, 512. Elizabeth M. Kerr, "*As I Lay Dying* as Ironic Quest," *William Faulkner, Four Decades of Criticism*, ed. by Linda Welshemer Wagner (East Lansing: Michigan State UP, 1973), 234.

[7] Gordon Price-Stephens, "The British Reception of William Faulkner—1929-1962. *The Mississippi Quarterly*, XVIII (Summer 1965), 155.

[8] William Van O'Connor, *The Tangled Fire of William Faulkner* (Minneapolis: U of Minnesota P, 1954), 50.

[9] Mary Jane Dickerson, "Some Sources of Myth in Faulkner's *As I Lay Dying*," *The Mississippi Quarterly*, XIX (Summer 1956), 138; Hyatt H. Waggoner, *William Faulkner: From Jefferson to the World* (Lexington: U of Kentucky P, 1959), 66; Richard P. Adams, *Faulkner: Myth and Motion* (Prin-

ceton: Princeton UP, 1968), 82.

[10] Olga W. Vickery, *The Novels of William Faulkner: A Critical Interpretation* (Baton Rouge: Louisiana State UP, 1961), 50,51.

[11] Robert M. Slabey, "*As I Lay Dying* as an Existential Novel," *Bucknell Review*, XI (December 1963), 16,15.

[12] Frederick J. Hoffman, *William Faulkner* (New Haven: College and University P, 1961), 61-62.

[13] James D. Hutchinson, "Time: The Fourth Dimension in Faulkner," *South Dakota Review*, VI (Autumn 1968), 95.

[14] Joseph Blotner, *Faulkner: A Biography*, (New York: Random House,

Chapter XI

GENERALISSIMO

How will you set about looking for that thing, the nature of which is totally unknown to you? Which, among the things you do not know, is the one which you propose to look for? And if by chance you should stumble upon it, how will you know that it is indeed that thing, since you are in ignorance of it?
—*Maurice Merleau-Ponty,* Phenomenology of Perception

I

Communication as the Third Mode of the Encompassing is inexhaustible: Addie Bundren reaching out from the far side of life to her family and Lena Grove greeting and being greeted by her son making his entrance into life. If we make allowance for the seemingly insurmountable differences between male and female, his continual attempt to force upon her his own flawed rhythms, especially the rhythms of sexual love, Byron Bunch shows us that a man can make a worthwhile effort to communicate with a woman. Communication between human beings on earth can hardly go further. We have left to consider, then, the most difficult of all communication problems, communication with the Eternal. The final test of the Encompassing, "the *act of faith*" (CF 148), like every other consciousness, "entails intentionality" (CF 144). The problem God and man must solve has been our problem from the beginning, that of consciousness but, in this instance, consciousness "given in the purest form in its *intention*" (CF 146). This is the act that "cannot be transcended," in which the modes of the Encompassing take on new meaning, illuminating for us not merely the presence of those who have died or are about to be born but Ultimate Presence (CF 148).

Presence necessarily implies an "appeal," as in Addie's voice from the coffin and in Lena's unborn son's signals from the womb. God's presence is also an appeal, but it offers no such perceptual certainties as a corpse or a fetus. Who is appealing when He appeals? To whom do we appeal when we appeal to Him? Is there "any justification" for believing that He understands the appeal and will act on it? What form will the action take (*CF* 145)? These questions that through the ages have baffled reflective men were answered with surprising ease in Yoknapatawpha. For some, God was present as an essence, the sort of "vaporized object" (*MB I* 255) which Pantheists discover in vegetation (*PF&R* 151) and which Ike McCaslin felt as he stood beside Sam's grave. Ike was one of the few white men in the county who did sense it. Rejecting any such abstraction as the Life Force, nearly everyone else demanded a Presence that could be heard, seen, felt, even though absent. For them, there had to be a "rudimentary . . . image," "a mere shadow" (*HV* 150), a "radical absence" to which they could relate (*B&N* 423), and this absent shadow, in many shapes, sizes, and forms, was God's Presence in Yoknapatawpha.

The Shadow had for Darl Bundren a down-home look, and he listened as Addie talked in plain language to Him (*AILD* 204). To Mink Snopes He was the God of Revenge—"*Old Moster jest punishes*" (*M* 398)—and to others precisely the opposite, a Gentleman. When Eula Snopes killed herself, Gavin Stevens took charge of the funeral arrangements and was prepared to preach the sermon. God would not mind this officiousness, Stevens assured himself, since he and the Lord were both privileged (*T* 342-43), and he believed that a daughter of someone as prominent as Judge Drake was entitled to the same privileges as he. In an effort to "protect" (*RFN* 163) her "first" child from her lurid "past" (*RFN* 162), according to Stevens, Temple "had struck, not a bargain, but an armistice with God," and as "at least a gentleman," God would "play fair" with her (*RFN* 163-64). Ratliff said that Stevens saw "God" as "anyhow a gentleman" who "wouldn't bollix up the same feller twice" (*M*

131). Horace Benbow was another Third who imagined God to be the best good-natured Man in the world. When Ruby Lamar expressed fear that Lee Goodwin might be executed or go to jail for a long time and thus she might not be able to pay the lawyer his fee (*S* 336), Benbow reassured her: "God is foolish at times, but at least He's a gentleman," implying that with two gentlemen on Goodwin's side the accused would go free (*S* 337). Quentin Compson also looked upon God as "a gentleman and a sport" (*S&F* 112), as did Bayard Sartoris, who said that in a poker game He "might have held His own with one" of the McCaslin twins, "but that with both of them" playing "He would have lost His shirt" (*U* 54). Charles Bon was another who imagined God as a sport who could lose His shirt, or at least remove it. When Henry Sutpen referred to one of Bon's friends as "a whore," Charles preached a little sermon. God was "young once" and doubtless would have tolerated and condoned houses of prostitution, but "now that He is old" (*AA* 115), He "is not interested." In any event, Bon told Henry, He would have to accept the responsibility for prostitutes, for although He did not make them, He did not prevent their being made, having fructified "the seed" from which they grew (*AA* 116).

Others in the county also wondered if their predicament was not as much God's fault as theirs. God seemed to be a gentleman in name only. Quentin Compson doubted that He would have been accepted by the elite of Boston (*S&F* 137-38), and this is the Shadow of whom Quentin's grandfather complained, questioning His Right to cause what no gentleman should cause, the suffering of others. The general was particularly incensed that God made no allowances for children. "If He meant that little children should need to *be* suffered to approach Him, what sort of earth had He created; . . . if they had to *suffer* in order to approach Him, what sort of Heaven did He have" (*AA* 198)? Temple also criticized this God. She was wary of trusting someone who had already treated her shabbily, and she asked why she had "to suffer everybody else's anguish just to believe in God. What kind of God is it that has to blackmail His customers with the whole world's grief and ruin?" (*RFN* 277). Whatever the Shadow was, according to General Compson and Temple, He was no Gentleman, and yet the general, as a prominent lawyer, and Temple, as the daughter of a judge, were both closely associated with the form God often took. When Temple had tried to pray at the Old Frenchman Place, "she could not think of a single designation for the heavenly father," and all that came to her was, "My father's a judge" (*S* 60).

In the stratified and fixed world of Yoknapatawpha, religion was not so much a question of being saved as of being judged, or, rather, the problem of being saved resolved itself in the act of being judged (*B* 56,57). Believers were looking for someone who could guarantee them their place in the community. They needed assurance that they belonged: they needed a savior, it is true, but they desperately needed a judge to put them in their place. They needed a Judge-Being (*B* 58-60) whom they "could deliberately place beyond the fundamental law of contingency, . . . who existed simply because . . . [He] had a right to exist and whose decrees conferred" upon them stability (*B* 56). They could not depend on mercurial Sartorises or the latter-day Compsons or upon any other Third, so they imagined One. This was "God as a judge" (*M&C* 75), a *Third* of Thirds, "omniscient, . . . omnipotent" (*PF&R* 152), from whose "judgment" "there could be no appeal" (*B* 57). He was the personified "Absolute, the ultimate I-Am" (*AF* 57), "the God of justice" (*SS* 153). He was a Being that *Looked* at them, put them in their place, One that could "never be looked-at" (*B&N* 423). Both "transparent . . . and mysterious" (*TR* 151), He was sacred, powerful, Yahweh, a hanging Judge before whom man was "just one more pinch of rotten and ephemeral dust" (*AF* 362), and unlike the Gentleman whom Bon imagined, He did not tolerate loose women. Jack Houston "lived . . . for seven years" (*H* 243) with a former prostitute who had treated him so well that he felt an obligation to marry her. Tired of her, he needed an excuse to leave, so he called upon the infallible old Judge. A marriage without children, Houston felt, would be no marriage at all. "The Babylonian interdict by heaven" made sterile those who sold their bodies, and Houston wondered how long his mistress would have to do penance before the "merchandised" organs would heal and the sentence be lifted. Going to the Judge, he learned that the time would never come, he accepted the verdict, and he left her (*H* 244).

The Old Judge was hard, proud, and demanding, but He had a soft spot. He was susceptible to flattery. Anse Bundren got to Him by humbly confessing that "the Lord giveth" and implying, as Addie lay on her death bed, that He could also take away (*AILD* 29). One of Anse's neighbors pleased the Old Man when he placed his crop in His hands, "*Ay. The Lord made it to grow. It's Hisn to wash up if He sees it fitten so*" (*AILD* 85). Others also knew how to work Him. When the "rich"lady (*AILD* 7) changed her mind and refused to take Cora Tull's cakes, the act was "His will," "His decree." Cora looked at the stiff-necked Addie Bundren, "the eternal and the everlasting salvation and grace . . . not upon her" (*AILD* 8), and afterward thought happily of herself, "bounding toward my God and my reward" (*AILD* 87). Those who knew God best and knew best how to handle Him were His earthly vicars. It was upon them, not upon church members that the burden of imagining God rested (*M&C* 101). In Yoknapatawpha the one with the biggest imagination was Whitfield. Before the courthouse was built in Jefferson or the town itself laid out or a church erected in it, a Whitfield was holding services in his "cabin" (*RFN* 28). One of the descendants, "a farmer, . . . stupid, honest, superstitious and upright" (*H* 231), was pastor of the Methodist church at Frenchman's Bend (*T* 343). He once gave cogent advice on how to break up the affair between Ike Snopes and the cow. The preacher had known of a similar case in which "the critter" had been killed and cooked and a piece eaten by "the fellow" who had "formed the habit." After that, Whitfield said, the fellow chased only "human women," but what he did not say was that the fellow might have been the Reverend Whitfield himself (*H* 231).

The opposite of his kinsman, Whitfield was smart and wore a smart-looking outfit with "his boiled shirt and his black hat and pants and necktie." He had a "gold" watch (*CS* 27). The "nightshirt" he used for baptism was made of "cloth" such as the "Archangel Michael" might have worn (*CS* 40), and after services he mounted his horse, "stiff," powerful (*CS* 29). He was stiff and powerful in more ways than one, as his nightshirt was a nightshirt in more ways than one. A ranting preacher with a "voice . . . bigger" than he was (*AILD* 86), he could do with God pretty much as he pleased, just as he did with Addie Bundren as he pleased. When he heard that "she was dying," he "confessed" his sin "to God" and was told to confess to Anse. It was "for that deceived husband, to forgive you: not I," God said (*AILD* 169). On the way to Addie's, Whitfield found the bridge under water, and again he petitioned Him, "just let me not perish before I have begged the forgiveness of the man whom I betrayed," and after he was safely across, he knew that he had been forgiven (*AILD* 170). He was further encouraged when at the Tulls' he heard that Addie was dead. "He is merciful," Whitfield believed; "He will accept the will for the deed. Who knew that when I framed the words of my confession it was to Anse I spoke them, even though he was not there" (*AILD* 171). Here lies the wonderful appeal of Whitfield's God. He knows what is best for us as we know what is best for ourselves. In His "bounteous and omnipotent love" (*AILD* 171), Whitfield found what every other believer in the county found, exactly what he intended. That is all he could find (*PF&R* 141,147,219).

The existence of the God of Yoknapatawpha, like the existence of the Loch Ness monster, implies the existence of that which is "unrealizable" (*B&N* 423). Those who believe in Him attempt to perceive a Subject that can never become an Object (*B&N* 281), a Subject that by its very "nature" can be grasped only in absence (*B&N* 423). Phenomenally, this absence can be nothing except what it is intended to be, an omnipotent, omniscient Presence, and believers invariably find that their needs and His sympathy are one (*PF&R* 324). Whether they are lost or saved depends on them: Miss Burden pleaded with the Judge to damn her "a little longer" (*LIA* 231) and received affirmation; Cora Tull felt sure of her ticket to Glory (*AILD* 70). The Reverend Tobe Sutterfield had no doubts that his purposes and God's coincided when he imagined that God approved of gambling. "We had to do a little of it, win a little money to live on," Tobe explained—a little grain for the horse and fatback "for us." God knew about it, and "that was all right with Him" (*AF* 198). The reason God did not send Tobe to the battlefront, away from the mansion where he lived in high style, was that His servant lacked courage. Tobe would have gone, if He had wished to send him, for then, Tobe believed, "it wouldn't matter to Him or me neither whether I was brave" (*AF* 202,203). Many others saw their purpose as God's. Bayard Sartoris had "outlived" his "time," the first of his clan to reach "sixty," and the purpose behind all of it, he believed, was the Lord's preserving one Sartoris as "a reliable witness to the extinction" of the clan (*Sart* 104). The "hand of God" could be seen in the trick Colonel Devries' nephews used to defeat Clarence Snopes (*M* 315), and it was visible in Monk Odlethrop's murder of the prison warden. Terrel explained to Monk that he and all the other convicts were "pore ignorant country folks" with "no chance" in the world, "that God had made [them] to live outdoors in the free world and farm His land for Him" (*KG* 57). That was "what God aimed for us to do," and killing the warden would release them from their confinement and coincide with His aims (*KG* 58).

Like Terrel and Monk, Doc Hines also felt the coalescing of God's purposes and his. To Doc and to God, as proved by Eve, all women were filth. The filthiest of all were white women who gave themselves to Negroes (*LIA* 111, 325). White prostitutes could not bear children (*H* 244), adultresses committed suicide (*T* 366), but Doc's own daughter had given birth to "a walking pollution in God's own face" (*LIA* 111-12).When Christmas was born, Doc heard God speak: "You wait and you watch [him], because I aint got the time. . . . I have set you there to watch and guard My will. It will be yours to tend to it and oversee" (*LIA* 325). What Doc tended to was God's purposes and his own at work in and through Christmas. The bastard had been placed on earth as "a sign and a damnation for bitchery" (*LIA* 111) and as a trap set to catch bitches (*LIA* 337). Over the years, Doc had lost sight of his grandson at work but not of God. Doc had kept in touch, inquiring after Christmas, God always answering that the bastard was "still walking My earth" (*LIA* 338), until in a frenzy of impatience, Doc did not ask but called His attention to him, "God's abomination of womanflesh," "the walking shape of bitchery and abomination . . . stinking in God's sight" (*LIA* 327). "That bastard, Lord! I feel! I feel the teeth and the fangs of evil!" Impressed with this eloquent plea, God himself admitted that the time had come to remove the "pollution and . . . abomination on My earth" (*LIA* 338), and when Doc saw Christmas and the mob, he knew that God's will and his had crested. No longer petitioning, he with God's blessing would execute, "Kill the bastard! . . . Kill him. Kill him" (*LIA* 302).

The victim also found his needs and God's to be one. At cross purposes with himself, Christmas was at cross purposes with God, and after the murder of Miss Burden, he used Him and His house in working out this conflict. There he would prove he was harder than God as he had proved he was harder than McEachern. Bursting into the Negro church, Christmas seized the preacher "by the throat" and slapped him (*LIA* 282), and when members of the congregation interfered, Christmas struck one of them and stepped "into the pulpit." He stood "muddy" and unshaven, disheveled exactly in the way God deplored. Looking down, He saw not His vicar in Sunday best but a "nigger" yelling and cursing Him in a voice rising "louder than" the screeches of "the women" (*LIA* 283). Then he stopped yelling, walked down the aisle, and laughed. God was hard, all right, but Christmas was harder, twice as hard, as hard as the Devil.

Like the Negro woman who recognized him, screaming as Christmas raged, "It's the devil!" (*LIA* 282), believers in the county, themselves in continuous conflict with others, attributed to God the same combative nature. These Manicheans could not imagine a God without an antagonist (*MB II* 162, *PF&R* 149,218,219). Miss Rosa Coldfield would have us believe that this adversary bore a closer resemblance to Colonel Sutpen than he did to Christmas, "faint . . . reek" of hell's "sulphur . . . still in hair, clothes and beard" of the "demon" (*AA* 8), "fiend," "devil" (*AA* 15). McEachern discovered the demon's face in Christmas' backside (*LIA* 130-31). Jason Compson, according to Stevens, found his "master" in "the Devil" (*M* 326). Women were especially devoted to him, since they were by nature evil (*S&F* 119). Temple discovered in the Memphis whorehouse what she had brought with her, "simple evil" (*RFN* 128). But the Devil in the imagination of Yoknapatawpha assumed more disguises than those of colonels, backsides, and women. He had as wide a repertoire as his Adversary; his best disguise was his Adversary (*PF&R* 224, *SG* 184-85). According to Mrs. Hines, the Devil and not God controlled her husband (*LIA* 326,327), and Miss Rosa was uncertain whether "God or the devil" had prompted Sutpen in the wrestling matches with his slaves, whether one of them were not taking "advantage" of the colonel's "vices in order to" curse the county (*AA* 28). This question was enough to move Flem Snopes. In a vision V. K. Ratliff had seen the biggest wolf have a go at the demon on his home grounds, the fiery pit from which Miss Burden had tried through the magic of prayer to deliver the reluctant Christmas (*LIA* 245). Flem found Hell as easy to invade as he had found Frenchman's Bend. In the chief role as Prince of Hell, the Devil had recognized the high caliber of Snopes (*H* 171) and had offered him all "*the gratifications*" and "*vanities*" (*H* 173). Flem was about as impressed with the Prince as he was with Jody

Varner. To "*the sound of frying . . . Christians,*" Satan then ran down a list of delicious "*satieties*" (*H* 174), but Flem kept on chewing, until in exasperation the Prince asked just what in hell Flem was after. Was it "*Paradise?*" Is that what "*you want?*" And Flem at last broke silence. "*I hadn't figured on it,*" he said; then, never one to miss an opportunity, he asked, "*Is it yours to offer?*" (*H* 175).

This question plagued the county (*PF&R* 204-20). In fact, Satan with all that persuasiveness and charm, all those gratifications and satieties, offered more by way of paradise than the testy old Judge with all those rules and regulations. "Evil is a part of man," explained the Reverend Sutterfield, "evil and sin and cowardice, the same as repentance and being brave" (*AF* 203), and believers in the county tended to lean a little more to the former than to the latter, except one. Ike McCaslin was as far removed from the Devil as he was close to God, and for a very good reason. God's ethic, Ike believed, was the land ethic, His one commandment, "Thou shalt love the land." Although Ike attributed several roles to Him, the Life Force, Adviser, and Humanitarian, Ike believed that He had a special interest in the South, the last stronghold of agrarianism, and that Ike was His chosen spokesman (*GDM* 282,285). He owned the earth with "man . . . His overseer" (*GDM* 257), Ike imagined. You will hold My earth, He told man, "mutual and intact in the communal anonymity of brotherhood" in MY name, and when man had other ideas, God disappeared, only to relent and return (*GDM* 257-59). He would give man another chance, Ike said, open to him a land undefiled, the pristine South with the Big Woods, abundant game, rich soil, perfect weather (*GDM* 283). But again it was the same story. God had created this New Eden, and man debased it, dared own another human being. He had usurped God's own prerogative (*GDM* 261). This was reason enough for God to destroy the whole race, Ike believed, but since man was His own creation, He would give him the privilege of destroying himself (*GDM* 282,285). Human beings, He had come to realize, understood "*nothing save when underlined in blood,*" the

War began, and once more God walked away in disillusionment (*GDM* 286).

Ike's God was as much his imagination as Stevens' God was Stevens' and Whitfield's, Whitfield's. Like Ike, He refused to accept the responsibility that was His, turning His back on man as Ike had turned his on the inheritance. Both Ike and God believed that because man and the world he lived in were not perfect, they were therefore worthless. Not everyone in the county, however, was content with this God, malleable though He be. A few Christians there would breathe human life into this imaginary Deity, accepting as true that He was once "God-Man" appearing on earth, that men had seen, heard, touched Him, but even though this story guarantees the "perceptible historical reality" (*PF&R* 337) of memory and recorded history, it was not without problems (*M&C* 21,31). God as man appeared as two Gods. One of them was preached by a chaplain to prisoners of war, the Christ who urged all, chaplain as well as soldiers, to be "brothers in arms." He moved his followers onward, crying out, "Do not despair" (*TS* 255)! A runaway slave found Him as she called out to Granny Millard, "Hit's Jordan we coming to. . . . Jesus gonter see me that far" (*U* 96). This was Jesus Christ militant, a born soldier. The Christ child, for Judge Allison, was this infant with scars on his feet and in his palms, surrounded with lead "effigies of . . . Roman soldiers in various stages of dismemberment" (*CS* 792). As the judge looked on, the infant "swept" the soldiers "flat" (*CS* 793). He would grow up "in thunder and lightning" (*AF* 81), roaming the battle fields and ordering the wounded "to rise up and live" (*U* 154). Grown, he looked much as Sutpen looked to Wash Jones: "*If God Himself was to come down and ride the natural earth, that's what he would aim to look like* (*AA* 282). He gave J. C. Goodyhay his orders. As a sergeant in the Marines in the Pacific (*M* 267), Goodyhay had gone to the rescue of another Marine fallen overboard during a landing operation (*M* 268), and both he and the man were drowning, when Jesus appeared, "looking like any other shavetail, . . . maybe a little older, . . . smoking a cigarette. 'Fall in, soldier,' He said" (*M* 280). After some effort and without assistance from Christ, Goodyhay came to attention. "About-*face!*" Christ ordered. "Forward *march!*" As Goodyhay moved off, the lieutenant pointed to the other Marine, and after trying "three times" to pick him up, Goodyhay succeeded, following Christ to the surface (*M* 281).

Others worshipped a Christ altogether different from Goodyhay's, the one preached by Reverend Shegog. This is the Christ of tears and forgiveness and mercy. For remembrance of Him and the blood He shed for our sins, He brings "de comfort en de unburdenin" (*S&F* 364). This is Jesus of Calvary, of the tree and the "thief en de murderer" (*S&F* 370), he who said to the thief, "Today shalt thou be with me in Paradise" (*Po* 172). He was crucified that others shall live. He died that others shall not die. He was the martyr of the lamb-like innocence (*PF&R* 338), the Christ child whose mother had suffered the birth pangs and who held him while the angels sang "him to sleep." One day while sitting in the doorway with Jesus in her lap, Shegog said, she saw the Roman soldiers passing. The look on their faces frightened her. We are going "to kill you little Jesus," they warned, and believers heard the weeping and the "lamentation." This is the Christ of women waiting outside the tomb where his body lay, and as Shegog told his story, they moaned, "Yes, Jesus!" "Yes, Jesus! Jesus!" (*S&F* 396) "Jesus! Little Jesus!" (*S&F* 370).

Doubtless, the most striking characteristic of the God and of the Christ of Yoknapatawpha is their close resemblance to deities of Christian orthodoxy (*PF&R* 15-143 *passim*, CF 184-93 *passim*). In the county we find not only "the 'sentimental, Protestant ethos'" of the South but in capsule "the orthodox Christian tradition" as it is revealed everywhere.[1] Anywhere and anytime there are God and Christ figures; we take for granted their kinship to those of Yoknapatawpha. This is what happened when the Generalissimo and the Corporal appeared in France during World War I. Like the God of Yoknapatawpha, the Generalissimo has been confused with his Adversary. Some have called him "the quintessence of secular wisdom and power,"[2] one "who functions as both Pontius Pilate and Tempter, and is functionally the supreme representative of Caesarism."[3] Another sees him as the God of Yoknapatawpha was seen, as a hybrid, "part God, part Pontius Pilate, part Caesar, and part Satan."[4] For still another, he is the *Third* of Thirds, representing "the voice of authority and power, . . . a symbol of authority, . . . and the defender of the *status quo*."[5] He is, others say, "a God-judge figure,"[6] and "we cannot understand him any more than we can understand God."[7]

We do not understand the corporal very well either. One critic sees *A Fable* as "a Christian allegory";[8] another critic disagrees. He is incensed at Faulkner's distortion "of the Christian story": Jesus was "celibate," turned "water into wine . . . at the wedding feast,"[9] and was buried quietly and with great dignity;[10] conversely, the corporal married a prostitute, arranged "a wedding for a girl whose doughboy has 'knocked her up,'"[11] and was carted unceremoniously to his grave.[12] There are other discrepancies. Christ himself restored the eyesight of "a blind person," while the corporal arranged "a surgical operation"; "the story of the Annunciation and the Virgin Birth is one of . . . poetic grace," while "in *A Fable*, the same story becomes one of . . . casual seduction."[13] These discrepancies are not surprising, for *A Fable* does not attempt to give us the Gods of orthodoxy (*MB 1* 258) but attempts to reveal one "powerful" enough to "usurp the legend" of those Gods.[14] It teaches us, as Albert Einstein, the existential-phenomenologist *par excellence*, has suggested, that we can "radically change" our "attitudes," move toward a "new way of thinking" (*FM* 201), toward "humanity in the encompassing framework of its potentialities," toward the reality that "man is what God created in His image" (*E&H* 73), not the other way around (*PF&R* 152). Most of all, it teaches us that "faith can take new forms" (*PF&R* 296), that there are holy men outside the Bible, that holy words can come from "mouths" other than those of "the primitive Christians" (*M&C* 100-101). Although the message does not minimize the power of jealousy and wrath and martyrdom and all the other magic, we learn that they are not all-powerful, that we no longer have to depend upon the least reliable and trickiest of all consciousnesses, the imagination, for the answer to the most important of all questions. The place to begin our search for the answer is not with the imaginary "God" of Yoknapatawpha, who "is dead" (*MMS* 13) precisely to the extent that the imaginary consciousness is dead, but with the least imaginary of beings, the philosopher.

II

Existential-phenomenology is the philosophy of "participation" (*CF* 56, *MB I* 137). The existentialist "philosopher" is an activist (*PF&R* 253,254); being-in-the-world means for him involvement in the world (*R&E* 135). He does not walk away from men at war, as Ike had imagined, or from men at anything else. Neither does he withdraw into himself as do the Stoics, hold out for the unattainable as do the idealists, bog down in endless detail as do the empiricists (*WW* 26,132-44 *passim*). He does not deny the efficacy of these philosophies any more than he denies the power of the emotions, but he denies that any one philosophy or any combination of philosophies is finalist (*WW* 110-19 *passim*). He wishes to let be "that which is" (*B&T* 22fn), his participation "negative insofar as it generates no new contents, but positive insofar as it establishes space for every possible content" (*R&E* 134). This openness, for the existential philosopher, is the existential-phenomenological *a priori*, the situation that cannot be contingent (*MB I* 137). Presiding at the trial of General Gragnon, the Generalissimo makes clear the *a priori*. Division commander of the regiment in which the mutiny began, Gragnon had been brought up in the strict confines of Catholicism and in joining the Army found himself at home, exchanging church bars for Army (*AF* 21). His Bible was the *Manual of War* (*AF* 250), and after the mutiny, Bible in hand, he argued before Corps that the regiment should be shot (*AF* 28). Corps rejected the argument, drifting into a hazy lecture on the rank and file, low-bred and ordinary, and how it had always acted in a cowardly fashion and always would (*AF* 30). Gragnon received permission to take his request to group (*AF* 34); the result of the appeal was more lectures on the failings of man in general and of soldiers in particular and permission to appear before the Supreme Council of the allied armies (*AF* 53,54).

Corps and group commanders had sat before a division commander, all of them abstractions speaking of abstractions, "merely mental operations that subserve certain determinate purposes" (*MB I* 164), regiments, companies, squads; and now Gragnon stood before a man, whose first move was to recover for him this impersonal mass of humanity as human beings. In a "pleasant," "almost warm" voice the General began, "The whole regiment. . . . Not just this ringleader and his twelve disciples." He himself would be willing, the General said in an effort to bring Gragnon into the world of flesh and blood, he himself believed that at least "nine of them"—the French soldiers—should be shot. They were "Frenchmen" and "still permitted themselves to be corrupted" (*AF* 233). Immediately, Gragnon suspected a trap. A ringleader was an individual, a man, and to admit that men were involved would be to admit that men would be killed, at his command. "'There was no ring leader,' the division commander said, harsh and rigid. 'The regiment mutinied'" (*AF* 233). The General was not discouraged. If he could not persuade his general to talk about men, perhaps he could convince him that he was not talking very well about the regiment. "Suppose we do" shoot it, the General asked, "What of the other regiments in your division?"

"'Shoot them,' the division commander said.

'And the other divisions in your corps, and the other corps on either side of you.'

'Shoot them,' the division commander said" (*AF* 234).

The trap this time, the either/or fallacy extended to absurdity, was easily set and as such would hardly have been worth the General's effort. It was not his wish to defeat Gragnon but to show him that he had defeated himself, that the regulations he lived by would not "swim or even float" (*AA* 275). But more: Gragnon caught a glimmer of why. Like Sutpen, another who placed more faith in logic than in life, a poor white as a make-believe planter, Gragnon the man of bad faith was a foot soldier masquerading as an officer. As the General turned from him, eyes averted as if he could no longer bear looking at the ersatz human being, and thanked the chief-of-staff for arranging the trial, Gragnon, who until this sound had remained "inflexible and composed," the automatic general with the automatic answers, came alive. Unmasking, he became the soldier he was, one of his own men. They had refused to obey the orders of their superior officers; he refused to recognize his superior officer. Without saluting he swung abruptly from the General, rushed toward the door, and disappeared through it, three stars joining the ranks (*AF* 234).

It was difficult for the General to reach Gragnon, the objectivist that lived outside himself; it was more difficult to reach his own son, the solipsist who could not get outside himself at all (*MB I* 135). Here is an "ego-centric" (*MB II* 8) who like the Communist Brunet was mired in the "sticky sap" of "*subjectivity*" (*TS* 251) and who seems to bear a closer resemblance to Charles Bon than he does to the Christ of the critics. Without elaborating the parallel, we know that both spent years attempting to avenge their dishonored mothers as well as trying to force their fathers to acknowledge them (*AA* 105,106,118, *AF* 298), that both masochistically battened on the knowledge that there was no escape either for themselves or for their fathers. In defiance Bon vindictively chose as his bride Sutpen's daughter and his own half sister (*AA* 118-19,353,354), and the corporal vengefully chose "a Marseille whore to mother the grandchildren of . . . [his father's] high and exalted blood" (*AF* 300). To the corporal, whose hatred was more virulent than Bon's, such private vengeance was not enough: he would not rest until the Generalissimo, like his mother, had been publicly shamed. After waiting some thirty years, the corporal had, during the third year of the war, finally caught his father in a vulnerable position. The morale of the German and the Allied Armies was at the time low (*AF* 69,70), and exerting only a little persuasion, he prevailed upon Gragnon's regiment of hard-pressed and obviously poorly trained front line troops to lay down arms (*AF* 25). This action, he correctly assumed, would bring him to the attention of the Commander-in-chief; but, more importantly, if the mutiny spread throughout the army, it would destroy the Commander's very *raison d'etre*.

The corporal failed in carrying out his plan. His father recognized him, but not publicly (*AF* 341); as for the mutiny, it was over almost as soon as it had begun (*AF* 346). That the corporal was not so successful as Bon was due to a father who, unlike the colonel, reasoned with his son instead of reacting to him; where Sutpen rejected Bon, refusing to discuss their conflict (*AA* 353-56), the General sitting beside his son on a hillside overlooking Paris put their conflict into perspective (*AF* 342). Objectively but compassionately, he pointed out that it was the age-old conflict between philosophical realism and subjective idealism. This idealism, the General indicated, is synonymous with emotionalism, which clearly had its uses. Appealing to the emotions of the run-down troops, specifically to their self-pity, the corporal had with little effort persuaded "three thousand" (*AF* 346) of them to accept the magical world he had set before them, had convinced them that they were too weak to fight (*AF* 343), and if he could persuade soldiers, whatever their morals, he could in no time persuade the canaille, extending his power over "half" "the earth" and, if he chose, in a year or two conquer the other half (*AF* 345). On the other hand, the Generalissimo continued, the conquest might be of short duration, and the reason for this possibility lay in the nature of the emotions.

The emotions are unstable. Emotional men existing on the first level of the Encompassing are always in one mood or another; they escape one mood only to become entangled in another (*B&T* 172-79). The soldiers in the corporal's regiment were no exception. Under arrest and looking for someone other than themselves to blame for their predicament, they found him, their pity for self turning into hatred for the corporal. Look at your followers now, the General suggested. Their cheers for you have turned into loud cries for your death (*AF* 343,346), and if this turnabout does not convince you of the "baleful effect" (*MB I* 46) of the emotions, look at your twelve disciples. Two of them have already deserted you (*AF* 346). The General had listened while Gragnon insisted that the ringleader of the mutiny never existed, implying that he was an illusion (*AF* 233). Now the General listened to his son cling to the illusion that he was still the ringleader. There were "still ten" (*AF* 346), the corporal said, who remain loyal to me. For one less patient than the General, this would indicate that the time had come to dismiss the illusion. Instead, in an effort to reach his son, he tried a new tactic. Down the hole they both went into the magic world where the General would release the ten and watch them desert the corporal, as had the regiment (No: "In ten minutes there would not be ten but a hundred. In ten hours . . . not . . . ten hundred but ten thousand. And in ten days—"), the son would take his father's limousine and escape in it (No: "There are still ten") (*AF* 346-47), and, most illusionary, father and son would open up vistas which no Caesar of Sultan or Kahn ever saw, a world beyond the dreams of "Rome, Cathay and Xanadu" (*AF* 348). "You will be God," the General proclaimed. For the corporal who in this wonderland was already God, the promise was meaningless, except for one thing (*AF* 349). It showed that the old "gray man" (*AF* 124) was exactly where he wanted him, on his knees begging for a truce and calling him God, and in a moment of pure delusion, the delusion of self as well as delusion of the father, the son said, "So we ally—confederate. . . . Are you that afraid of me?" (*AF* 349)

The General answered. De-fusing the conflict, removing it from the narrow conflict of personalities like the low quarrel between Sutpen and his son, between Sutpen and Miss Rosa, General Compson and Colonel Sartoris, Mink and Houston, the latter-day Ike and Cass, the General said, "I . . . respect you; I dont need to fear you" (*AF* 349). Man is neither a fearful monster nor a fearful coward, the General went on. He is just foolish: this is what is wrong—and right—with him. There isn't anything he won't try (*AF* 352-54)—Ike Snopes to diddle a cow (*H*230), Flem to be a banker, Sutpen a planter, Quentin Compson his sister's lover, Lucas Beauchamp a white man, Ike McCaslin a red one, Gragnon a general, you a god. Nothing can stop man. He may finally evict himself from the earth, as Ike said that he would do and as the God of Yoknapatawpha hoped that he would do, but this would not mean his end: there are the other planets he will mess up, just as he messed up this one (*AF* 354). That's your "quality-mark" as man, this "deathless folly" (*AF* 352), the General said, that made him proud. "Because man and his folly—" (*AF* 354), and with this sound the pieces of the corporal's chaotic life fell into place. For the first time this bastard who had roamed the world, coming from nowhere and headed for oblivion, found himself a home. His foolishness was not his alone, a right reserved for himself but something he could share with all men: "'Because man and his folly—' 'will endure.' the corporal said" (*AF* 354). The General had seen Gragnon break out of the encrustations of Army Regulations into humanity, and now he listened as his solipsist son broke out of himself toward him, and yet, at least in the effort to reach his son, there was an added dimension. The bond between them transcending the military was the strongest between human beings, "the family bond" (*MB I* 242, *HV* 95,96, *MMA* 58-59).

Nowhere does this bond count for more than in a traditional society such as Yoknapatawpha, where family offers a protective shield against all outsiders as well as furnishing a guarantee for its own continued existence (*HV* 77). Even Mink Snopes (*M* 5) and Nub Gowrie (*IID* 200) were disturbed at the lowering of the shield. In a traditional society, a society dominated by Thirds, men and women are joined together by an "association of individual interests," property interests (*HV* 87). Their first duty, the duty of Bayard Sartoris, III, and Narcissa Benbow, for example, was to provide an heir that could consolidate these interests (*Sart* 75-77), all three, father-son-mother, "a mere link in an endless chain" called family (*HV* 95). Here the act of love runs a poor second to the act of "procreation" (*HV* 99). It was of little importance whether Sutpen and Rosa, General Compson and his wife, Colonel Sartoris and his cared for each other. The point was a son, but, more, a son willing to preside over still another consolidation, indeed, a son who would be willing . . . (*Sart* 87). In Yoknapatawpha, there were plenty who were willing, producing "generation after generation" (*Sart* 375) of the line called Sartoris or Compson or Edmonds.

Commanding fathers and obedient sons who, in turn, became commanding fathers were the framework in the Yoknapatawpha family structure (*HV* 125-27). Young Bayard Sartoris had taken his degree in law because "Father decided I should" (*U* 253); similarly, Gavin Stevens decided for his nephew. Stevens had been trained by his father from whom he had inherited the office of county attorney, and now came Chick running errands and emptying ash trays (*IID* 21). Training was not confined to Thirds. Some "fifteen miles" from Jefferson in the hill country (*KG* 200), Anse MacCallum had five well-trained sons (*CS* 54), who farmed cotton, raised cattle (*CS* 57), hunted (*KG* 200), made whiskey (*Sart* 313), and occasionally worked at horse trading (*KG* 201). Anse was undisputed, if benevolent, ruler of his household and presumably of the weather. When young Bayard Sartoris doubted Buddy's prophecy of mild weather, Buddy convinced him, "Pappy said so" (*Sart* 316). Res Grier felt the same way about his father. When Res wished to prove something to his son, he would begin, "Now, take your Grandpap" (*CS* 111). The first question entering the minds of Anse's sons (and doubtless Res Grier's too) was what their father would think, and even after Anse's death his authority, like that of Colonel Sartoris, persisted. In the 1930's when the question arose whether to comply with the AAA regulations, the boys talked it over and decided that "father would have said no" (*CS* 57). Buddy MacCallum received from his sons the same filial devotion he and his brothers had shown Anse. At the beginning of World War II, neither would report to his induction center until Buddy gave permission(*CS* 60).

In a traditional society, looks are important. Not only should families think alike, there should be a marked family resemblance (*MB: I* 246), and although the members of the MacCallum family were different in personality (*Sart* 315,316), all of them, like Snopeses, bore an "iron kinship" (*H* 165), the unmistakable physical stamp of the old man (*CS* 55), faces "aquiline and spare, reserved and grave" (*Sart* 334). Through their veins ran true-blue blood. Buddy's advice to the twins when they left for World War II was, "Obey them, but remember your name and don't take nothing from no man" (*CS* 53). Buddy's advice was echoed by the mother of Pete Grier who told him when he left "our blood is good as any blood anywhere, and don't you never forget it" (*CS* 87). Ab Snopes warned Sarty, "You got to learn to stick to your own blood or you ain't going to have any blood to stick to you"(*CS* 8). The uncles of Buck Thorpe sounded like Ab when they said that all they needed to take their nephew from Fentry, no matter who had raised him, was blood relationship. "He is our kin. We want him home" (*KG* 102). Kin in a traditional society means, then, to look alike, think alike, act alike. It is a relationship subject to proof, expressed in "judicial," "sociological," "biological terms" (*HV* 99), a mode of treating family members as if they were "puppets" (*HV* 72) whose sole purpose is to produce reasonable facsimiles of themselves (*MB I* 246). "Human life" in these facsimiles goes "on recurring like animal life, immutable for countless generations" (*FM* 267-68, *PF&R* 312-13), Sartorises and Snopeses alike, carbon copies; missing is a sense of the "actual and . . . vital" (*MB I* 246), which the General pressed upon his son. "Like everyone," the General loved "death as much as life, since both the one and the other are part of our lot"; yet, with him, "the style of death gives way to a style of life" (*Sit* 337). In eloquent tones he poured forth this existential-phenomenological affirmation: "Nothing—nothing—nothing . . . is as valuable as simple breathing, simply being alive" (*AF* 350). Charles Bon, Christmas, Dewey Dell's expected child, Lena's child, none of them had reason for shame, just because they were born out of wedlock. Life is "metasociological" (*MB I* 243). Take it, the father urged his son; "merely knowing that you are alive" (*AF* 350) is the only prerequisite for life—of no import are marriage vows, faces identical, blank, black, with delicately carved nostrils—and the corporal qualified, if for only a brief time. As he and the General came to the end of their talk and returned to the limousine, the General said, "Goodnight, my child," and the child answered, "Good-bye, Father," and for the first time was contradicted. The Father refused the finality: "'Not good-bye,' the old general said" (*AF* 356).

For the General it was never good-bye, to anyone. He was a friend for and of life, holding the same respect for all sons as he held for his own, greeting American, Englishman, Frenchman, German, the illustrious and the lowly, "my child" (*AF* 275), "Yes, my child" (*AF* 237), "Good morning, my child" (*AF* 207), "Thank you, my child" (*AF* 279), "Get in, my child" (*AF* 341), "Now, my child" (*AF* 342), remembering

> the name and face of every man in uniform whom he had ever seen—not only those out of the old regiment into which he had been commissioned from St. Cyr, and the ranking commanders of his armies and corps whom he saw daily, but their staffs and secretaries and clerks, and the commanders of divisions and brigades and their staffs, and regimental and battalion and company officers and their orderlies and batmen and runners, and the privates whom he had decorated or reprimanded or condemned, and the N.C.O. leaders and

degreeless file-closers of sections and platoons and squads whose inspection-opened ranks he had merely walked rapidly through once thirty and forty years ago. (*AF* 229-30)

It was as if he were spiritual father to the world (*MB I* 248), "calling . . . all 'my child,'" his son, his "personal aide," "his chauffeur," and "his ancient batman" (*AF* 230), the old soldier who had served him nearly all his military life and who walked in the famed funeral cortege (*AF* 244,245). Only one had known the General longer, the Norman who had stood number two in the General's class at St. Cyr (*AF* 246).

The relationship between these two was at a far remove from the sentimental attachment of a high ranking officer for his factotum or that of a philosopher-general dealing with a recalcitrant division commander or a philosopher-father and a stubborn son. The Norman served the General as a valet of sorts, as an efficient quartermaster general, as a putative son, but all this is of little moment in view of his major service, that of preaching the General to the world. The subject of the sermons had revealed that of all men he was the least self-centered and thus the most philosophical, but for the Norman this miracle was not enough. Even the General's imperfections were perfections in disguise.

Rapacity is that part of man which, on the lowest level of the Encompassing, leads him to use other men for his own ends. This is the rapacity of the Gragnons and Bidets, whose careers were nourished on the blood of their troops (*AF* 54). The more aggressive and ambitious Snopeses operated on this level. Their "natural heritage of cold rapacity" was that of generals, "as instinctive as breathing, . . . rapacity raised to the absolute *nth*" (*T* 35). It was the motor driving the Hares and Masons and Harpes, who took the "heritage of simple rapacity and bloodlust and converted it into a bloody dream of outlaw-empire" (*RFN* 226), and of the ambitious "carpetbagger" Redmond, driven by "a blind rapacity almost like a biological instinct" (*RFN* 238). For the General it was biological instinct, rapacity that uses another to create life, not exploit it. His lust for the corporal's mother was in one respect the lust of any male, Lafe for Dewey Dell, Lucas for Lena, but mere physical attraction, the corporal's half-sister said, was "nowhere near enough." The General's passion was "something much bigger, . . . much more splendid, much more terrible" (*AF* 287), something which had "a purpose, . . . aim, . . . purity" (*AF* 286) and which came clear years later in the person of the corporal. He furnished proof that a human being can remain open to another, even one obsessed with destroying him.

On a second level of the Encompassing, rapacity becomes a civilizing force (*AF* 259), energizing "giants," "milestones of the rise of man—the giants who coerced compelled directed and . . . led his myriad moil," the Caesars, Alexanders, Marlboroughs (*AF* 181), and in Yoknapatawpha those who turned a wilderness into Yoknapatawpha county. First there were the Indians who roamed the rich land but who did nothing with it, except grow a little corn, hunt, and fish, and then came giants, arrogant, clever, if not very intelligent, who took the land from the Indians and did do something with it. Cotton economy, that "edifice intricate and complex," was "erected by [their] ruthless rapacity and carried on" by their "savagery not only to the human beings but . . . animals too" (*GDM* 298). They tamed the land by brute force. The General did not share their weaknesses. More powerful than a hundred Caesars and a thousand Sartorises, he never savaged man, black or white, individually or collectively. His rapacity was the well-spring of life itself. It was rapacity in name only, the Norman said, the never-failing,

> else man must deny he breathes. Not [this] rapacity: its whole vast glorious history repudiates that. It does not, cannot, must not fail. . . . Not [this]rapacity, which, like poverty, takes care of its own. Because it endures, not even because it is rapacity but because man is man, enduring and immortal; enduring not because he is immortal but immortal because he endures: and so with rapacity, which immortal man never

> fails, since it is in and from rapacity that he gets, holds, his
> immortality—the vast, the all-being, the compassionate,
> which says to him only, Believe in Me; though ye doubt
> seventy times seven, ye need only believe again. (*AF* 259-61)

The immortality of rapacious man, at least on these levels of the
Encompassing, whatever his accomplishments, sounds suspi-
ciously like the immortality of foolish man: his "rapacity" (*AF*
260) and "his folly . . . will endure" (*AF* 354). The survival of
man-existing-as-man depends upon this foolish rapacity, but
the General believed that man would do more than survive. He
expressed this thought to his son. Coming to his senses the
corporal had, in his moment of lucidity, believed that "man and
his folly" would "endure." "'They will do more,' the old
General said proudly. 'They will prevail'" (*AF* 354).

To endure means to "survive," "last," "continue." To prevail means all this and more. It means "to surpass," "go beyond," "transcend." Like consciousness, it releases life from
stasis—the endurance of the "rock" (*AF* 239), "ground" (*AF*
199), a "monument" (*CS* 149)—for movement and, ultimately,
for a movement that surpasses itself. It is the Encompassing encompassing, as it were, being encompassed. Cass Edmonds was
hinting at this movement when he said that "you always wear
out life long before you have exhausted the possibilities of
living" (*GDM* 186), and Gavin Stevens, speaking better than he
knew, said that "life" is not only "inconclusive" but "inconclud-
able" (*T* 317); "it must be before itself, in advance of itself, to
have been at all" (*T* 318). It is, wrote Nietzsche, that which "hath
to be surpassed" (*Z* 53,63): it will, it has to prevail. On this earth
it prevails as existential-phenomenological myth.

On one level myth is "the objective aspect of the Encompassing . . . [assuming] the form of . . . tangible presence" (*M&C*
14). Most often it is a story, not unlike that of the General seen
through the eyes of his classmates. An orphan descended from
impeccable aristocratic parents, he was heir to incredible
wealth, and from the moment he entered St. Cyr there was no

doubt about his brains (*AF* 246). He graduated number one in his class, "with the highest marks ever made at the Academy," and was immediately offered a "captaincy" in the quartermaster corps (*AF* 249), which he refused in favor of "field service" in Africa (*AF* 250). According to his classmates his action was easy to understand. First, it was the typical "gesture" of someone "powerful and potent enough to afford even discretion and modesty" (*AF* 250), but of more significance, no quartermaster had ever become General of the Armies. Too, he had placed himself beyond the range of the incessant snipping of his fellow officers, envious and afraid of him (*AF* 251). In due time he would in one or two long strides make it from a junior officer stationed at the tiny desert outpost to marshal of the French Army (*AF* 244,249,250). The General's classmates have given us an extremely clever man of large ambitions, another Odysseus, and they were wrong. They were wrong, or, rather, they were right in the wrong way. The General was ambitious, clever, powerful, a man, as the Norman knew, who could easily have "insisted on becoming a marshal" in a few years, who could have used his personal "power and influence" to overcome "the power and influence" (*AF* 258) of "the long rigid mosaic of seniority" (*AF* 251), but he was also something else, something, the Norman believed, like a saint.

Existential-phenomenological myth at the religious level is man's way of being at once human and divine. Though often a story, myth is less concerned with empirical realities than with expressing transcendent insights, and yet, it does not stray so far into the transcendent that we lose sight of the empirical (*M&C* 14). It is history but sacred history. We are mistaken in thinking that this history is a "cloak" thrown "over a general idea" (*M&C* 15), the vehicle for "universal concepts," an excuse to establish universal religious laws. Saints as "mythical figures" are "unique. They cannot be interpreted rationally; they . . . interpret each other" (*M&C* 16). The Norman, as existential-phenomenological mythologizer, uses this interpretation in helping us understand the General. Some saints, he suggests, are little more than magicians entertaining spellbound audiences (*R&A* 71-74). The Tanzanian medicine man, the Hopi rain dancer, the Aztec high priest are, in one way or another, performers, the transcendent degraded to "superstition" and "sorcery" (*M&C* 19). They are "mythical forms [filled] with banal content" (*M&C* 16), and, according to the Norman, so was St. Simeon. In an effort to show that the General was not a saint of this low order, the Norman tells us that he had "sought a desert not as Simeon, . . . not merely to acquire a roosting-place for contempt and scorn but . . . as Anthony" (*AF* 259), who after fifteen years had come down from the mountain top with plans for a great monastery.[15] The General came out of the desert with even grander plans. He would provide, the Norman believed, a home for all men.

The Norman as mythologizer is not concerned with the *corpus sanctorium*, a fingernail clipping here, a thighbone from there, a lock of hair from some other place, fragments assembled as St. Simeon, St. Anthony, St. Andrew (*M&C* 13,17, *PF&R* 110,283,305,343). He comes "to grips with the living existential-phenomenological contents" (*M&C* 20), as he continues to reveal the General's living destiny, not the "destiny and end" (*AF* 261) others prophesied for him. The General's destiny would be a saint's but different from that of a mere saint, one who passes "out of enmity to amazement: to contempt: to unreality, and at last out of . . . race and kind altogether, into the dusty lumber room of literature" (*AF* 263). The General would establish no sect, leave behind no sacred "monuments" (*AF* 260). Almost before he was cold in his grave, he would be forgotten, but he would return in "a new time, a new age, a new century," the Norman prophesied, the Second Coming from "wherever it is you are going, in order to return from it when the time, the moment comes, in the shape of man's living hope" (*AF* 263).

Great myths as "existential-phenomenological truth" come to life only in a transformation such as this (*M&C* 20), and in order to understand it, we must turn for a moment to the existential-phenomenology of hope. More often than not, men treat hope as they treat myth. Just as myth is no more than a story, hope is frequently nothing more than "a practical little problem of possibilities" (*HV* 29). Sutpen's hope that Bon would be killed in the War and thus be eliminated as a son-in-law was on this level: Bon's hope was the opposite from Sutpen's but of the same "low order" (*HV* 29). At other times, hope is merely a "*response*" to distress (*HV* 30); we find ourselves trapped, we wish to be free, and hope is the magic that will free us. Awaiting execution for the murder of Temple Drake's child, Nancy Mannigoe comforted herself with this magic. She would not "let go of" hope, "the hardest thing of all to break, get rid of, . . . the last thing of all poor sinning man will turn aloose" (*RFN* 272). This is the hope Gavin Stevens held out to Temple, who shared the blame with Nancy. "You never really give up hope," he told her (*RFN* 163). A third level of hope is that which *refuses* to respond to distress; it resists "the temptation to despair" (*HV* 36). Man can bear anything, the division runner said, "provided he has . . . his integrity," provided he is "tough and enduring enough not only not to hope but not even to believe in to" (*AF* 203). A more "positive philosophy of hope" (*HV* 50) offers us the possibility of maintaining our integrity but without rhetorical flourishes. Modest and unassuming, hope of this order "is linked to a certain candor, a certain virginity untouched by experience" (*HV* 51). "'There must be a way,' and . . . 'I am going to find it'" becomes "simply: 'It will be found'" (*HV* 51-52). Lena Grove's hope of finding Lucas Burch was such. At Frenchman's Bend when Armstid expressed doubt that Lena would find Lucas, she quietly replied, "I reckon I'll find him. It wont be hard" (*LIA* 11). For the Lena Groves, it is never hard. She had left her brother's house under the same circumstances she faced at Frenchman's Bend (*LIA* 5,6): What direction had Lucas taken; how would she be able to follow him? As the sweet and amiable girl refused to consider the what, she was "not" at all "interested in the *how*" (*HV* 51). She shunned elaborate inferences and deductions, appealing instead "to the existence of a certain creative power in the world" (*HV* 52), the power of those innocent enough to hope (*T* 203). Mrs. Armstid was paying tribute to it when she ordered her husband to give her hard-earned "eggmoney" to Lena (*LIA* 19).

And yet hope at this level is still "not compatible with hope in its purest form" (*HV* 36). Whether it is Bon hoping or Lena, hope is restricted by its object. To hope in this mode means "to hope that . . . " (*HV* 45, *MB II* 181). It means to treat the "transcendent" phenomenon—this "principle hidden in the heart of . . . events," the "radical refusal to reckon possibilities" (*B&H* 79)—as if it had to depend upon some power other than its own, "the hoping machine," Gavin Stevens called it (*LIA* 390). Hope here is an objective to be attained, a design to be worked out (*HV* 45). If the design fails, hope fails; if the design succeeds, hope disappears. "True hope" (*HV* 57) moves away from "the problematical . . . to a new ground: a ground on which . . . [objects] lose their meaning" (*PE* 20). The Norman expressed this hope when he prophesied that the General would die to live again, that he would return in a "century [different] from that one when man discovered God for a second time and then lost Him [a return] postulated by a new digit in the record of . . . hope" (*AF* 262). The new digit, a quantum leap, is to "hope in" (*HV* 60).

Hope at this level is all-encompassing. It involves man and himself, man and other men, and man and men and God. When the Norman announced that the General will be to men their "living hope" (*AF* 263), he was not demanding or expecting, he was announcing, "I hope in thee for us" (*HV* 60). In this annunciation, a new dimension in the "metaphysic of hope" (*HV* 29), "hope . . . akin to life" (*MB II* 184), the subject-object dichotomy has disappeared (*M&C* 31): "Between . . . 'thou' and . . . 'us'" God and man and men, "is . . . 'Thou' . . . [,] the union which holds us together, myself to myself, or the one to the other, or these beings to those other beings, . . . the very cement which binds the whole into one" (*HV* 60-61): (on the existential-phenomenological level, the cement of nothingness that binds together the intention and consciousness). Instead of listening anxiously for threats of hellfire, on the one hand, and to promises of heaven, on the other, both equally illusory (*AF* 354), we are free, the Norman says, to live in God, our living hope, and this is as much as he can tell us. He cannot tell us what we wish most to know, "the shape" of that hope (*AF* 263).

In order to understand the reason that he cannot tell us, we must return once more, for the last time, to the problem of consciousness. Husserl gave us a hint of the problem when he wrote that we can describe consciousness and that we can describe the object but that consciousness-of-something is at once clear and ambiguous (*I* 345-49). To repeat: we can describe consciousness, as this study has shown, and we can describe the phenomenon of which we are conscious, as the study has also shown, but how do we describe consciousness in the act of being consciousness—the living, moving, ever-creating consciousness? Long ago, we gave up on the most profound of all consciousnesses, the Consciousness (of) God, objectifying Him variously as Santa Claus, Revenger, a Gentleman (*PF&R* 144,145,330). Our efforts in this direction led Marcel to write, "When we speak of God . . . reduced to our absurd, human proportions . . . it is not of God that we speak" (*CF* 36). God himself warns us of our desecration in His greatest commandment, "Thou shalt not make unto thee any image or likeness" (*PF&R* 136). Our consciousness of Him must be "given" to us "in the purest form in its *intention*" (*CF* 146); thus to experience God means turning away from all that interposes itself between us and God. On all impedimenta, we should perform the *epoche*, leaving only the expression (of) God, and for the expression, we turn to ciphers, the universal language of existential-phenomenological myth.

Ciphers should not be confused with symbols. A Faulkner critic writes "that the degree or integrity produced by symbols results not from what the symbols represent, but from the motivation of the writer."[16] Ciphers neither represent anything nor are they motivated by anything. Their integrity lies in that they *are*. Stated crudely, ciphers are infinite possibilities (*PF&R* 103,108,134,288), the ground of which is Nothingness. They are consciousness in its purest manifestation, the intending undefiled by the object intended. They cannot be perceived, conceptualized, imagined. Ciphers of God, then, have no content, no criteria of verification(*T&S* 55-62, *PF&R* 126,143,324,325). They are an "illuminating" (*PF&R* 108) of "the indestructible, the immutable, the source, the encompassing of all encompassing" (*PF&R* 255). "Just as light can be [revealed] only through the medium of that which it illuminates" (*MB II* 135), cipher can be discovered only through that which it illuminates. The quality "peculiar to light" is the quality peculiar to existential-phenomenological cipher, "that of being illuminating" (*MB* 133).

This is also the quality peculiar to the Myth (of) Hope, our Consciousness (of) God, which never strays very far from illumination, whatever the level of the Encompassing (*HV* 29-33). Even when hope is a response to despair, ourselves plunged into "the darkness of illness, of separation, exile or slavery," we feel "deprived . . . of a certain light for which . . . [we] long" (*HV* 30). Temple Drake enslaved at Miss Reba's felt the longing. She saw her hopes disappear as the light faded, "the final light condense into the clock face, and the dial change from a round orifice in the darkness to a disc suspended in nothingness, the original chaos" (*S* 180-81). Hope-as-light of this relatively low order involves a "physical agent," just as "physical light" involves an agent (*MB II* 136), the rays of the sun, for example. It is this light and, correlatively, the dim hope that Marthe was bemoaning as she described the narrow little valley in which she had been brought up. The light was blocked by a peak, which was not "high, . . . just higher than any of our men . . . ever went. Not higher than they could but than they did, dared" (*AF* 288). Here we can understand the specifics of light, the physics, just as we can understand the specifics of hope. Another level of light-as-hope escapes physics and chemistry, the hope, for instance, of "the woman who is expecting a baby" (*HV* 31)—Lena Grove, "tranquil and calm" (*LIA* 16), "literally inhabited" by hope-as-light (*HV* 31), "an inwardlighted quality" (*LIA* 16).

There is finally the hope and, correlatively, the light that "infinitely transcends all possible verification because it exists in an immediacy beyond all conceivable mediation" (*PE* 15 *HV* 66-67). It is the "metaphysic of light" (*MB II* 134) that is the "metaphysic of hope" (*HV* 29), "the light . . . enlightnening every man who comes into the world" (*MB II* 136). It is given to man as consciousness is given to him, and like consciousness, it "feeds on itself," "*a light whose joy is in giving light, in being light*" (*MB II* 133). It is this light—the existential-phenomenological cipher-shape of man's living hope—which the Generalissimo discovered in and to man:

> The windows were open, curtain and casement, so that there came into the room not only the afternoon light and air, but something of the city's tumult too—not sound, because the voices . . . didn't reach here. It was rather a sense, a quality as of the light itself, a reflection as of light itself from the massed faces below, refracted upward into the room through the open windows like light from disturbed water, pulsing and quivering faintly and constantly on the ceiling where nobody . . . would notice it without they chanced to look up. (*AF* 228-229)

He looked up. The human sound as light, a holy synesthesia, had begun to beckon even as the General had approached GHQ in Paris where he would listen first to General Gragnon (*AF* 13-15), one "incapable of hoping," to whom "hoping" was "baseless [,] . . . the diet of weaklings" (*AF* 22), and then to his son, the "champion of an esoteric realm of man's baseless hopes" (*AF* 348), but most, he listened to the cipher sounds from the city.

> He just stood in the window above the thronged motionless *Place* where the patient mass of people lay against the iron fence. . . . He just stood there, a little back from the window and a little to one side, holding the curtain slightly aside, visible if anyone in the *Place* had thought to look up. . . . And now the mass beyond the fence itself began to move, flowing back across the *Place* toward the diverging boulevards, emptying the *Place*, already fading before it was out of the *Place*, as though with one long quiet inhalation evening was effacing the whole . . . mist of man. (*AF* 237-39)

The inhalation never occurred, man never effaced so long as there was the light:

> The old general dropped the curtain and began to turn from the window. . . . Then he stopped. It was as though he didn't anticipate the [other] sound so much as he simply foreknew it. . . . It came up, . . . beginning not as sound at all but rather as light, diffused yet steady from across the plain beyond the city: the voices of men, . . . growing not in volume but in density as dawn itself increases, filling the low horizon beyond the city's black and soaring bulk with a band not of sound but light, . . . still filling the horizon even after the voices themselves had ceased with a resonant humming like a fading sunset . . . against which the black tremendous city seemed to rush skyward in one fixed iron roar out of the furious career of earth toward . . . the fixed stars. (*AF* 242-243)

there, "an unreached hub of light [fluttering] toward the infinite distance of Transcendence," "the fulfilled silence": the "existential [-phenomenological] experiences of thinking the unthinkable"—"the irreplacable thinking experience," "the magnificent phenomena of thinking"—a "springboard to fulfillment," a humanist miracle, where "thought is asked to venture into empty space with nothing to hold onto, no ground to stand on": where existential-phenomenology is at its purest, where "Being is Nothingness" (*PF&R* 125,255,256, *HV* 29-68 *passim*), where will be found, if they ever are found, the answers to these profound questions:

> How will you set about looking for that thing, the nature of which is totally unknown to you? Which, among the things you do not know, is the one you propose to look for? And if by chance you should stumble upon it, how will you know that it is indeed that thing, since you are in ignorance of it? (*PP* 371)

Notes

[1] Walter F. Taylor, "William Faulkner: The Faulkner Fable," *The American Scholar*, XXVI (Autumn 1957), 471.

[2] Taylor, 471.

[3] Philip Blair Rice, "Faulkner's Crucifixion," Frederick J. Hoffman and Olga W. Vickery, eds., *William Faulkner: Three Decades of Criticism* (New York: Harcourt, Brace and World, 1960), 377.

[4] Walter J. Slatoff, *Quest for Failure: A Study of William Faulkner* (Ithaca, N.Y.: Cornell UP, 1960), 221.

[5] Olga W. Vickery, *The Novels of William Faulkner: A Critical Interpretation* (Baton Rouge: Louisiana State UP, 1961), 194,195.

[6] Walter K. Everett, *Faulkner's Art and Characters* (Woodbury, NY: Barron's, 1969), 16.

[7] Slatoff, 221.

[8] Taylor, 477.

[9] *Ibid.*, 474.

[10] *Ibid.*, 475.

[11] *Ibid.*, 474.

[12] *Ibid.*, 475.